CIVIL WAR BROCKPORT

A Canal Town and the Union Army

WILLIAM G. ANDREWS

THE History PRESS

Published by The History Press
Charleston, SC 29403
www.historypress.net

Front cover: Courtesy of the Library of Congress.
Back cover image: The illustration reproduces a painting by Rochester's John William Wagner that depicts the 140th NYVI at Little Round Top. Colonel Patrick O'Rorke is leading the charge. Captain Milo Starks, commander of Brockport's Company A, appears in the lower right corner. The soldiers are members of his company. *By permission of the artist.*

First published 2013

Manufactured in the United States

ISBN 978.1.62619.122.8

Library of Congress CIP data applied for.

Notice: The information in this book is true and complete to the best of our knowledge. It is offered without guarantee on the part of the author or The History Press. The author and The History Press disclaim all liability in connection with the use of this book.

This book is dedicated to the memory of Monika

Contents

Preface

The 1964 Town of Sweden Sesqui-Centennial Celebration commemorative booklet, in its brief account of the town's involvement in the Civil War, said: "A full volume could be written, and perhaps will be someday, describing the role played by our people at home and at the front during those tragic years of 1861–1865." Well, Wilbur W. (Doc) Hiler and your committee, here it is—nearly half a century late.

The purpose of this book is to portray, as well as possible, the role of the Brockport, New York area in the American Civil War. It argues that Brockport was intensely involved in the war and that, in some respects, that role was important. The first four chapters look at activities in the village that were related to the war. The next ten report in detail the experiences of the first Union army company recruited in Brockport. Part III provides shorter accounts of the other seven companies formed in the Brockport area. The final chapter gives some information about Brockporters who served in units not enlisted in Brockport. All of those activities formed the experience of the community during the war, and memories of them continued to influence its life for a long time after the war's end.

This project began in 2005, after I completed my *Early Brockport* book. That work traced the history of the village through 1865. In researching the Civil War years, I discovered 189 long letters from Brockport soldiers in the *Brockport Republic* weekly newspaper from April 1861 through September 1864. (The *Brockport Republic* file for October 1864–October 1865 is missing.)

It occurred to me that those letters could form the basis for another book. So, I did not include anything about the war in *Early Brockport*.

However, when I had finished Part I below and turned my attention to the letters, I discovered that they did not, in fact, provide the basis for a coherent portrayal of the careers of the Brockport companies. For Part II, I supplemented the letters from Brockporters with letters from other Monroe County members of that regiment that were published in Rochester newspapers. In that way, and by drawing on some other sources, I could provide a very complete account of the experiences of a typical Union army regiment with a substantial complement of Brockporters, relying heavily on firsthand accounts. The Brockport company was broken up early in the war and its members scattered throughout the regiment. So, the regimental activities became the Brockport experience. Because I treat the other Brockport companies more briefly, I rely much less on firsthand accounts, and I do not use them at all in Part IV.

Put another way, Part I recounts the war-related lives of the home folks; Part II brings to life the day-by-day experiences of Brockport soldiers; Part III describes the highlights of the careers of the other Brockport companies, whose daily lives were much like those described in Part II; and Part IV completes the panoply of the full extent of Brockport's involvement in the war.

My most unexpected discovery in working on this project was the number of Brockporters who served in units that were not recruited in the Brockport area and the wealth and diversity of their experiences. When the careers of those 233 men in 113 army units, the U.S. Navy, the Medical Corps, and the Veterans Reserve Corps are added to those of the eight Brockport companies, they cover almost every aspect of the war. For a small village to receive the reports of its men from such a range of experiences must have brought the war home in a very vivid, immediate, and substantial way.

I have taken as the geographic scope of this work what seems to me to have been the circulation area of the *Brockport Republic*. The *Brockport Republic* seems to have been the main means of public communication in the towns of Sweden, Clarkson, and Hamlin at that time (until 1861, Hamlin bore the name Union), and its influence seems to have spilled over into adjacent towns. It seems to have formed a kind of loose-knit community in its orbit. Also, Brockport seems to have served as the focus of public activity for that area. It was the port for shipping its agricultural and industrial products. It was a kind of market center for that "community." The companies that were formed in Brockport drew heavily on that community beyond the limits of the village. Also, I have included on my roster men from towns adjacent to those three who served in Brockport companies. Therefore, when I refer to Brockport and Brockporters in the pages that follow, I usually mean that community, the Brockport area.

My most important research sources have been the *Brockport Republic*; the American Civil War Research Database website (ACWRD); the United States census reports for 1860 and 1870 and the New York State census for 1865, as available on the Rochester/Monroe County Public Library website and at the New York Public Library; the 1865 reports of the town clerks of Sweden and Clarkson to the NYS Department of Military and Naval Affairs on the contributions of their towns to the war effort (provided to me by Jim Foltz of the NYS Archives and Record Administration); Frederick Phisterer, *New York in the War of the Rebellion, 1861–1865*, Albany, 1912, 5 vols.; and the regimental histories listed in my bibliography. I received valuable help from Mary Smith, Town of Hamlin historian emerita, and Eunice Chesnut, historian of the Western Monroe Historical Society. I also benefited from the hospitality of the Drake Library at the College of Brockport in consulting its microfilm file of the *Brockport Republic*. Wayne Mahood and Brian Bennett, who know Civil War literature much better than I, reviewed the manuscript and made many helpful suggestions.

Finally, I would be remiss if I did not acknowledge that it has been a pleasure working with Whitney Landis and Janet Long, editors at The History Press, who guided me through the production process with real care, efficiency, and positive attitudes.

WILLIAM G. ANDREWS
Brockport, NY
May 2013

Abbreviations

ACWRD = American Civil War Reseach Database (website)
AGNY = NYS Adjutant General's Report
BD = *Brockport Democrat* (weekly newspaper, 1870–1925)
BR = *Brockport Republic* (weekly newspaper, 1856–1925)
They merged in 1925 as the *Brockport Republic-Democrat*, 1925-1971
CTCR = Clarkson Town Clerk's Report, 1865
CWTI = *Civil War Times Illustrated*
Davis Report = Detailed Account of Aid Afforded by Towns… (Sweden)
DMNA = New York State Department of Military and Naval Affairs website
NY Cavalry = New York Volunteer Cavalry
NYHA = New York Heavy Artillery
NYLA = New York Light Artillery
NYVI = New York Volunteer Infantry
OR = *The War of the Rebellion: A Compilation of the Official Records of the Union and Confederate Armies*
RDD = *Rochester Daily Democrat*
REE = *Rochester Evening Express*
ROEM = Return of Officers and Enlisted Men who have been in the military or naval service, Monroe County
STCR = Sweden Town Clerk's Report, 1865
U&A = *Rochester Daily Union and Advertiser*

Part I

The Homefront

Chapter 1

Brockport Goes to War

Understanding the atmosphere in the Brockport area at the outbreak of the Civil War helps greatly to get an accurate picture of the attitudes and activities of Brockporters during the conflict. The situation of the village in the early 1860s predisposed its residents to become intensely involved in the cause of the Union. They exuded self-confidence and had expressed political leanings consonant with the unionist and antislavery crusade. That confidence and commitment certainly facilitated their involvement.

Brockport before Sumter

Brockport at the dawn of the 1860s was a thriving industrial village on the Erie Canal, brimming with self-confidence. It throbbed with the vigor of youth. Barely a generation had passed since it was founded in 1822 and chartered in 1829. Many original settlers still walked its streets. In its first thirty-eight years, it had grown from a handful of pioneer settlers to a village of 2,238 inhabitants in the 1860 census, within the town of Sweden, which had a total of 4,045 residents. The town of Clarkson had a population of 2,093, and the town of Hamlin had 2,460 for a three-town total of 8,598. Brockport had always been the most populous village in Monroe County and was unrivalled as a center of social and commercial activity in the neighboring towns. (For details, see my *Early Brockport* 248.)

Yet the village also basked in the glow of substantial accomplishment. It had, in a sense, presided over the completion of the Erie Canal. The last section of that great waterway was opened between the village and Buffalo. The canal was the world's greatest engineering feat of the nineteenth century and the transportation facility that made possible the rise of the United States as a continental power and as the greatest nation in the history of the world. Also, it had been midwife to the industrial revolution in agriculture, for here had been manufactured the first farm machines. Brockport workmen had solved a problem that had plagued Cyrus McCormick for fifteen years when they produced reapers in quantity for the first time.

That accomplishment had far-reaching consequences for the Union in the Civil War. According to a writer in *American Heritage Magazine,* each reaper freed five farm workers for service in the Union army. The United States (almost entirely in the North) produced 165,000 reapers during the war. The calculation of 165,000 x 5 may be a bit of an exaggeration, but it must, nevertheless, be true that the reaper—and Brockport's contribution—played an important part in winning the war.

Brockport's location on the canal not only enabled it to profit from its transient traffic but also to become the shipping and marketing center for a large area of hinterland. That status was enhanced by its hosting of the Monroe County Fair annually. One of the toll stations on the canal was located in the village, meaning that the toll receipts were deposited in Brockport banks, further boosting the economy. In 1860, "business on the canal" was "enormous," with toll receipts up 49 percent over 1859. (*BR* 11/8/1860, 12/6/1860)

The railroad had reached the village in 1852 and had become almost as great an asset as the canal, taking over passenger traffic completely and shipping nearly as much freight from the village. (*BR* 12/13/1860) Brockport claimed to have the busiest railroad station on the Niagara Falls line and was blessed with a new passenger depot and a new Main Street bridge as a result. (*BR* 8/22/1861)

The economy was booming. The *Brockport Republic* (*BR*) boasted that the village "has never been more prosperous," that every storefront was filled, "and there still are demands for more." All dwellings were occupied, and there had been "no business failure in the past three years." (3/25/1859, 12/6/1860, 4/11/1861) It estimated that the grocery, shoe and boot, clothing, and dry goods retailers in the village did an aggregate business of $235,000 to $255,000 annually, a very substantial amount in 1860 dollars for a community of 2,200 inhabitants. (4/5/1860, 5/3/1860) It predicted confidently that such success "must indicate our approach to metropolitan greatness." (6/14/1860)

The village was home to at least six farm implement manufacturers. They reported the best reaper business "in at least three years," and the two largest of them undertook major expansion programs. (*BR* 11/22/1860) Also, the Cary & Brainerd Co. was achieving considerable success building pumps for fire engines (*BR* 11/1/1860), and the village was a major player in the lumber business. In 1860, it received 3.4 million board feet of lumber on the canal and shipped 5.8 million pounds of barrel staves. (*BR* 12/13/1860)

Brockport's self-image was further enhanced by the presence in its midst of several residents of distinction. The only two men (Dr. Davis Carpenter and Elias B. Holmes) to have served in the United States Congress while residing in Brockport, were active members of the community. Henry Selden of Clarkson had been lieutenant governor and became a judge on New York State's highest court. Among his fellow townsmen Captain James Warren was Monroe County sheriff and Simeon Jewett was sufficiently prominent politically to have been considered for the vice presidency of the United States under Lincoln. Another village resident, Mary Jane Holmes, was well established as America's most popular woman novelist, and her home on College Street was a major tourist attraction.

Another factor predisposing Brockporters to become heavily involved in the war effort was its Republicanism. Horatio N. Beach had founded the *BR* late in 1856 as part of the effort by the Republican Party to become established throughout the North. By the 1860 elections, Lincoln Republicanism had become the dominant political current in the Brockport area. Honest Abe carried the Town of Sweden by 571 to 264, a 68.4 percent majority. (*BR* 11/8/1860) The village had previously been caught up in the struggle over "Bloody Kansas." Susan B. Anthony; Clarinda Nichols, who was a former Brockport resident and had become a leader in the anti-slavery cause in Kansas; and an escaped slave spoke to public meetings in the village on that issue. (*BR* 3/15/1860, 5/10/1860)

However, the villagers do not seem to have been much involved in the anti-slavery movement closer to home. An early resident recalled only two abolitionists in the community, neither of them important politically. (Smith/Husted 17) In fact, Brockport's Whig Congressman in the late 1840s, Elias B. Holmes, spoke disparagingly of abolitionists on the floor of the House of Representatives, while arguing against the extension of slavery into the new territories acquired by the Mexican War. (June 7, 1848, speech 10–11, 14) Moreover, not one scintilla of evidence indicates that the Underground Railroad ever had a station in the three-town area. None of the reminiscences about that period mention one, when it would have been a matter of pride. None of the histories presents any support for such speculation.

In the period leading up to the Civil War, therefore, Brockporters seem to have been caught up in their successes and only marginally interested in the events that were precipitating the approaching holocaust. Their political positions were solidly in the mainstream of Northern opinion. However, at least one voice was anticipating trouble. After Lincoln's election but well before the Fort Sumter crisis, with southerners threatening secession, Editor Beach advocated the formation of "a military company" in the village. (*BR* 11/22/1860) In any case, by the time hostilities erupted, Brockporters were well conditioned for involvement in an armed conflict to preserve the Union, though they probably did not see it as an anti-slavery crusade.

THE IMPACT OF WAR

It should come as no surprise, then, that war fever gripped Brockport very quickly after the firing on Fort Sumter and held on for four years with an intensity of involvement that probably was not matched in any other American conflict. One of Beach's editorials suggests the mood that prevailed in the village in the aftermath of Sumter:

> *All ordinary themes of conversation now succumb to that of war. Ask the first man you meet about the health of his wife, and he answers "war." Ask the farmer about the state of the roads or his crops, and he answers "war." Ask the merchant about trade, and he replies by asking "what is the latest war news?" And so on through all the social and business intercourse between individuals, war is the great, prominent and all-absorbing topic.* (BR *4/25/1861)*

Some Brockporters struggled mightily to find suitable ways to manifest that spirit. They pledged financial aid for the relief fund, even offered to enlist, including some who were beyond military age. In one early War Meeting, John A. Latta, a merchant, expressed his frustration thus:

> *I feel patriotism burning in my bosom. What shall I do? What can I do?—I have no property.—I asked my wife to-night what we should do, and she said—wear plainer dresses and eat plainer food, and give fifty dollars and I will do so, and secure that sum for the object, against all contingencies.* (BR *4/25/1861)*

The intensity of involvement that both required and generated that spirit was partly because the war was fought entirely on American soil. The proximity of the fighting gave it special immediacy. Moreover, it made possible relatively easy travel between the homefront and the battlefront. Fathers visited their sons in camp and soldiers were able to come home on leave.

The war also had unusually great impact on the homefront, because the Union forces suffered a higher casualty rate than have our troops in any other American conflict, 29.2 percent, compared to 6.6 percent in World War II and 2.4 percent in the Vietnam conflict. Even though a larger share of the male population served in World War II, a larger share of the male population was casualties in the Civil War, 5.7 percent, compared to 1.6 percent in 1941–45. So, the tragedy of war hit home with greater frequency. The loss of family members, friends, and neighbors ratcheted up the intensity of involvement. (These figures were calculated before the recent substantial boost in historians' estimates of the casualty rate.)

Most evident, however, were the recruitment efforts. Unlike American wars in the 20th and 21st centuries, the Civil War was fought mostly with units that were recruited community-by-community across the land. The task of mustering the great armies that the conflict required fell mainly to the villages, towns, cities, counties, and states. Every municipality was expected to raise from among its inhabitants companies of men who had grown up together and would fight and die together. As the war dragged on, the casualty lists grew, and the pool of potential recruits shrank, that effort became increasingly onerous, difficult, and unpleasant.

A fourth factor was the virtual absence of military censorship. Soldiers wrote home freely about their experiences. Newspapers, like the *BR*, published many letters from the training camps and the battlefields. In fact, Editor Beach boasted that he had at least one correspondent in each unit containing Brockport men, and he printed at least 189 letters from them during the conflict. He instructed them as follows:

> *We desire our correspondents...to give as many facts as possible of general public interest. Description of movements, the names of the disabled soldiers and the cause of their disability, the names of the promoted or dishonored, the particulars of battles, &c, as they would write to their friends. Description of the country through which they pass or in which they are located, will be in order. (*BR *8/28/1862)*

A final factor that intensified the impact arose because Uncle Sam provided less well for his soldiers than in later conflicts. The troops were often short of supplies. This was especially true of the military hospitals. Because of the relative ease of communication and transportation between the homefront and the war front, Brockporters were well informed about those problems. Consequently, the home folks pitched in with drives to provide clothing, blankets, food, medicine, and other provisions. Those efforts mobilized civilians who, otherwise, might not have been involved.

All of this contributed to create a situation in which Brockporters were, and sensed that they were, deeply involved in a Herculean enterprise. How else can one account for the tremendous effort exerted on behalf of the Union, which will be described in the pages that follow?

A WAR MEETING

One of the main ways that Brockport organized its war effort was to hold so-called War Meetings. These were large public assemblies with the main purpose of encouraging men of military age to enlist in the Union Army. The village's first War Meeting was held in the Concert Hall on Saturday evening, April 20, five days after Lincoln's first call for volunteers. No indication was given as to how it had been summoned, but it seems to have been a largely spontaneous response to the president's appeal, organized by some of the community's leading citizens. Also, the village had a tradition of holding such unofficial public meetings. (*Early Brockport* 53–55) Because it seems to have become somewhat of a template for the many meetings that followed, it deserves description at some length.

The excitement engendered by the War Meeting seems to be a fair indication of the initial intensity of the war spirit in the village. *BR* editor Beach exulted at great length, taking up nearly five long columns of type:

> *On no occasion since the village was founded, has there been such an union of sentiment and outburst of enthusiasm…The people came together as one man—actuated by a single purpose, and all zealous for its accomplishment. The hall and passageways were densely packed with patriotic citizens, a goodly number of whom were ladies. Previous to the assembling of the people, all along Main Street the Stars and Stripes were proudly floating, and our old cannon, "Garibaldi"—that has done execution on many*

battle-fields—spoke in sonorous tones. [Garibaldi later blew up announcing one of the meetings.] *(*BR *4/25/1861)*

Formality was conferred on the meeting by the election through acclamation of a president, ten vice presidents, and three secretaries, from among the most distinguished men in the community. Then five-member committees on resolutions and "on volunteers" were appointed, though the appointer was not identified. That was followed by a "spirited" rendition of "America" by the Glee Club.

The speechifying began when Jerome M. Fuller, an attorney, was "loudly called for" by the audience. His two sons were among the first volunteers. One of them, Eugene P., was recruiting Brockport's first infantry company. Fuller's "brilliant and patriotic address [was] often interrupted by bursts of applause."

Henry P. Norton, another attorney who chaired the resolutions committee, succeeded him to present four resolutions. The first resolved that "we pledge our fortunes and our lives, and whatever else we hold most dear" to the Union cause and ended with the sentiment that Lincoln expressed so much more eloquently at Gettysburg two and a half years later: "the issue of this conflict is to determine, for all time to come, whether human liberty and free representative governments shall have an abiding place in the world."

That language suggests one reason for the fame of the Gettysburg Address. Lincoln expressed a belief that had been widespread in the North throughout the war. A man unknown to history in an insignificant little canal town at the very outset of the war persuaded his neighbors to resolve that the Union armies had a sacred mission that transcended national boundaries. The fate of "human liberty and free representative governments" throughout the world hung in the balance and could be redeemed only by troops such as those being recruited that night in Brockport.

The second resolution declared the rebellion to be treasonous and called "upon all loyal citizens…to come to the rescue of the Constitution and the Union." The third commended "the patriotic men who are coming forward…as volunteers in defence of their country." The fourth authorized the chair to appoint a committee of five "to raise by subscription such funds as may be necessary" to provide relief to the indigent families of the volunteers. Note that the abolition of slavery was not mentioned.

Elias B. Holmes and Horace J. Thomas spoke in support of the resolutions. Holmes had been a two-term Whig member of the United States House of Representatives, 1845–49, and was married to a daughter of Hiel Brockway, co-founder of the village. He was 54 years old and a leading lawyer and businessman. He was also a farmer and raised prize show horses. He was the principal owner of a packet line on the canal, 1840–55, and a director of the Rochester & Niagara Falls Railroad. He died in 1866. Thomas was a leading lawyer who had just returned from Albany with a captain's commission.

Then "loud calls were made for Eugene P. Fuller, Esq." He had a lieutenant's commission in Captain Thomas's company. Lieutenant Fuller complained that 39 Brockporters had signed a paper "proposing to organize a military company," but that only 17 of them had signed the enlistment form.

Henry W. Seymour "was called for" and spoke. At age 26, he was ripe for military service, but despite saying that night that he was "willing to take my part and lot in the contest," he never served. Seymour, the youngest of the leaders, was the son of William E. Seymour, Brockport's leading citizen, and nephew of James Seymour, co-founder of the village. Henry had been admitted to the bar, but never practiced law, being engaged at various times in manufacturing, lumber milling, and farming. After moving to Michigan in 1872, he served as a Republican in Congress, 1888–89. J. D. Decker, Esq., followed him to the podium, "in response to calls." He, also, vowed to "rally around the old flag," but did not sign up until July 1862, when he received a second lieutenant's commission.

Then the four resolutions were "unanimously adopted" and a committee of five appointed "to raise funds for the maintenance of the families of volunteers." The Glee Club sang "The Star-Spangled Banner." Captain Thomas returned to the platform, "read the list of volunteers, and invited others to step forward." The response was so enthusiastic that 24 more young men stepped forward and the Brockport company now numbered 41. "During the enrollment, the martial band, with its warlike music, stirred up the multitude to a great degree of excitement" and, with three cheers for "those who had enrolled," the meeting adjourned until the following Tuesday, when it would meet in the Presbyterian Church, which could accommodate a larger crowd.

For the adjourned meeting, the Presbyterian sanctuary "was filled in every part by an excited and enthusiastic audience, composed about one-third of patriotic ladies." The recruits for the new company—now numbering fifty—occupied reserved seats at the front, preceded by a martial band. The Glee Club sang, "[m]artial drums were beaten near the altar, patriotic songs were sung by the choir and people and upon the altar table men were enrolled as volunteers… During the meeting, Mr. Jenner's little cannon was repeatedly fired in front of the church." The finance committee reported on its fund-raising efforts. Unlike the earlier meeting, this one opened with a prayer by the Reverend Joseph Kimball.

A series of short speeches followed, interspersed by martial and patriotic music. As usual, speakers took their turn only when called for by the crowd.

BROCKPORT'S FIRST TROOPS

The principal response to that first War Meeting was the recruitment of a military unit that became Company K of the 13th New York Volunteer Regiment of Infantry. In fact, both the War Meeting and the recruitment were responses to President Lincoln's April 15, 1861, call for 75,000 volunteers to serve enlistment terms of three months. Seventeen regiments with 13,280 men (Phisterer I: 57) were to be raised in New York, the largest number of any state. By April 25, 75 volunteers had joined the Brockport unit. (*BR* 4/25/1861 says 77, but lists only 75 names) The 13th consisted of ten companies, each having 100 men when full. Eight companies were recruited in Rochester and one in Dansville, Livingston County. So, Brockport was the only community in Monroe County, except Rochester, to raise a company in response to Lincoln's first appeal.

By May 13, the company had traveled to the training base at Elmira with the rest of the regiment. By the time they left to be mustered in, they numbered 99. However, six men refused to take the oath, six had deserted, and two were medical rejects. The classes and residences of the 85 who remained were: (*BR* 5/16/1861)

RESIDENCE	OFFICERS	NON-COMS	PRIVATES	TOTALS
Brockport	3 (100%)	6 (85.7%)	28 (37.3%)	37 (43.5%)
Sweden	—	—	10 (13.3%)	10 (11.8%)
Clarkson	—	1 (14.3%)	11 (14.7%)	12 (14.1%)
Hamlin	—	—	11 (14.7%)	11 (12.9%)
Rochester	—	—	6 (8.0%)	6 (7.1%)
Kendall, Orleans Co.	—	—	3 (4.0%)	3 (3.5%)
Ogden	—	—	2 (2.7%)	2 (2.4%)
Murray, Orleans Co.	—	—	1 (1.3%)	1 (1.2%)
Albion, Orleans Co.	—	—	1 (1.3%)	1 (1.2%)
Knapp's Corners	—	—	1 (1.3%)	1 (1.2%)
Webster's Mills	—	—	1 (1.3%)	1 (1.2%)
	3	7	75	85

Note: The identity of the officers and non-coms was reported in *BR* 4/25/1861, but the residences were reported in *BR* 5/16/1861. As there were some changes in the interim, this chart is not perfectly accurate. For instance, Monroe Copps was 2nd corporal on 4/25, but does not appear on the 5/16 list. Webster's Mills was later named Kendall Mills.

Company K was very much a Brockport area, and, especially, a Village of Brockport unit. All the officers and non-coms and 82.4 percent of the men came from the three Brockport area towns and only seven privates (9.3%) came from outside Monroe County. Indeed, only the recruit from Albion lived outside the Brockport area as defined in the Preface above. The village provided all the officers, six of the seven non-coms, and more than three times as many men as any other municipality. This dominance changed drastically for the later companies recruited in the village.

So, within ten days of Lincoln's first appeal, the basic pattern of Brockport's involvement in the war had been laid. War meetings would be held almost monthly, those in need because of the war would be aided by private donations and governmental appropriations, and seven more companies would be recruited. The village responded with alacrity and enthusiasm. Little did Brockporters—or anyone else—know how long the conflict would last, how great its toll would be, and what effort would be required before the foe was vanquished. Yet, that commitment never lagged. Brockporters supported the war effort in many, substantial ways until peace returned.

Chapter 2

The Mobilization System

The recruitment efforts set in motion by the war meetings were probably the most important Civil War activity undertaken in the Brockport area and the one that had the greatest impact on the lives of Brockporters. Of course, the recruits themselves were affected the most. However, those activities were a very pervasive element in the daily lives of all Brockporters.

Although the recruitment efforts in the village were mainly organized locally, they were direct responses to actions taken at higher governmental levels and were largely determined by them. Their timing, rhythm, and intensity were set by decisions and actions upstairs and can be understood only in that context. Therefore, we shall look at that national, state, county, and town framework before describing what happened in the village. That framework consisted mainly of four components: voluntarism, conscription, bounties, and commutation fees.

Voluntarism

Americans had a long tradition of voluntarism, both civilian and military. In all armed conflicts before the Civil War, voluntarism had been the main means of recruiting non-professional soldiers. In the Civil War, the initial recruitment policies of the national government conformed to that tradition. At the outset of the war, on April 15, 1861, President Lincoln issued a call for 75,000 volunteers to serve for three months, anticipating an early end to the conflict. That total was distributed among the states and within states to lower governmental units proportionately to their populations. Patriotic fervor was expected to be sufficient inducement to enroll. The expectations were sound and the call was filled quickly. (Geary)

Lincoln's April 1861 call set a precedent. He or the Provost Marshal General issued similar appeals throughout the war. They always implied that a sufficient number of men would respond voluntarily. As the quotas filtered down to the local level, they became the main stimulus for recruitment efforts and determined their rhythm. The main calls were:

April 15, 1861	75,000 for 3 mos.
May/July 1861	592,748 for 3 yrs.
July 2, 1862	300,000 for 3 yrs.
August 4, 1862	300,000 for 9 mos.
June 15, 1863	100,000 for 6 mos.
October 17, 1863	500,000 for 3 yrs.
March 14, 1864	200,000 for 3 yrs.
April 23, 1864	85,000 for 100 days
July 18, 1864	500,000 for 1, 2, or 3 yrs.
December 19, 1864	300,000 for 1, 2, or 3 yrs.

At least superficially, voluntarism seemed sufficient to fill the quotas until the summer of 1864. By August 5 of that year, 356 men had been "furnished" by the Town of Sweden. Only two had been "DRAFTED…under the President's levy of 1863" and "entered the service personally" and three had been drafted and provided substitutes. (Davis Report) The progress of voluntary enlistments was followed closely, as the more men who volunteered the fewer would be drafted or required to hire substitutes. For instance in late September 1864, the *BR* reported that "there is a prospect that the quota of the county will be filled by enlistments. On Tuesday Sweden was twenty-one short of its quota. Clarkson, Parma and Riga are reported to have full quotas…P.S.—We have heard that Sweden now only lacks four of its quota." (9/29/1864)

CONSCRIPTION

By July 1862, the horrors of war had become evident and voluntary enlistments were lagging. Appeals from on high were not sufficiently productive and conscription became necessary. Though it was adopted belatedly and reluctantly and was the object of much controversy, confusion, and dysfunction, conscription played a major role in the Union's recruitment system thereafter.

The reluctance to adopt conscription was based partly on the belief that patriotism required voluntary participation in the war effort. The *BR* expressed that sentiment soon after adoption of the 1862 law: (8/7/1862)

> *The order for a draft created quite an excitement in this community, and has greatly stimulated volunteering. In fact there is a great pressure upon every able bodied man to enlist who has no good reason for remaining at home. The pressure, in the form of public opinion, will compel every individual of the class named, who has any respect for himself, to enlist.*

Congress enacted the first general military conscription law in American history in July 1862. Although this very controversial break with tradition was not implemented, (Geary) it seems, nevertheless, to have inspired patriotic fervor in the village:

> *The President's order for a draft instead of chilling the ardor of the people added fuel to the patriotic fires that were already brilliantly burning. Mechanics have left their workshops and places of labor, farmers have lain down the scythe and the hoe to take up the sword and the rifle, lawyers have discarded Coke and Blackstone for a study of military tactics, and men of all avocations have left them to study and practice the art of war. Who will have the temerity to say that the loyal heart is not true to the best interests of the country? The fires of patriotism are hotly burning throughout the loyal North, and the valiant band now going forth will never return until they have accomplished the labor they have set out to perform. Mark that. The days of the rebellion are numbered, and we believe the numbers are few. (*BR *8/14/1862)*

In anticipation of the draft law, New York State enacted a militia law that grouped area towns and Rochester wards into regimental and company districts. Monroe and Wayne counties constituted a regimental district and its Fourth Company District covered the 7th and 12th Rochester wards and Sweden, Clarkson, and Hamlin. The commander of that district was Captain I.S. Hobbie, "a manufacturer of wooden water pipe" and "a gentleman." (*BR* 6/19/1862)

The conscription machinery was set up in mid-1862. The federal law required all able-bodied male citizens, 18 to 45, to register. Draft quotas were distributed among the states, congressional districts, counties, and towns in proportion to the number of enrolled men. Enlistments after July 2, 1862, were credited to the quotas. The list of exemptions was long, including honorably discharged servicemen and those on active duty, ministers of the gospel, elected officials, government employees, Shakers and Quakers, professors and teachers, canal boat captains, prison employees, physicians, surgeons, and nurses, and "idiots, lunatics, paupers, habitual drunkards, and persons convicted of infamous crimes." (*BR* 8/21/1862)

Because voluntary enlistments met the needs of the Union army in 1862, the draft was not actually put into effect, at least in New York State, until mid-1863. Then the Provost Marshall's office reported that, by then, it had enrolled 196 married and 167 single men in the Town of Sweden, 95 married and 117 single men in Clarkson, and 126 married and 94 single men in Hamlin. (*BR* 7/23/1863) Based on those figures, the 1862 quotas were: Sweden 99, Clarkson 94, and Hamlin 54. (*BR* 7/16/1862)

The law on the draft remained a stick behind the door because the quotas it set were filled, almost entirely, without resort to it. By August 5, 1864, only two men had been conscripted from the Town of Sweden, although the town's quotas had totaled 315 as follows: (Davis report, *BR* 7/28/1864, Geary 81, *U&A* 2/11/1865)

Under the President's calls of July and August 1862 for 600,000 men—125.
Under the draft of 1863—69.
Under the Proclamation of February 1, 1864, for 500,000 men—86.
Under the Provost Marshal General's call of March 14, 1864 for 200,000 men—35

As the war dragged on and mobilization became increasingly difficult, Congress passed in March 1864 the Enrollment Act to create a more effective conscription system run directly by the national government. It established an elaborate administrative structure, including local enrollment boards, headed by federal officers, in 185 Congressional districts. (Geary 73) Under that act, by August 5, 1864, 600 men had been enrolled in the Town of Sweden, 104 names had been drawn, 21 of them passed the medical examination, and 16 paid the $300 commutation fee. (Davis Report)

The effects of that law were felt in Brockport in response to President Lincoln's July 18, 1864, call for another 500,000 troops. The quotas for the Brockport area were: Sweden 94, Clarkson 49, and Hamlin 56. (*BR* 7/28/1864) The quotas could be filled by volunteers, draftees, or substitutes for draftees. If enough volunteers did not come forth, the draft would be used.

This led to close attention to the recruitment effort. Some extraordinary measures had been taken to fill the quotas. For one thing, Canadians were imported. The names of 38 men appear on the STCR with this notation: "These Recruits were obtained at or near Sackets Harbor and Rec'd Town and County Bounty & were credited to the Town of Sweden." They all enlisted in September 1864. As Sackett's Harbor is near the Canadian border, it seems likely that they were Canadians.

Another 46 men are listed with this note: "Could not obtain any other facts in relation to him or the following Recruits except that they were credited to the Town of Sweden." (STCR) For two names the only information given is that they enlisted in Rochester and received no bounties. All the others enlisted in Rochester. Forty-two responded to the July 1864 draft call and received both town and county bounties. The other two enlisted on March 21, 1865, and received only a county bounty. In all 44 cases, they were substitutes and the names of their "principals" are listed with theirs. Many of the most prominent men in the community were "principals."

Finally, 45 names follow this note: "This and the following Recruits were obtained through the firm of C.P. Avery & Co. and credited to the Town of Sweden." (STCR) No residences or enlistment places are given for them. Forty-one of them enlisted on April 5, 1865, and four on April 25 or 26, 1865, after the war had ended. No service unit is indicated for 21 of them, but 24 joined the navy.

The Clarkson Town Clerk's Report of 1865 (CTCR) does not list the names of substitutes, but concludes with a note that, following a vote by a town meeting on August 26, 1864, it raised by taxes $24,280, which was "paid by said town and [to?] Volunteers hired from Canada and elsewhere." Also, in "the Spring of 1865...the sum of $5000 was again raised by volunteer subscriptions to make up the quota." (CTCR) Moreover, the Monroe County Board of Supervisors in December 1864, reported that it had paid bounties to 15 substitutes credited to the Town of Clarkson and 13 credited to the Town of Hamlin, but none to substitutes for the Town of Sweden. (*REE* 12/20/1864) The Hamlin Town Clerk's Report is not available.

Also, the county Board of Supervisors sent "enlisting agents...to go South and enlist negroes for filling the quota of the county." The agents were "remunerated by a fee of $50 for each Negro they enlist and get credited to the county." One of the three agents was Brockporter Dr. L.H. Reynolds. (*BR* 8/4/1864) In the event, enough volunteers had come forward by late September that "Sweden now lacks only four of its quota." (*BR* 9/29/1864)

Another device employed in 1864 to bolster recruitment was the so-called Representative Recruit. A person not liable to be drafted could hire a man to enlist and be recognized for the civic-spirited act with a certificate and identification in the recruit's official records. Although the plan fizzled nationally, eight Clarkson soldiers (but none in the other two towns) were "Representative" upon re-enlistment in 1864. (Geary 133, ROEM)

December 19, 1864, the Provost Marshal General issued another call. The quotas were not distributed to the towns until February 10, 1865. After deducting volunteers already enrolled, the figures for the Brockport area were: Sweden 38, Clarkson 27, and Hamlin 2. (*U&A* 2/11/1865) The draft was scheduled to begin February 15, but was deferred to give the towns more time to recruit volunteers. (*U&A* 2/15/1865) The drawing finally began February 28 at the Provost Marshal's office in Rochester for the congressional district comprised of Monroe and Orleans Counties. Each day, names were drawn for a Rochester ward or a town (or sometimes two of them), beginning with those that had the largest quotas. Each quota was reduced by 25 percent and that figure doubled to get the number of names to be drawn. Thus, Ridgeway, the first town drawn, had a quota of 93, so 140 names were drawn. This allowed for the large number of men who would be rejected for medical or other reasons or would fail to report. (*U&A* 2/28/1865)

The draft proceeded haltingly, because the first draftees had to be examined by physicians from the surgeon general's office before more names could be drawn. Sweden's turn came on March 3. (*U&A* 3/3/1865) The town had 372 enrollees and a raw quota of 50, reduced to 38. So, 76 names were drawn, with the aim of producing 38 soldiers. The names of only six of the 76 appear on my roster. Oscar Chase had served in the 105th NYVI from December 6, 1861, until he was discharged for disability on December 29, 1863. George Smith had served in the 108th NYVI from July 19, 1862, until May 28, 1865. Sylvester Edwards served in the 8th NY Cavalry from October 14, 1862, until discharged for disability on May 13, 1865. (ACWRD; STCR gives different dates) The 105th had been recruited in late 1861 and the 108th in mid-1862. Therefore, those three names must have been drawn for second tours of duty.

By the time the Sweden names were drawn, everyone realized that the war would end soon and that the draft was only a formality. Probably, the Sweden draftees never saw service or joined a unit. The names that the provost marshal drew, other than Chase, Edwards, and Smith, appear on my lists only in postwar connections and may have been recognized as veterans, though they never really served. No names for either Clarkson or Hamlin were ever called, because the war ended.

In sum, the draft had little direct effect on the Brockport area. Although records are incomplete for Clarkson and Hamlin, it seems that only one man from Clarkson and two from Hamlin were actually drafted and entered the service. Two men from Sweden were drafted and entered the service and three were drafted and furnished substitutes under the 1863 draft and no men were drafted under the 1864 draft. (Davis Report) However, the draft probably had very substantial indirect effect, especially after the President's call of July 14, 1864. Before that time, it seems likely that many men volunteered to escape the draft. Thereafter, it was the major stimulus for the substitute system. It worked as it did, in large part, because of the way the conscription system interacted with the bounty system.

The effect of the 1863 draft is suggested by this table giving the results for the Congressional District that included Monroe County: (*BR* 10/1/1863)

Whole number enrolled	2,859
Physically disabled	962
Mentally disabled	13
Only son of widow	94
Aged and infirm	150
Elected officials	23
Fathers of motherless children	31
Fathers and sons in military service	32
Aliens	395
Substitutes	291
Paid commutation	438
Improper enrollment	276
In service	61
Accepted	92
Not reported	406

To summarize, 59.5 percent of those enrolled were exempt for one reason or another, 11.8 percent were improperly enrolled, 25.5 percent obtained substitutes or paid the commutation fee, and 14.2 percent failed to appear. Thus, only 3.2 percent of those enrolled were actually drafted. If the draftees, substitutes, and recruits hired with the commutation fees were all mustered in, the draft had a 28.7 percent return.

The three western towns had a total enrollment of 825, of whom 222 (26.9%) were accepted, pretty close to the average for the Congressional District. The breakdown by town was Sweden 364/104 (28.6%), Clarkson 212/58 (27.4%), Hamlin 249/60 (24.1%). (*BR* 8/13/1863). Those numbers seem to have included substitutes and hired recruits.

BOUNTIES

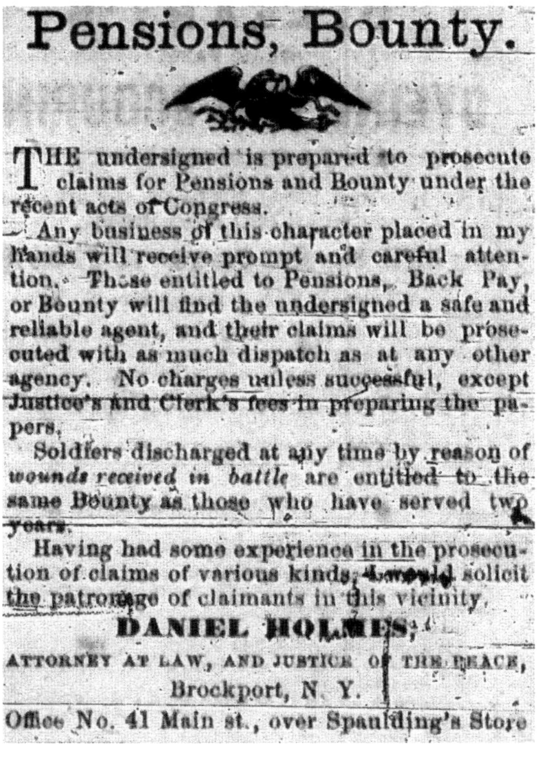

Advertisement in the February 25, 1864 *Brockport Republic* by lawyer Daniel Holmes.

Bounties were the carrots to conscription's stick. The draft was seen as a dishonorable last resort. Bounties were paid only to volunteers, not draftees. Men whose names were called for the draft had two days in which to volunteer and collect the bounties. They could escape the stick by grabbing the carrot. Moreover, their neighbors pressured them to enlist. Communities felt dishonored if they could not fill their quotas with volunteers. Moreover, other soldiers regarded conscripts as inferior. As a result, only six percent of Union soldiers were draftees. (Geary 84)

Enlistment bounties were a long-standing recruitment tool for American and European armies. So, the national government began offering $100 bounties for volunteers, to be paid upon discharge, within a month after Lincoln's first call for volunteers. (Geary 12) This was more an expression of community gratitude than inducement, though, of course, enlistees probably saw it both ways. In late 1863, the amount was increased to $300 for new enlistments and $400 for re-enlistments. (Geary 16)

Those bounties attracted little notice in Brockport, however. The first reference to them in the *BR* did not appear until March 13, 1862, when "Daniel Holmes, Att'y at Law, and Justice of the Peace," advertised that he would represent discharged soldiers, war widows and other heirs in collecting "ONE HUNDRED DOLLARS BOUNTY MONEY" and "arrears of Pay."

NEW YORK STATE

Although the national government provided the framework and the timing of the recruitment system, the states played important roles as well. The actual formation of the military units was almost entirely a matter for the states. Though the states did not participate in the commutation system and did not help to wield the "stick" of the draft system, they did add "carrots" to the bounty system.

The Regular United States Army at the outbreak of the Civil War was composed of only 16,367 officers and enlisted men and many of them resigned to join the Confederacy. (Faust) Therefore, the Union Army was overwhelmingly formed of regiments mobilized by the states in response to calls by the national government. The practice for organizing those units was for prominent members of each community to secure officer commissions from the state government, often through political influence and, then, to recruit the appropriate number of soldiers to fill whatever size units they had been commissioned to command. Typically, an important politician would be commissioned a colonel and undertake to recruit a regiment of about 1,000 men from a congressional district or large county. He would, then, "issue permits" to lower-ranking leaders. They conferred captains' and lieutenants' commissions and mandates to muster companies of about 100 men each at the local level.

New York State entered the bounty business in July 1862 in response to the Congressional enactment of a conscription law. To draft an army was unpopular. Monetary inducements might attract enough recruits that the draft would not be needed. Therefore, Governor Morgan took it upon himself, without summoning the legislature, to "offer a State Bounty of $50 for each recruit,...trusting to the next Legislature to legalize and endorse his action."

The legislature confirmed his action in September, but rescinded its approval when enlistments exceeded the state's quota. However, in February 1863 it re-confirmed Morgan's action and in April 1863 passed a law providing $150 re-enlistment bounties and $75 for first enlistments. (Phisterer 35, 41)

In the wake of Morgan's 1862 action, the *BR* reported that:

> *Soldiers were never offered more liberal pay than those who enlist in the volunteer force. The private receives his regular pay of $13 per month, $100 bounty from the General Government, and those from this State will now receive a special bounty of $50 under the arrangement just decided upon by Gov. Morgan. Besides this, $2 is given for every volunteer...This makes the aggregate pay of a private as follows per year:*
>
> *Regular monthly pay......$157.00*
> *Government bounty......$100.00*
> *Special State bounty.......$50.00*
> *Enlistment pay.............$2.00*
> *Total for one year..........$309.00*
>
> *This gives, besides rations, clothing, etc., monthly wages of $25.75. In all probability if the enlistments are kept up briskly, the war will end within the year. As a pecuniary matter merely, can one man in ten do better than to enlist?* (BR *7/31/1862)*

In February 1865, as the war was drawing to a close, the state legislature raised the amounts to $250 for drafted men, $300 for one-year new enlistments, $400 for two-year hitches, and $600 for three-year hitches. However, administrative problems prevented its implementation until the war had ended. That act also guaranteed that the state would reimburse localities for their expenditures on bounties. (Phisterer 54, 55) Of course, the state levied on the counties the taxes to pay the bounties. In 1863, that amounted to $50,920 for Monroe County. (*BR* 10/15/1863)

MONROE COUNTY

At the time Morgan acted, Monroe County's Board of Supervisors voted to raise $100,000 for bounties, in case the state legislature did not support

Morgan. (*BR* 7/17/1862) On August 19, it offered $100 bounties on top of the federal and state amounts. (B. Bennett 31) In December 1863, It raised the amount to $300 and issued $373,000 worth of bonds to pay for them. The bonds were to be repaid with three annual special property tax assessments. (*BR* 12/4/1863, 12/10/1863, 12/31/1863) At the same time, it authorized the payment of $300 bounties to substitutes of drafted men to be paid from a $375,000 bond issue. (*BR* 12/24/1863) One hundred dollars was to be paid to each soldier upon being mustered into service and the balance before he left the state for the war zone. (*BR* 12/10/1863) By July 1864, it was paying bounties of $400 to substitutes, but still paying local volunteers $300. By March 1865, the county raised the amount for substitutes to $600 and was paying some hired volunteers $400 and others $600, but the bounties for local volunteers remained $300. (STCR)

Local recruits received county bounties in these amounts: two of $50, 32 of $100, one of $200, and 21 of $300. This means that 56 (23.6%) of the 237 local recruits in the STCR received county bounties. So, the county spent $9,800 on Sweden recruits.

Forty-five substitutes for Town of Sweden residents received county bounties of $400 each and two substitutes got $600 each for a total of $19,200. Recruits from outside the area, mainly, apparently, from Canada received county bounties in the following amounts: one of $200, 39 of $300, 21 of $400, and 23 of $600 each for a total of $34,100.

In sum, then, the county spent $9,800 on 56 Sweden recruits, $19,200 on 47 substitutes for Sweden draftees, and $34,100 on 45 hired recruits for a total of $63,100. The town spent $26,927 on 44 local recruits, $26,575 on 45 substitutes, and $18,291 on thirty hired recruits for a total of $71,793. The combined totals spent by the two jurisdictions for the Town of Sweden was $134,893,

Looking at the system from the point of view of the individual soldier, the total bounties from the county and town ranged from $50 (2 local recruits) to $1,000 (41 substitutes). Other amounts received by local recruits were $100 (31), $200 (1), $300 (13), and $915–919 (5). Other amounts for substitutes were $900 (2) and $925 (2). Four of the hired outsiders received $300 total, 21 drew $400, 26 got $600, and the remaining 35 received between $914 and $919. In addition, almost all recruits were paid bounties of $50 by the state and $100 by the federal government. The average annual wage for a common day laborer at that time was about $200 and for a skilled worker was about $300. So, the total bounties for most of the substitutes and hired outsiders were the equivalent of four to six years' earnings.

TOWN BOARDS

The local municipalities also paid bounties, though they were slower to act. The village government never did offer bounties and the Town of Sweden was quite reluctant. In May 1862, the Town Board resolved that "in the judgement of this board they have no legal right to impose a tax upon the taxable inhabitants of the Town for the purpose of paying Three hundred dollars to each individual that may be drafted." (Minutes, May 4, 1863)

However, enactment of the Enrollment Act and the President's call of July 18, 1864, for another 500,000 men effected a change in heart by the Town. Twenty-six leading Brockporters petitioned for a special Town Meeting "for the purpose of taking into consideration and devising means for the relief of such persons as may be drafted or volunteer into the military service of the United States." That meeting "of the electors and legal voters of the Town of Sweden" was held on August 31, 1864. Five men (Jerome Fuller, Robert Staples, F.P. Root, Asa Rowe, and Samuel H. Davis) drafted two resolutions and presented them to the Town Meeting. They requested that the town raise by taxes enough money to pay $500 to each volunteer, draftee or substitute who joined the military or naval service and was credited toward the quota of the Town of Sweden. An amendment by the Town Meeting raised the amount to $600. Both motions were adopted. (Minutes)

That action authorized the Town to issue to 96 men "scrip" of values ranging from $10 to $600. The most common amount was $600 (71). There was one bounty of $10 and one of $200. The other 23 ranged between $400 and $575. The total was $54,125—this in a town that had an annual budget that averaged less than $1,250. Thus, the appropriation was 43.3 times the average town budget.

Only nine local recruits (3.8%) received Town bounties, in amounts between $615 and $619, for a total of $5,551. All of them also received county bounties. Eight of those local recruits were embedded in the STCR with the hired recruits, as though they also were hired, though they had local addresses. Seven of the bounty recipients enlisted in August 1864, one in August 1862, and one in September 1865, five months after Appomattox.

Two substitutes for Sweden residents received town bounties of $500, three drew $525 each, and forty got $600 each for a total of $26,575. Hired recruits from outside the area received town bounties in the following amounts: one of $400, one of $600, and 28 of $614–19 for a total of $18,291.

Somewhat different figures emerge from the STCR, which lists the town and county bounties paid to each man.

TOWN BOUNTIES

AMOUNT	# PAID TO LOCAL	# PAID TO SUBSTITUTES	# PAID TO HIRED	# PAID TOTAL VOLUNTEERS	AMOUNT PAID TOTAL VOLUNTEERS
$400	1	0	1	2	$800
$500	0	2	0	2	1,000
$525	0	2	0	2	1,050
$600	1	40	1	42	25,200
$614–19	42	0	28	70	43,218
Totals	44	44	30	118	71,268

COUNTY BOUNTIES

AMOUNT	# PAID TO LOCAL	# PAID TO SUBSTITUTES	# PAID TO HIRED	# PAID TOTAL VOLUNTEERS	AMOUNT PAID TOTAL VOLUNTEERS
$50	2	0	0	2	$100
$100	32	0	0	32	3,200
$200	1	0	1	2	400
$300	21	0	39	60	18,000
$400	0	45	21	66	26,400
$600	0	2	23	25	15,000
Totals	56	47	84	187	63,100

When the Town and County bounties for each man are added together, this is the result:

AMOUNT	# PAID TO LOCAL	# PAID TO SUBSTITUTES	# PAID TO HIRED	# PAID TOTAL VOLUNTEERS	AMOUNT PAID TOTAL VOLUNTEERS
$50	2	0	0	2	$100
$100	31	0	0	31	3,100
$200	1	0	0	1	200
$300	18	0	4	22	6,600
$400	0	0	21	21	8,400
$600	0	0	26	26	15,600
$900–25	9	4	35	48	44,011
$1,000	0	41	0	41	41,000
Totals	61	45	86	192	119,011

The bounties were to be paid to 41 volunteers and 48 substitutes. In another five cases, the notation said "cash borrowed," presumably to pay a substitute, and two cases were unspecified. The names of neither of the men whose "capacity" was unspecified appear in my list of Union army veterans from the Brockport area, so they must have been substitutes. Four of the five "cash borrowed" men are absent from my list. A "George L. Smith" is identified as "cash borrowed" and a "George Smith" served in the 108th NY Volunteer Infantry from Brockport, but I cannot tell if they are the same person. In any case, it seems that more than half the bounties were paid to substitutes. Among the men who hired substitutes were some of the most prominent civic leaders. They included former Town Supervisors Reuben Stickney and Robert Staples; leading industrialists Byron Huntley, Franklin F. Capen, and George H. Allen; lawyers Daniel Holmes and Horace J. Thomas; leading merchants the three Benedict brothers; and banker John R. Kingsbury.

Clarkson took no action on bounties until mid-1864. On August 16, "a town meeting…pretty thoroughly discussed…what action should be taken in regard to the draft" (*BR* 8/18/1864) and an official special town meeting on August 26, authorized the Town Board to "raise by tax upon said town the sum of $500 to pay to each volunteer or drafted man upon the Call of the President…which required in order to fill the quota of said town the sum of $24,280.00 which was raised by tax and paid by said town and Volunteers hired from Canada and elsewhere." In response to another Call by the President in the spring of 1865, "$5,000 was again raised by volunteer subscription to make up the quota." (CTCR) Unlike the STCR, the CTRC does not list any bounties, either town or county, paid to local residents and does not include any substitutes or "Volunteers hired from Canada or elsewhere."

Hamlin held a town meeting in August 1863 to consider offering $300 bounties but took no action. A year later, August 13, 1864, a "somewhat informal" town meeting "to ascertain the will of the electors relative to the draft" agreed "that there be raised by a tax upon the property of the town a sum sufficient to pay each substitute or drafted person that enters the military service to the credit of the quota of the town $600 for three years or $400 for one year." (*BR* 8/18/1864) A week later, an official special town meeting "in issuance of a call made by the Town Clerk (he having previously been notified by twelve Freeholders of said Town to make such call)" confirmed that decision, 184-81, but voted to raise the money by "town bonds," rather than a property tax. (Mary Smith, *BR* 8/25/1864) No record of the disbursement of those funds has survived.

Local level in the Brockport area meant a recruitment base in the village, drawing on the Towns of Sweden, Clarkson, and Hamlin with a sprinkling of recruits from other neighboring towns. An official list of Town of Sweden men "subject to do military duty" contained 342 names. For purposes of the draft, they were divided into two classes: 18–30 years of age and those aged 30–45. (*BR* 7/3/1862)

Commutation Fees

A fourth element in the national recruitment system—after volunteerism, bounties, and conscription—was the commutation fee. The Enrollment Act of 1863 provided that any draftee could buy exemption by paying a $300 fee to the government. Although this provision had precedent in earlier militia acts and was used by other countries, it was highly criticized as favoring the wealthy. It was widely used by draftees. Half of those who were found to be eligible for service bought their way out. (Faust) It was rescinded in July 1864.

The recruitment system was complex and cumbersome. It produced many anomalies. For instance, some men enlisted, collected their bounties, and deserted, only to enlist again in another place and repeat the cycle. One Brockporter enlisted and deserted three times, presumably collecting his bounties en route. Also, some provisions of the law were never implemented and others proved ineffective. The draft, bounties, and substitutes system was criticized widely at the time and by historians since then as favoring the wealthy. However, if the local municipalities were as forthcoming with their tax money as were Sweden and Clarkson they pretty much leveled the playing field. The next chapter will examine how the system actually worked in the Brockport area in terms of the resulting recruitment of soldiers.

Chapter 3

Brockport Mobilizes

War Meetings

The most obvious recruitment means in the Brockport area was the "War Meeting," the first of which was described in detail previously (pages 20–22). Besides their primary purpose of encouraging military-age men to enlist in the armed forces, they also fired up the war spirit in the community. They resembled the religious "revival meetings" that were a popular feature of small-town American life at that time. During the period ending in October 1864 for which issues of the *BR* exist, at least 31 War Meetings were held in 38 months.

Most War Meetings were held in churches. Other venues included the Concert Hall, the Village Hall, and the corner of Market and Main Streets. Similar meetings were held in Sweden outside Brockport and in Clarkson, and Hamlin. For instance, four meetings were held in three weeks in Hamlin in July 1862. Occasionally, also, Brockporters went as a group to War Meetings elsewhere. Thus, "about one hundred persons" went from Brockport to an assembly in Adams Basin in July 1862. (*BR* 7/31/1862)

The meeting would begin with exhortatory orations, filled with patriotic appeals. It was almost essential that there be prayers and that clergymen be among the speakers. Martial music and hymns were also included. At least once, the meeting took the guise of a "Soldiers Ball." (*BR* 1/13/1864, 1/17/1864) Many War Meetings concluded with a ritual call for volunteers, usually accompanied by the hymn "Just As I Am," much like the call for salvation that ended the typical revival meeting.

Brockport's second War Meeting was held on August 22, 1861, in the Methodist church, "without any general notice." (*BR* 8/29/1861) Jerome Fuller gave "an address upon the war," preceded by a prayer and choir singing. The chairman of the meeting and principal orator, Elias B. Holmes, spoke for two hours. He argued that the southern rebellion was unjustified and all good citizens must support the war effort. Especially, he "said it was the duty of every man to enlist in the cause of his country who was so situated to do it without a great sacrifice of business responsibilities." (Presumably, that excluded the speaker, a prominent businessman. Also, business concerns seemed to prevail over family matters.) He concluded by reporting on his five-week visit to Washington observing some 75,000 troops, including the 13th NY Volunteer Infantry with its Brockport company. He assured his listeners that, though "some of its soldiers were poorly clad," they were "well provided with food."

A third War Meeting on September 8 in the Presbyterian church heard principal speaker Eugene P. Fuller recruit for his regiment. (*BR* 9/12/1861) At a September 19 meeting, Colonel Samuel J. Crooks and Fuller recruited men for a company being raised by George Guenther that would be part of Colonel Crooks's 8th New York Cavalry regiment. (*BR* 9/26/1861) A November meeting filled "Concert Hall to its utmost capacity" to hear appeals on behalf of "the Irish Regiment now being organized in Western New York." Elias B. Holmes, five clergymen, and a Brockport Collegiate Institute professor spoke. The Reverend Daniel Moore, "the originator of the Irish Regiment...had been authorized...to raise an Irish Regiment, and...had issued twelve permits to persons to raise companies." Captain Thomas G. Murphy had opened a recruiting office in the village and "strongly intimated that when they had aided in successfully subduing the great rebellion, they would be well qualified to lend a helping hand in freeing their mother isle from its subjugated position." (*BR* 11/14/1861) A second meeting to benefit the Guenther company met in the Baptist church a month later. (*BR* 12/12/1861)

In July 1862, Lincoln's call for another 300,000 men precipitated another War Meeting. Elias B. Holmes and Dr. Davis Carpenter addressed "the large though not crowded" assembly in the Baptist church. Carpenter had served in Congress as a Whig, 1853–55, was 61 years old when the war broke out, and was another of Hiel Brockway's many sons-in-law. He was a physician and senior partner in a drugstore and had held numerous village offices. Jerome Fuller and Kimball also spoke. (*BR* 7/17/1862) Carpenter and Fuller got into an argument, the former advocating abolition and the latter protesting that slavery was irrelevant to the struggle. The dispute "disgusted" the "better part of the audience."

Holmes reported that the towns of Sweden, Clarkson, and Hamlin were required to furnish a company toward the county's quota of 1,000 men. The meeting adopted unanimously five resolutions, urging the state legislature and the Board of Supervisors to raise by taxation the money required to support those troops, promising to pay their share in "treasure" and "volunteers," and vowing to attend a mass War Meeting in Rochester the following Tuesday. Several prominent Brockporters led the Rochester meeting. Similar meetings were held that week in Hamlin and Adams Basin.

The War Meetings were sometimes quite entertaining, with martial music and fancy dress drills by military units. For instance, in July 1862, the Rochester Light Guard Zouaves and Perkins's Cornet Band came from Rochester by special train to perform at a meeting. "The Zouaves went through the evolutions in a manner highly creditable to their military knowledge and very pleasing to the large concourse of people drawn together by the novelty and the music." (*BR* 7/31/1862)

Besides importing from Rochester the Perkins's Cornet Band and from Bergen its Brass Band, Brockport formed its own "martial band" and Glee Club. (*BR* 8/7/1862, 8/14/1862) Attendance was encouraged on the grounds that "all who participate will have a fine time." (*BR* 1/17/1864)

The number of men who responded to the call for volunteers varied greatly. They were reported at various meetings as a "number" (*BR* 11/14/1861), "some recruits" (*BR* 11/21/1861), "twenty three" (*BR* 8/14/1862), and 24, (*BR* 4/25/1861) At some meetings, no specific recruitment effort was made. (*BR* 8/21/1861) Editor Beach justified those meetings:

> *The good results of calling the people together and laying before them facts pertinent to the welfare of our country are not always immediately apparent, but the good seed sown springs forth and bears fruit in due time. Often have war meetings been held when no recruits were obtained; but the spirit of patriotism was set to work, and perhaps in one, two, three days or a week thereafter the effects of the meetings are shown in the enlistment of patriotic young men. (*BR *7/31/1862)*

The substance of the War Meetings consisted almost entirely of appeals to patriotism. The North was defending the Union, "our great nation," the Constitution, Old Glory, democracy, our honor, our freedom, etc., against traitors and ingrates. Historical figures and events were invoked:

Washington, Jefferson, Jackson, the American Revolution, etc. Secession was illegal and unconstitutional. If the North lost the war, its freedoms would be destroyed and it would be ruled by "tyrants." Slavery was rarely mentioned. (*BR* 4/25/1861, 8/29/1861, 11/14/1861, 11/21/1861, 12/12/1861, 7/17/1862, 7/24/1862, 7/31/1862, 8/7/1862, 8/14/1862, 8/21/1862, 8/28/1861, 3/12/1863, 3/19/1863, 11/26/1863)

Most of the Clarkson and Hamlin War Meetings were precipitated by President Lincoln's call for 500,000 troops in July 1862. The earliest such assemblies reported in the *BR* were "large gathering(s)" held in Clarkson's Presbyterian church on November 16 and 21, 1861. The "Holley martial band" accompanied the speechifying on the 16th. (*BR* 11/21/1861 11/28/1861) Another "very large" Clarkson meeting was held on July 19, 1862, in a schoolhouse in the eastern part of the town. (*BR* 7/24/1862) A week later "a large gathering of the citizens of Clarkson on the green in front of the Presbyterian church…was called to aid recruiting in Captain Fuller's company." (*BR* 8/7/1862)

The first Hamlin meetings met in July and August 1862. At one "Captain Fuller got three recruits." Another was held for "the benefit of Capt. Pond's company" in Simmons Hill Baptist Church and a third for Captain Starks's company at Hamlin Center. Nine recruits were obtained at each of the latter two meetings. (*BR* 7/17/1862 7/24/1862 7/31/1862 8/14/1862)

Other Recruitment Efforts

The War Meetings were not the only recruitment efforts. Recruitment agents and their offices were a common feature of Brockport life. Often, the prospective officers of the unit being recruited served as the recruitment agents. For companies being recruited in Brockport, they tended to be local men. Frequently, however, agents came from Rochester to recruit soldiers for units based elsewhere.

Prominent members of the community supported those efforts. Elias B. Holmes was reported to be making "it his every day business to impress upon men a belief of their duty to their country" rendering "efficient aid to all persons engaged in the recruiting business." (*BR* 9/5/1861)

Carpenter, Thomas Cornes, and Henry W. Seymour also played leading roles in the recruitment efforts. Cornes was English by birth, a butcher by trade, and a large real estate owner. He was President of the Village

Board in 1858, 1860, 1864, and 1865 and a trustee in 1857 and 1861. Conspicuously absent from the recruitment efforts were William E. Seymour and Dayton S. Morgan, the partners in the foundry that had manufactured the first McCormick reapers and that remained Brockport's largest employer.

BROCKPORT'S COMPANIES

Eight companies were recruited in the Brockport area: Company K of the 13th NYVI, Company H of the 8th NY Cavalry, Company B of the 24th NY Light Artillery, Company F of the 105th NYVI, Company H of the 108th NYVI, Company M of the 3rd NY Cavalry, Company A of the 140th NYVI, and Company C of the 22nd NY Cavalry. (*BR* and Marcotte 20) In addition, at least 18 recruitment agents for other regiments came to the village in search of men. Also, on at least one occasion, "2 or 3 ladies" volunteered as nurses. (*BR* 4/25/1861)

Captain George Henry Barry, co-organizer of Company H, 8th New York Cavalry, wounded at Culpeper, Virginia. *Photo courtesy of New York State Military Museum © Historical Data Systems, Inc.*

After the Union disaster at the First Battle of Bull Run (July 16–21, 1861) had doused the initial burst of optimism, President Lincoln and Congress responded by calling for additional volunteers. New York's governor called for 25,000 men. (Phisterer 57) This led to a veritable frenzy of recruiting activity in Brockport.

From late September until mid-December—barely two and a half months—the village saw at least eight organized recruiting drives. George Guenther, a native of England, recruited a company for the Colonel Sam J. Crooks 8th New York Cavalry and was slated to be its Captain with Brockporter Charles Warren as First Lieutenant. Guenther had joined the 13th as a private, but had been discharged for ill health. (*BR* 8/29/1861, 10/24/1861) He had returned to Brockport in late August and, by October 24, had recruited forty men and the unit was organized. Captain George H. Barry and Quartermaster Frederic H. Barry operated a recruiting office for another company in the same regiment, which was "accepted and sworn into service" with 32 men by the same date. (*BR* 9/26/1861, 10/3/1861, 10/24/1861) The two proto-companies merged as Company H. By late November, the 8th Cavalry was fully formed and camped in Washington, D.C. (*BR* 11/28/1861)

Other recruitment efforts in Brockport during that autumn included a recruiting advertisement for the "Ira Harris Guards Cavalry Regiment" (*BR* 9/26/1861), the enlistment of "2–3 men" for the United States Light Cavalry 3rd Regiment. (*BR* 8/22/1861), and recruiting offices of "Lieut. Bassett…for Col. Stewart's regiment of engineers and mechanics," (*BR* 9/5/1861, 9/26/1861), Lieutenant W.W. Tice for "the artillery service," (*BR* 10/24/1861) Captain Benjamin Maxon and Lieutenant S.B. Northrup for a company in Col. J.M. Fuller's regiment, (*BR* 11/14/1861) and Captain Thomas G. Murphy for an "Irish Regiment." (*BR* 11/14/1861)

A month later, Murphy had signed up "about 20" recruits and Maxon had "nearly 40." (*BR* 12/12/1861) By the end of February 1862, Abram Moore had become captain of the Maxon recruits, now numbering "over 100 men," and forming Company G (later F) of the 105th NYVI, and in a staging camp at Leroy. The seven companies in the regiment had 450 men. (*BR* 1/30/1862, 4/3/1862, *BR* 2/27/1862) In March 1862, Murphy's "Irish Regiment" was "consolidated with Colonel Fuller's regiment" under Fuller's command, despite his earlier expressed opposition to the merger. (*BR* 2/6/1862, 3/20/1862)

After that long spurt of recruitment activity, nothing further of note occurred until the summer of 1862, precipitated by two more calls from the President. The first, on July 1, asked for 300,000 volunteers for three-year enlistments. The second, a month later, summoned 300,000 reserve militia for nine-month terms. The New York State share of each of those calls was 59,705 and Monroe County's was 1,556. However, the state enlisted 78,004 in the first enrollment and 1,781 voluntarily responded to the second call. So no draft took place. (Phisterer I: 57, B. Bennett 23) The Brockport area quotas for the two calls were Sweden 125, Clarkson 64, and Hamlin 76. (*BR* 8/21/1862)

Those calls precipitated another flurry of recruitment activity in the village. From late June until late August, no fewer than nine companies recruited

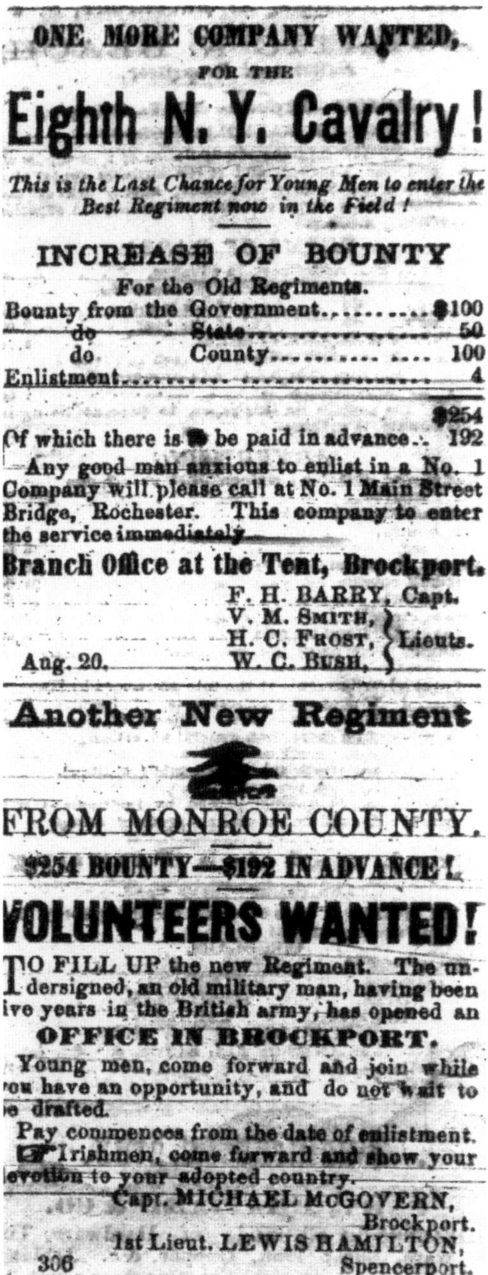

ONE MORE COMPANY WANTED,
FOR THE
Eighth N. Y. Cavalry!
This is the Last Chance for Young Men to enter the Best Regiment now in the Field!

INCREASE OF BOUNTY
For the Old Regiments.

Bounty from the Government	$100
do State	50
do County	100
Enlistment	4
	$254

Of which there is to be paid in advance .. 192

Any good man anxious to enlist in a No. 1 Company will please call at No. 1 Main Street Bridge, Rochester. This company to enter the service immediately.

Branch Office at the Tent, Brockport.
F. H. BARRY, Capt.
V. M. SMITH,
H. C. FROST, Lieuts.
Aug. 20. W. C. BUSH,

Another New Regiment
FROM MONROE COUNTY.
$254 BOUNTY—$192 IN ADVANCE!
VOLUNTEERS WANTED!

TO FILL UP the new Regiment. The undersigned, an old military man, having been five years in the British army, has opened an
OFFICE IN BROCKPORT.
Young men, come forward and join while you have an opportunity, and do not wait to be drafted.
Pay commences from the date of enlistment.
Irishmen, come forward and show your devotion to your adopted country.
Capt. MICHAEL McGOVERN, Brockport.
1st Lieut. LEWIS HAMILTON, Spencerport.
306

Two recruitment advertisements in the February 21, 1862 *Brockport Republic*.

in Brockport. (*BR* 8/7/1862) Eugene P. Fuller, now a captain, returned to the village in late June to enlist a company for the 108th New York Volunteer Infantry. (6/26/1862) By late July, it had filled up with 101 recruits and left for Washington. (*BR* 7/31/1862) Also in July, a Rochester company "denominated the New York Reserve" solicited Brockporters. (*BR* 7/10/1862) Captain F.E. Pierce recruited eighty men for a company in "the Monroe County Regiment," attending War Meetings in Kendall Mills and Sweden Center, as well as Brockport. (*BR* 7/31/1862, 8/7/1862) The *BR* (8/21/1862) carried advertisements for Captain F.H. Barry's 8th New York Cavalry and for Captain Michael McGovern of Brockport and 1st Lieut. Lewis Hamilton of Spencerport who were recruiting for "Another New Regiment From Monroe County." A week later, Barry had enlisted "40–50" men and McGovern 20–30. (*BR* 8/28/1862). Finally, Captain Abijah Gray recruited for his "sharpshooters company" and a War Meeting was held "to induce enlistments in Captain Barnes' company, of Rochester." (*BR* 8/14/1862, 8/21/1862, 8/28/1862)

In early August 1862, Captain Milo L. Starks began recruiting another "Brockport" infantry company, using the law office of Jonah Durward Decker, who became the unit's second lieutenant. Starks was a single, 26-year-old Sweden farmer. He was tall and dark "with an intimidating appearance." His father, Israel, was a Baptist deacon. (B. Bennett 39, *BR* 8/7/1862)

Starks's company was supposed to have joined the 108th NYVI, but that regiment had filled up. Therefore, it became Company A of the 140th NYVI, Brockport's most distinguished Civil War unit. A series of War Meetings promoted his company. An assembly at the Presbyterian church in Brockport signed up 23 men, (*BR* 8/14/1862) "a large gathering of the patriotic farmers at the West Sweden Baptist Church" produced 14 recruits and $100 to aid further recruiting, (*BR* 8/14/1862) and a "war picnic" on F.P. Root's farm in Sweden, accompanied by vocalists, the Brockport Glee Club, the Martial Band, the Bergen Brass Band, and numerous speeches produced "Fifteen first rate men," bringing Starks's total to 85. (*BR* 8/14/1862) By August 21, his company had filled up and left for Rochester. The composition of the company by rank and residence was:

RESIDENCE	OFFICERS	NON-COMS	PRIVATES	TOTAL
Sweden	1 (33.3%)	3 (18.8%)	16 (20.0%)	20 (20.2%)
Dutchess County	1 (33.3%)	—	—	1 (1.0%)
Clarkson	1 (33.3%)	7 (43.8%)	30 (37.5%)	38 (38.4%)
Brockport	—	2 (12.5%)	16* (20.0%)	18 (18.2%)
Ogden	—	2 (12.5%)	—	2 (2.0%)
Rochester	—	1 (6.3%)	1 (1.3%)	2 (2.0%)
Hamlin	—	1 (6.3%)	7 (8.8%)	8 (8.1%)
Fairport	—	—	1 (1.3%)	1 (1.0%)
Clarendon	—	—	1 (1.3%)	1 (1.0%)
Unknown	—	—	8 (8.8%)	8 (8.1%)
	3	16	80	99

*Joseph A. Perry "Reported to have cut off one of his toes for the purpose of escaping military duty, and finally fled to Canada. He got his bounty." (*BR* 9/25/1862) If he is subtracted from the Brockport count, it amounts to only 17.3% of the total.

Thus, less than one-fifth of the "Brockport company," including none of the officers and only two of the 16 non-coms, were village residents and the largest group, by far, was from Clarkson.

Brian Bennett has provided birthplace information on the 140th from the companies' descriptive books. It shows that Company A had, by far, the largest numbers of American-born, New York State–born, and Monroe County–born. Here is his table, in percentages:

BIRTHPLACE	COMPANIES									
	A	B	C	D	E	F	G	H	I	K
United States	85	10	38	54	59	46	33	52	68	33
New York State	80	8	34	4	16	27	49	28		
Monroe County	57	6	18	35	20	32	13	20	41	25

By the time the 140th was formed, the horrors of war had become fully evident. The likely consequences of so many young men bound for the bloody battlefields must have been realized by their neighbors. Therefore, the royal sendoff given by the villagers is quite understandable.

> *The departure of Captain Milo L. Starks' company from this village for Rochester took place yesterday with great éclat. Capt. Starks company for high educational attainments and excellent morals will not be excelled by*

Captain Milo L. Starks, commander, Company A, 140th NYVI, later major on the field staff, four wounds at Gettysburg, killed at Laurel Hill. *Provided by Ashley Allen.*

> *any body of men in the field, be they from where they may. The company left by the 9:45 morning train. About an hour before the time of departure the fire bell was rung for the firemen to assemble, they volunteering to do escort service. The firemen soon assembled, and being headed by the always present martial band marched to the Concert Hall where Capt. Starks' company was in waiting. The firemen and company then marched up Main to Market St., where all formed into lines and were ambrotyped by W.H. Fuller, the popular artist. A procession was then formed, the martial band in front, followed respectively by the firemen, Capt. Starks' company, citizens on foot and in carriages. Besides the persons in line, the sidewalks were crowded by pedestrians and the street was full of teams. The depot was soon reached and the throng* [estimated at one to two thousand] *filled the long platforms in front of the passenger and freight depots and the space between them. Capt.* [Starks's] *company after being marched in line along the railroad tracks between the buildings, was permitted to break ranks, and for about half an hour received warm tokens and expressions of love and friendship. Many of the partings and farewells were very effective, and the whole scene was one calculated to beget many solemn emotions. The train came, and the soldiers were marched on board. As the train passed along, the soldiers cheered from the cars and the people responded heartily. (*BR *8/28/1862)*

Their departure from the village did not end the festivities. On September 17, as the troops were preparing to leave Rochester, Brockporters traveled to the city to honor their heroes with a luncheon that was "laden with all the luxuries of the season." The Reverend P.J. Williams, principal of the Brockport Collegiate Institute, delivered a "short but eloquent and soul-stirring speech" and entrusted "an elegant sword and a splendid sash and revolver…to the bravery and honor of Capt. Starks." Starks responded "in words of deep feeling, saying that his life was a stake laid down for the safety of the Republic, and that should it be swept off in the grand game, he knew that those whom he left behind would feel proud that he died in his country's cause." Then two young ladies of the village presented gifts of oiled silk nightcaps to every member of the company and the "men acknowledged the gift in three hearty cheers for the fair donors." (*RDA* 9/18/1862 per Brian Bennett)

The village's sendoff of Company K was the more poignant for it having seen off in similar fashion Captain Nathan P. Pond's Company M for the 3rd New York Cavalry regiment just two days earlier. The *BR* had reported on August 7 that Pond had gone to Albany in search of "a captain's commission for the purpose of raising a cavalry company." Yet, by August 25, his unit was completely formed with 105 members and on its way to Rochester. Its composition by residence was:

RESIDENCE	OFFICERS	NON-COMS	PRIVATES	TOTALS
Brockport	2 (50.0%)	3 (20.0%)	28 (32.6%)	33 (31.4%)
Rochester	2 (50.0%)	1 (6.7%)	—	3 (2.9%)
Miscellaneous*	—	7 (46.7%)	24 (27.9%)	31 (29.5%)
Hamlin	—	—	17 (19.8%)	17 (16.2%)
Sweden	—	1 (6.7%)	6 (7.0%)	7 (6.7%)
Ogden	—	2 (13.3%)	5 (5.8%)	7 (6.7%)
Clarkson	—	—	4 (4.7%)	4 (3.8%)
Parma	—	1 (6.7%)	—	1 (0.9%)
Kendall	—	—	1 (1.2%)	1 (0.9%)
Knowlesville	—	—	1 (1.2%)	1 (0.9%)
	4	15	86	105

* The *BR* identified this category as "Rochester or some of the eastern towns in the county." (9/4/1862)

Thus, within 48 hours, 145 men from the three towns plus 11 from contiguous towns left Brockport, bound for the bloodiest war in our history. In contrast to the Starks company, Brockporters were much the most numerous group in Pond's company. Clarkson and Sweden had very few members among the cavalrymen. Add to them the men who had left with the Fuller company less than a month earlier and those who enlisted in the Pierce, Barry, and McGovern companies by August 28. The *BR* did not publish the residences of the men in those four companies, but if their recruits from the three towns comprised the same portion of their companies as of the other two, the total number of Brockporters who left for the front or made the commitment to do so in the month ending August 28 must have been 350–400. Even that number is probably incomplete, as they do not take into account Brockporters who enlisted in other companies, including the New York Reserve and the Gray and Barnes units, during that month. Given the departures that had preceded them, the impact on the community can be well imagined.

The *BR* reported no further recruiting efforts in Brockport during the remainder of 1862. However, Brockporters continued to recruit. In December, Lieutenant Ira Holmes, a village banker in Captain Pond's Company M of the 3rd New York Cavalry Regiment, returned to western New York to recruit men for his regiment and met with "excellent success." He had offices in Rochester and Buffalo, but not, apparently, in his hometown. He enlisted 85 men in six weeks, but 15 of them deserted before being mustered in. His efforts earned him promotion to captain and he set sail for North Carolina on March 11 with the remaining seventy men (*BR* 1/1/1863, 2/12/1862, 3/12/1863)

Also, Brockporter Captain William Henry Joslyn's office in the village in April, gave "all persons desirous of avoiding the draft an opportunity to do so in the easiest branch of the military service." (*BR* 4/2/1863) Joslyn was recruiting Company H of the 21st New York Cavalry. Only ten Brockporters joined that unit.

Not until November 1863 was another company recruited in Brockport. Captain Franklin Edwards enlisted men for Company C of Colonel Samuel J. Crooks's 22nd New York Cavalry. This was Colonel Crooks's second regiment. His command of the 8th New York Cavalry had been so disastrous that he had been forced to resign. Yet, he was given a second chance with the 22nd. (Marcotte 85–85, 188–89) The *BR* later alleged that Crooks's second effort "had the opposition of the Enrolling Board, a portion of the city press, and many prominent citizens." (*BR* 3/10/1864)

Apparently, Crooks was a better recruiter than commander. By January 1864, he had raised 900 men. (*BR* 1/7/1864) Franklin Edwards, the prospective captain of the Brockport company had earlier been rejected from the 13th NYVI on medical grounds. One of his comrades in that unit reported: (Sphinx in *BR* 9/23/1861) "Poor fellow! he wanted to go so bad that he cried nearly all day afterwards, and wanted someone to assume his name, and go before the Inspector and be examined. Let it be published that Franklin D. Edwards is a brave man, and would have made a good soldier, had it not been for this defect." His defect had disappeared or it did not matter for an officer or the standards had declined with the passage of two bloody years of war.

A draft call on February 1, 1864, aided the Crooks/Edwards recruiting. The national quota was raised to 500,000, with New York's share set at 81,993. The new draft quotas for the Brockport area were Sweden 51, Clarkson 30, and Hamlin 31. (*BR* 12/24/1863, Phisterer I: 58)

The offer by the national, state, and county governments of generous bounties with an early deadline also helped. (*BR* 11/26/1863) The county Board of Supervisors had just voted to pay volunteers $300, (*BR* 12/4/1863) which raised the total amount of all bounties to $650–750 per recruit—at least three years' wages for a common laborer. (*BR* 12/4/1863) Captain Edwards's company was "the first to be paid the bounty." (*BR* 12/10/1863, *BR* 1/7/1864)

Finally, and perhaps most importantly, Captain Edwards spread his recruiting net much more widely than his Brockport predecessors. Although his unit is among the "Brockport companies," only one of its 85 members was a village resident and only 39 came from the three Brockport area towns. It included 14 from the town of Riga, 11 from Rochester, and 20 from outside

Monroe County. This contrasted sharply with the three earlier companies for which this breakdown is available. The percentages of Brockporters had been 82.4, 84.9, and 58.1, compared to 45.9. The percentage of men who came from outside Monroe County had been 10.6, 2.0, and 2.9. Now, it was 21.4. Apparently, the recruitment pool in the three towns was running dry.

The composition of the company by residence was:

RESIDENCE	OFFICERS	NON-COMS	PRIVATES	TOTALS
Sweden	1 (100%)	12 (50.0%)	9 (15.0%)	22 (25.9%)
Riga	—	3 (12.5%)	11 (18.3%)	14 (16.5%)
Clarkson	—	4 (16.7%)	8 (13.3%)	12 (14.1%)
Weston, Oneida Co.	—	1 (4.2%)	1 (1.7%)	2 (2.4%)
Brockport	—	1 (4.2%)	—	1 (1.2%)
Hamlin	—	1 (4.2%)	3 (5.0%)	4 (4.7%)
Rome	—	2 (8.3%)	7 (11.7%)	9 (10.6%)
Rochester	—	—	11 (18.3%)	11 (12.9%)
Benton, Yates Co.	—	—	1 (1.7%)	1 (1.2%)
Potter, Yates Co.	—	—	1 (1.7%)	1 (1.2%)
Kendall, Orleans Co.	—	—	2 (3.3%)	2 (2.4%)
Murray, Orleans Co.	—	—	2 (3.3%)	3 (2.4%)
Milo, Yates Co.	—	—	1 (1.7%)	1 (1.2%)
	1	24	57	83

Very likely because so few members were local, the Edwards company did not get the same send-off as its predecessors. However, in Rochester the "people turned out largely to see the regiment off." (*BR* 3/10/1864) Two weeks later, the regiment was in Washington. (*BR* 3/24/1864)

Despite the diminution of the pool of men eligible for military service, another recruiting effort was undertaken in the village in early 1864, responding to another draft call with a goal of 200,000 men. New York had a quota of 32,794 and furnished 44,207. (Phisterer 58, Statistical Record 6) Captain A. Lester Cady, enrolling in Hamlin, was "quite successful in obtaining new recruits" for Company B of the 24th New York Independent Battery. (*BR* 3/17/1864) An advertisement announced that he "desires a few good men to whom the largest bounties will be paid" to join "one of the best branches of the service." (*BR* 3/10/1864)

In addition to the companies that were recruited in Brockport, a number of Brockport area men joined units recruited elsewhere. Among them were eight "persons, belonging in this village" who "joined Capt. Lewis' company of dragoons, at Rochester." (*BR* 4/25/1861)

Besides the recruitment of companies for specified regiments, at least one effort was made to form a "rifle company—to be entirely independent of State and Government authorities—for the purpose of becoming familiar with military tactics." Its members were to pay for their own uniforms and arms at a cost of about $60—three months pay for a common laborer. They would decide individually whether and how to enlist and would be governed by majority vote. Three-member committees were elected to raise funds and to solicit members. "Several persons signed the roll of membership." (*BR* 5/2/1861)

The *BR* said nothing further about that organization, but 16 months later, it reported that "young men of this village are very laudably engaged in getting up a military organization with the design of acquiring military knowledge." Apparently, they were preparing for eventual army duty, but not to form an independent company. (*BR* 9/11/1862)

Hamlin got off to a rough start in the Civil War. The *BR* reported in August 1861 that "the Hamlin military company" had been "accepted by Governor Morgan" and its "members had signed a regular enlistment paper," but before being mustered had suffered "a great scare—some of them taking the shortest route for Canada, others going through a 'double quick' motion of making themselves invisibly scarce." (8/8/1861)

One month later, another company was organized in Hamlin, Company B of Battery B, Rocket Battalion of Artillery. In September 1862, 100 men had been "selected for a military company for Hamlin." (*BR* 9/22/1864) Aaron Lester Cady had enlisted 24 Hamlin and Clarkson men. They marched through Brockport on October 24, 1862, en route to be organized at Buffalo two days later and mustered in at Albany December 7. The unit consisted of "nearly one hundred men," with Jay E. Lee its captain and Cady (for whom Brockport's Grand Army of the Republic post was named) its first lieutenant. Lee was a Hamlin native residing in Perry when the company was formed. Their "lauded weapon having proved a failure," being "as likely to fly back toward the battery that fired them," light artillery replaced rockets in May 1862 and in November 1, 1862, it became the 24th Independent Battery, Light Artillery. (Phisterer 1612–14, *BR* 10/24/1861, 10/31/1861, 5/8/1862, Marcotte 167–71; see pages 247–52)

This chapter has described the recruitment process as seen by Brockporters. Its main purpose has been to describe the impact of those activities on their lives. In summary, recruitment had considerable impact, though by fits and starts. Periods of intense activity were followed by long stretches when nothing much happened. Parts II and III cover the recruitment of the eight Brockport companies briefly, but deals mainly with their experiences thereafter.

Chapter 4

Support for the War Effort

Nobody in the greater Brockport community could have been unaware of the recruitment drives when they occurred. Attendance at the War Meetings was large and the whole population joined in giving the troops celebratory sendoffs. The readers of the *BR* were kept fully informed. Editor Beach gave as much as 100 column inches of type to report on each of those activities. The voters approved the levies for bounties, sometimes even taking the initiative, and the taxpayers assumed a heavy financial burden. The civic leaders were much engaged in organizing the efforts. However, the men of military age were the focus of all the attention, had their lives most disrupted, and had the most at stake in those efforts. Nevertheless, the recruitment drives were far from the only activities that involved the homefront in the war effort. This chapter describes the principal other ways in which the home folks joined that effort.

Military Drills

The war affected Brockporters, especially in the early months, through military activities other than the recruitment efforts. "Local events of a war character" were "numerous." (*BR* 4/25/1861) The enlistees began their military service and even their training in the neighborhood. For instance, two days after Company K of the 13th NYVI was recruited, it "assembled in very full force, as per a call issued, at the Village Hall," elected its officers, and "under the command of their officers, marched down to the canal bridge, and back to the Village Hall…During its march, it was loudly cheered by the citizens in the street."

Three days later "they took up their quarters on the Fair Grounds" where they "were very comfortably provided for."

> *They occupied Floral Hall as barracks having fitted it up with beds and blankets that had been furnished them. Matters looked quite comfortable and somewhat warlike. Capt. Carpenter of the Wide Awakes* [a paramilitary arm of the Republican Party] *was drilling the troops upon the race track. They seemed to be doing well for raw recruits. (*BR *5/2/1861)*

Five days later, they "appeared to have made considerable advancement in military knowledge. They have kept up the drilling every day." That routine continued for two weeks, until they left for Rochester.

Thus, the villagers not only organized in their midst the recruitment of their sons and neighbors, but also, witnessed the first two weeks of their training. If they walked to the end of Fair Street they could watch the marching, provided they could tolerate the vulgarity of the drill sergeant.

Reports on Soldiers' Behavior

Another indication of the pervasiveness of the war's presence in the lives of Brockporters comes from the way the *BR* handled the behavior of their soldiers. Editor Beach was merciless in parading before the community the misconduct of his neighbors. He reported in detail on desertions from the Brockport companies and the fates of the miscreants. For instance, his report on the mustering of Company K of the 13th NYVI names six men "who refused to take the oath." Two of them "had previously deserted, been captured and taken back." Six others were named as having deserted earlier and had not been retaken. Those who refused the oath received this treatment:

> *The rest of the company formed around them, and one at a time was put upon a large piece of canvass, (made for the purpose) which the members would straighten up and then slack down, tumbling the renegade into every conceivable position. When* [Duane] *Draper was put upon the canvass,*

> *a quantity of water was thrown on, and when he tumbled down, it nigh smothered him. After the cowards had been put through this course of treatment, they were driven around the camp and out of it. The boys say that Brockport should be made too hot for such a graceless lot. (*BR *5/16/1861)*

Thus, the "cowards" were held up to the scorn of their families and neighbors. This may have had the desired effect of making Brockport "too hot" for them in at least two cases. Draper and Michael Toole rejoined the company a week later. Beach commented that if they "prove faithful now, they should be forgiven for their past seemingly cowardly conduct." (5/23/1861) He did not disclose the fate of the others, but, certainly, the report of their offenses and punishment brought the war to the homefolks in still another way.

PRIVATE ENLISTMENT BOUNTIES

As the war dragged on and its horrors became increasingly evident to everyone, and, especially, to men of military age, the payment of bounties for enlistment became a major and controversial issue. The governments—federal, state, county, and town—bore much the greatest burden of the system. But, especially early in the war, some bounties were paid voluntarily by prosperous Brockporters, another way in which the village participated in the war. In July 1862, two Brockport businessmen put up $25 and four others offered $20 each to the first ten volunteers. (*BR* 7/24, 7/31/1862) In August, another businessman offered $25 and a recruiter named McGovern offered $100 extra for each recruit, though no source of his money was mentioned. (*BR* 8/7/1862, 8/21/1862) Sometime before August 5, 1864, about $300 more was raised by popular subscription "to pay commutation for Benjamin Purdy after getting the money he skedadled." (Davis Report)

In a few special cases, Brockporters rewarded their soldiers in more tangible ways. For instance, some of Lieutenant Fuller's friends took the occasion of his return to the village to recover a couple of early deserters and bring back a few new recruits to present him with a "splendid new sword" that had cost $25. E.B. Holmes, as usual, stepped forward to present it and to make a few "appropriate" remarks. He called the weapon "a slight token" of the "appreciation and remembrance" of his friends. Lieutenant

Fuller accepted the gift as a "memorial of your kindness and generosity" and assured them that "you will never be dishonored by me while in the service of my country." The martial band, several friends, and the soldiers he had come to collect accompanied him back "to the cars." (*BR* 5/23/1861) Similar sword presentations were held, with less fanfare, for Captain Abram Moore, commander of Company F of the 105th NYVI; (*BR* 3/6/1862, 3/20/1862), Captain Milo Starks and Lieutenant J.D. Decker of Company A of the 140th NYVI; and Captain F.H. Barry of the 8th NY Cavalry. (*BR* 8/14/1862, 9/25/1862)

Private Relief Efforts

The second most important way in which the villagers were involved in the war effort, after recruitment, was private relief efforts. These took four principal forms: aid for indigent families of Brockport soldiers, aid for widows of deceased soldiers, supplies for Brockport soldiers, and supplies for Union Army hospitals. These undertakings were spontaneous volunteer actions by the townspeople. As with the War Meetings, some leading citizen noted a need and issued a call and the Brockporters showed up in large numbers for full and free discussion of the matter. It was local democracy at its best in the old New England town meeting style. Moreover, the decisions called for real sacrifices. Governmental leaders often played important roles, but in their private capacities.

Indigent Families of Soldiers

The need for volunteer work and donations to provide assistance to the families of soldiers was recognized at the same time as the recruitment drives began. At the first War Meeting, a resolution was passed creating "a committee of five… appointed by the chair, to raise by subscription such funds as may be necessary to give suitable aid, in their discretion, to the families of volunteers enlisting in behalf of the government in this emergency, in case they should need assistance in the absence of their natural protectors." (*BR* 4/25/1861)

That same meeting appointed a Finance Committee, composed of five leading men in the community, one (J.H. Warren) being from Clarkson.

When that meeting resumed on Tuesday, it was announced that two men had been added to the Finance Committee, that $5,095 had been raised by subscription, and that the Village Board had appropriated $500 for the same purpose. By Thursday, the pledges had reached $7,730, including the village appropriation. They ranged from $10 up to Elias B. Holmes's $1,000. Sixty-six names of men and businesses were listed. Three men pledged $500, one $300, five $200, and one $150. The most common pledge was $100, of which there were 23. Editor Beach, for all his bombast, was in the $50 category, with eight others. The remaining 22 ranged from $10 to $40. (*BR* 4/25/1861) During the following week, 27 more pledges, ranging from $10 to $300 and totaling $1,940, were added, bringing the grand total to $9,670. (*BR* 5/2/1861) By May 23, the fund had reached $10,856, including $500 from D.S. Morgan, and $150 more was added by mid-June. (*BR* 5/23/1861, 6/13/1861)

Each of the volunteers' families was to be paid $35 per week from that fund. (*BR* 5/30/1861) If that intention was, in fact, realized, the soldiers' families received at least ten times as much from private charity as from the Board of Relief. The number of families was not given. (*BR* 3/30/1861) Apparently, those efforts succeeded, for Editor Beach mentioned several times that no "soldier's wife or children, or widow and orphans suffer in this community for the want of the necessaries of life." (*BR* 4/21/1864)

By May 2, barely two weeks after Lincoln's call for volunteers, Brockport's Finance Committee began operating. It had elected a treasurer, appointed a disbursements sub-committee, opened a bank account, assessed five percent of the pledged amounts to be paid by the donors within one week, and asked Captain Thomas for a list of families of his men who might need assistance. (*BR* 5/2/1861) A second assessment of five percent was levied on May 23 and a payment of three percent, to be the final payment if the men were released upon expiration of their three-month enlistments, was assessed in early August. (*BR* 5/23/1861, 8/8/1861) The fifth installment, which was levied on the donors in October 1861, called for five percent slices of the pledges. The August 1862 installment called for only three percent. (*BR* 10/24/1861 8/8/1862)

On May 23, the first disbursements from the fund were reported. The donations were used, not only for payments to the families, but also for related expenses. In fact, in the initial disbursement, only $139 of the $624.91 total went to "Families of Volunteers." Other expenditures included $4 for use of the Concert Hall, $28 for "carriage hire," $38.08 for forty pairs of shoes, $13.87 "Expenses of recovering deserters," and $322.80 for clothing and blankets. The ladies were reimbursed $154.23 for the cost of the materials they had used. The balance went for various expenses incurred in running the program. (*BR* 5/23/1861)

Of course, it is one thing to make a pledge and quite another to make a payment. The amount due on the first installment was $511.75. The amount actually collected was $418.75. Therefore, 81.8 percent of the assessment was, in fact, paid. Moreover, the amount collected covered only 67.0 percent of the costs incurred by that time. (*BR* 5/23/1861)

Another early problem with the fund was that it was deposited about May 1 with the Brockport Exchange Bank, which declared bankruptcy on August 5. The Republic did not say whether the relief fund lost money as a result. (*BR* 8/8/1861, 8/15/1861, 9/12/1861, 11/14/1861, 1/23/1862, 7/17/1862)

Hamlin established a similar fund about the same time. A public meeting on April 30, 1861, voted to raise by private subscription "funds for the support of volunteers' families in town." A 15-member committee was appointed to solicit donations and twenty men pledged a total of $900 during the meeting. By June 6, 1861, 101 donors had contributed $2,931 and by mid-October the funds were "being judiciously distributed" to the families. "As the Hamlin volunteers belong to the Brockport company," suggested Beach, "either the Hamlin fund should be united with the Brockport fund, or the Hamlin folks should pay their portion of the expense of fitting out the volunteers." He said that nine of the 77 soldiers were from Hamlin. (*BR* 5/9/1861 6/6/1861 10/17/1861)

Aid to Soldiers

The evening before their departure, the new recruits for Company K of the 13th were honored guests at a meeting in the Concert Hall. The "ladies of the village and vicinity…aided by three gentlemen" had labored for five days making for them, "Eighty-one pair of drawers, seventy-seven shirts, seventy-seven pin balls, one hundred and fifty towels, and seventy-seven needle books" plus "fine teeth combs and brushes for seventy-seven" and testaments at a cost to the donors of $162.83. (*BR* 5/2/1861) After some of the usual speechifying, the company roll was called and the recruits stepped forward, one by one, to receive their packages. "The distribution of the clothing occupied many minutes, and afforded a few comical, and many mirthful incidents. At the close of the distribution, the volunteers gave three deafening cheers for the ladies," and then they "marched back to the Fair Grounds, followed by many relatives and friends. Many adieus were said there, and all would have passed off satisfactorily to the friends of the volunteers, but for the profane and brutal language in which they were addressed—which was entirely uncalled for—by the Orderly Sergeant." (*BR* 5/9/1861)

The next day, the volunteers left Brockport for Rochester by train, escorted to the depot by a line of firemen and "several hundred citizens." At the train station, E.B. Holmes gave Captain Thomas eighty dollars to be distributed to the men.

The pin balls proved to have unexpected utility for the soldiers. A Brockport visitor to their camp in Elmira reported that, "many of the boys are now short of tobacco and money, and when they gamble are obliged to use the pins presented them by the ladies for stakes." (*BR* 5/16/1861)

That early surge of willingness to contribute to the Union cause through volunteer effort did not end with the subscription of monetary pledges to aid the soldier's families. That same week, the "ladies of the village met in large numbers at Beach's Hall...and commenced preparing articles for the use of soldiers." Within a week, they had prepared 77 packages of clothing and other supplies for Captain Thomas's company. (*BR* 5/2/1861) By November, they were meeting every Wednesday and Friday to work on their project and sent off a box of blankets in December, with mittens soon to follow. (*BR* 11/21/1861, 12/5/1861) The liberality poured out for the boys of Company K does not seem to have reappeared as other Brockport companies were formed. Late in 1863, an item in the *BR* solicited mittens for Captain Pond's company, but no other such efforts were reported. (*BR* 11/26/1863, 12/4/1863) Rather, Brockport's relief work was directed toward the families of the soldiers and to the sick and wounded in military hospitals.

Some funds to support this effort were raised by a concert by the "renowned ballad singer James G. Clark..., one-third of the proceeds being given to the local Soldier's Aid Society." (*BR* 2/25/1864) The same "best ballad singer in the State" performed in Clarkson in September 1863, with a "portion of the proceeds...given to the Aid Society." (*BR* 9/10/1863)

The "citizens of Clarkson" also participated in that effort. The *BR* reported in August 1864 that they "are contributing liberally of articles for the Western army," having "sent off many packages." (*BR* 8/28/1864) Also, the "ladies of West Clarkson" sent "two valuable packages of hospital stores to Washington." (*BR* 9/4/1862)

AID TO SICK AND WOUNDED SOLDIERS

The soldiers in hospitals were the object of the third, and most important, leg of Brockport's private relief program. It began in October 1861 with the formation by Brockport women of "a benevolent movement," later called the Ladies Union Aid Society (LUAS), still later, Soldiers Relief, and, finally, the Brockport Christian Commission or Christian and Sanitary Commission, to furnish "many necessaries not provided by the army regulations, to the wounded soldiers of St. Louis." (*BR* 10/24/1861) They were donated to the Western Sanitary Commission, which operated 29 army hospitals from its base in St. Louis. (*BR* 2/13/1862) The work of the LUAS was supplemented by similar groups in Clarkson, West Clarkson, and Sweden Center and by Brockport's Baptist Benevolent Society. (*BR* 9/4/1862)

A week later, the ladies had "been zealously at work" and had readied for shipment "a large quantity of double gowns, night shirts, drawers, pillows, and other bedding and clothing, and also quantities of wines. Jellies, farinas, &c." Some of the clothing went to Brockport's Company K of the 13th regiment. The rest went to St. Louis. (*BR* 10/31/1861) A member of the Sanitary Committee in St. Louis acknowledged receipt of "two boxes of goods" from the ladies, noting that the "government furnish only sheets and pillow cases" but "no socks, shirts, drawers or flannels." (*BR* 12/5/1861) The ladies sent another large shipment in December. Among its more notable items were 12 pairs of drawers, 26 shirts, 27 pairs of socks, 14 double gowns, 12 pillows, 24 bottles of wine, 17 pillowcases, plus spices, canned fruit, blankets, etc., etc. (*BR* 1/2/1862) Two weeks later, they sent another large box of drawers, shirts, socks, pillows, gowns, and sundry other items. The ladies of Clarkson contributed 32 pairs of mittens, two pairs of socks, and one shirt to that shipment. However, the ladies announced that they had exhausted their fund and would cease their endeavors for the time being. (*BR* 1/16/1862) At the same time, the Baptists sent to the same place two cases "containing shirts, drawers, socks, etc., etc., and delicacies for the sick." (*BR* 1/16/1862)

Eight months later, the ladies had resumed their endeavors, "holding one or two meetings each week." (*BR* 8/7/1862) They made a shipment to the Chesapeake General Hospital on August 8, 1862, that included "dried fruit, tea, and onions" and lint, which was used as dressing for wounds. The recipients passed a resolution of gratitude for "a large box filled with articles of luxury, comfort and convenience…for the relief of soldiers, of Brockport, Monroe County, N.Y." (*BR* 8/21/1862)

The source of the new funds is not given, but one possibility is the inter-denominational Union Mite Society, which held weekly meetings at which five cents was collected from each member for the Soldiers' Relief Fund. Absentees were expected to send in their money. (*BR* 10/9/1862) Also, the fund continued to receive donations in kind. In March 1863, the ladies announced that they had shipped 51 packages of "articles contributed by liberal persons of this village and neighborhood" to the "hospitals of the Army of the Potomac." (*BR* 3/17/1864, 3/24/1864)

In June 1864, the ladies reorganized and began meeting weekly and issuing monthly reports. The society was open to all and its members gathered at Concert Hall each Friday afternoon to receive donations. They had recruited students from the Brockport Collegiate Institute who donated seven dollars and "prepared nearly four barrels of toasted bread" that were shipped to hospitals.

The ladies unleashed, as their secretary and treasurer, their heaviest weapon, "authoress" Mary Jane Holmes. She was Brockport's most famous resident, being America's best-selling woman novelist. In her first report, she appealed for support through donations of money and of "everything which can conduce to the comfort of the sick and convalescent." She listed the contents of the "boxes and barrels" that they had sent to various military hospitals since the outbreak of hostilities:

> *244 shirts, 86 sheets, 329 towels, 108 pillow cases, over 300 pocket handkerchiefs, together with pants, socks, slippers, fans, lint, bandages, pillows, corn starch, cocoa, chocolate, farina, tea, sugar, nutmegs, onions, wines, jellies, canned fruit, dried fruit, cologne, tobacco, books, papers, envelopes, housewives, pickled cabbage, pickled potatoes, bottles of horse-radish, pickled cucumbers, and 80 pairs of mittens. (*BR *6/9/1864)*

She concluded her report with a fervent and highly emotional call for "hearty cooperation, in sending immediate relief to our suffering heroes. Shall they appeal in vain?"

In her next report, she described her visit to a military hospital in Rochester:

> *Could you see how thankful they are for a handful of berries, pop corn or cherries, you would gladly deny yourself that they might be fed. One boy…sobbing, writhing, whose agonized suffering from a gangrenal wound awoke our keenest sympathy, had begged two days for a piece of cake. I*

> *need not tell you how quickly the contents of Mrs. Stover's basket were bro't forward and the poor fellow regaled with sponge cake, the big tears dropping as he ate.* (BR *7/21/1864)*

She reported that, in the previous seven weeks, the ladies had collected $33.86 in donations, mostly from themselves, and had spent $29.05 for supplies and shipping, leaving a balance of $4.81. They had delivered to St. Mary's Hospital in Rochester two baskets of specialty foods, plus shirts, buttons, handkerchiefs, old linen, lint, bandages, socks, a pillowcase, and a "comfortable." Also, they had made 32 flannel shirts and 19 sheets for the Sanitary Commission in Rochester and 20 cotton shirts and some hospital supplies for the Christian Commission in Philadelphia.

Mrs. Holmes's account shows how the ability of Brockporters to visit the sick and wounded in hospitals easily accessible from the village provided still another way that the war came home vividly and pervasively.

Aid to Widows and Orphans

The system to assist the widows of deceased soldiers was quite different from the others, being more carefully organized. Six two-member teams were appointed to solicit "donations of food and clothing" in different neighborhoods on a specified day. Three committees were appointed, one to organize the system, another to receive the articles, and a third to arrange for their distribution. Only two widows were identified as prospective beneficiaries initially. (*BR* 2/27/1862) The first round of solicitations of "articles and cash" produced about $90, but Editor Beach confidently predicted that it would soon reach $200. (*BR* 3/6/1862)

Aid to Freedmen

One war-related charity that did not attract the interest of Brockporters was aid to the "poor freedmen of the South." The *BR* reported that the people of Lockport had collected about $1,200 and "several boxes of clothing." Editor Beach commended the Lockporters, but never mentioned a similar drive in Brockport. (3/3/1864)

PRESSURE ON THE TOWN BOARD

Not only did the good people of Brockport undertake, quite spontaneously, the relief efforts described above, but, also, they pressed the Town government to do a better job. As usual, they did so through an open public meeting, "Pursuant to a call read in the village churches on Sunday." Apparently, the volunteer system had broken down and the efforts of the Town Board were deemed inadequate. The chair of the meeting who, ironically, was the Town Supervisor, announced that its object "was to consider whether the Town Board have not authority to provide more liberally for the families of soldiers, and if they have not to organize a volunteering system of relief." (*BR* 12/24/1863)

The meeting concluded that the Town had the authority to spend money that way, but lacked authority to borrow money for that purpose. It appointed a committee to petition the state legislature to amend the law to permit such action. Also, it called for a committee of women "to canvass the village and town and report to the Town Board the condition of the soldiers' families." A follow-up meeting the next Monday named eight women to that task. (*BR* 12/31/1863) The *BR* did not report any results from the decisions made.

VILLAGE BOARD

The Village Board became involved earlier than the Town Board. On April 21, 1861, only nine days after the firing on Fort Sumter, it allocated "Five Hundred Dollars from any funds in the Treasury not otherwise appropriated for the purpose of defraying the expenses of Volunteers & for the necessary support of their families during their absence, to be appropriated in such manner as the finance committee appointed at the public meeting on Saturday last shall direct."

However, there is no evidence that those funds were, in fact, expended. The annual report of the Board, published on April 2, 1862, included among its expenditures: "For Volunteers..........100.00." (Minutes of March 31,1862) No later minutes or annual report mentioned such an expenditure.

The minutes of the Village Board during the conflict mention no other business having to do with the war. However, after the war ended, some Civil War–related action was taken. The Board voted to "take charge of any monies that may be raised for the purpose of erecting a Monument to the memory of the late President, Abraham Lincoln & of the soldiers who have fallen in the present war, and will expend the same in accordance with the desires of the contributors." (Minutes of May 2, 1865)

Also, it agreed to make "arrangements for the Funeral Obsequies of the late Major Milo Starks, of the 140th Reg't N.Y. Vols." (Minutes of May 19, 1865)

TOWN BOARD

The Town Board meeting minutes do not mention Civil War business until May 2, 1863, more than two years after the outbreak of hostilities. However, thereafter, they devote more space to that than to all other matters combined. Almost all their attention thereafter until the end of the war was devoted to two topics: relief for the families of soldiers and the payment of bounties.

The former topic arose in response to a recent act of the state legislature, "giving authority to the different City's and Towns…to provide for the Familys of Indigent Volunteers and other Persons who are or may be called into the service of the United States."

The Board resolved, "That those Volunteers and other persons ordered into the service of the United States leaving families in needy circumstances should have and they are hereby assured that their families will be liberally provided for."

Another resolution levied a property tax of $500 for that purpose. A third resolution appointed Samuel H. Davis, John A. Latta, and Daniel Holmes a committee to administer the funds. They were instructed "to inquire into the situation and condition of such indigent family's and grant such releaf as in their judgement their several circumstances may require." (Board Minutes of August 17, 1863)

Finally, the Board agreed to raise additional funds for that purpose if needed.

At a special meeting on September 4, 1862, the Board appointed Davis and Holmes "a committee to confer with the Bankers in regard to raising moneys for Indigent families." (Minutes) The Board regarded this matter as urgent, for the very next day, it voted, on motion by Holmes, to borrow the $500 until March 1, 1864, from the Brockport banking house of Waters Bishop & Co., and at another special meeting on September 14, adopted this "guide in the distribution of the Relief Fund": "That the wife shall be allowed Three dollars per week and Fifty Cents for each Child but that the above amount may be varied according to the Circumstances of each case." (Minutes)

Also, it agreed to have the "Board of Relief" "meet on the last Monday of each Month at 10 oclock A.M. to consider applications for relief" and to require applicants "to present to the Board a statement verified by oath showing their circumstances, number of family & that the same be certified to by two credible persons known to the Board." The Board of Relief first met on September 28, but no applicants appeared. (Minutes) From August 17 until its annual meeting on October 1, the Board transacted no business, except to set up the Board of Relief system.

The second meeting of the Board of Relief on October 26, granted $28 per week to 14 wives of servicemen. Three received $2.50 per week, nine $2.00, one $1.50, and one $1.00. (Minutes) At their third session, November 30, it "cut off" two grantees, one "unless she presents an affidavit satisfactory to the board."

At the December 28, 1863, and January 25, 1864, meetings, the Board repeated the affidavit requirement and agreed to pay her $2.00 per week if the applicant met it. At their May 30 meeting, they were finally satisfied and allocated that amount to her. The other wife who had been cut off reappeared on the December 28 list with the same amount as on the initial allocation.

Clearly, the Board of Relief took its task seriously. It required new applications with affidavits every month from every applicant, except that it did not meet in October 1865. It changed allocations frequently, both up and down, as though it believed that the needs of the women changed. Some women were dropped from the list and then reappeared. Others disappeared forever. New names were added almost every month. It made three lump-sum allocations of relatively large amounts (two of $10 and one of $7.50). The regular weekly amounts ranged from $1.00 to $3.50, with $2.00 being the most common amount. Sometimes, an "extra" amount, ranging from $3.00 to $7.50 accompanied the weekly allocation.

Forty-five women received money at least once. The list began with 14 names in October 1863 and fluctuated significantly monthly until May 1864. Then it grew steadily to a peak of 31 in January and February 1865. Thereafter, it declined to 28 in April and May and, after Appomattox, to 16 in June and nine in July and August. Its list had only four names the last four months before it declared itself defunct at its January 1866 meeting.

The total amount received by the women varied greatly. Catherine Clark received the largest amount, $227.50 in 27 monthly allocations and two "extra" payments totaling $10. In 1860, she was a 32-year-old farm wife, married to 40-year-old Owen, with four children 11 and under. Her husband enlisted in Company H of the 140th NYVI on August 13, 1862, and was killed at Waldon Railroad, Virginia, on August 19, 1864. (ACWRD) Four other women received similar, but lesser, amounts. Four women were on the list only once each.

The Board functioned without a fixed budget. Its mandate was to provide for the needs of the war families by raising through taxation the money required. It reported to the annual meeting of the Town Board on February 28, 1865, that it had been appropriated a total of $3,804.50, and had expended $1,988.80. The Board voted it another $1,250 for a grand total of $5,054.50. The Board minutes do not record a final financial report by the Board of Relief, so the exact amount of its expenditures cannot be determined. To give those figures some context, the annual expenditures of the Town of Sweden approved at the Board meeting of October 3, 1863, were $1,307.50. The corresponding figure for 1864 was $1,187.23. Thus, the funds expended for the relief of the needy families of servicemen was about double the regular operating budget of the Town.

If the CTCR is accurate and complete, its Town Board took no action to provide relief to the indigent families of soldiers until 1863. In that year, its "Board of Relief raised by tax and disbursed the sum of $250 to families of Soldiers." In 1864, the amount raised for that purpose was $550 and in 1865 "to the close of the Rebellion" $335. (*BR* 12/10/1863, CTCR) Hamlin appropriated $250 for the same purpose in 1863, (*BR* 11/4/1863) but no information is available for 1864 and 1865.

The activities recounted in this and the previous three chapters make clear that the war effort had become the leading preoccupation of the Brockport community. It did not take over its life completely, as should be obvious from reading about the Civil War years in my *Early Brockport*, but it overshadowed everything else. All Brockporters were aware of that effort. The enlistees and their families were affected most deeply, but when the participants in the war meetings, the relief drives, the troop sendoffs, the small boys playing war, the friends and neighbors of the soldiers, etc., etc., are taken into account, practically all Brockporters were involved to one extent or another. The lives of the soldiers were, of course, most completely disrupted by the war and their experiences became important parts of the consciousness of those they left behind for they were shared through the *BR*, letters and furloughs home, and the everyday converse in the community. To those experiences, then, we turn now.

Part II

THE 13TH NYVI

Chapter 5

Recruitment and Training

Prefatory Note

The purpose of Part II is to present an account of the experiences of some Brockport soldiers in the Civil War that is as complete and vivid as possible at this distance in time. Many Civil War regiments have been the subjects of regimental histories. So far as I have been able to learn, that is not the case of the 13th, though Robert Marcotte's *Where They Fell* includes the 13th in its history of Monroe County's role in the Civil War. So, one purpose of Part II is to fill that gap. Its focus, as far as possible, is on Brockport's Company K and, after its dissolution, on the Brockporters who were dispersed throughout the regiment. The only significant sources of information on Brockporters in the 13th are some newspaper accounts and some letters from soldiers that were published in the *BR*. Also, letters by soldier-correspondents from other communities who were closely associated with Brockporters are used, even though they were published in Rochester newspapers. In this and the following chapters, the excerpts from the soldiers' letters are italicized. Quotations in roman typeface come from other sources. No attempt was made to modernize or correct the spelling.

The letters by Brockport soldiers and their comrades written in the immediate aftermath of the events they report, can convey the actions and atmosphere more vividly and, presumably, more accurately, than could any summary or paraphrase. Therefore, they will form most of this chapter. Where they are repetitious, uninteresting, or trivial, only extracts will be included. Also, brief descriptions of their context and some connective tissue should ensure clarity and continuity.

The purpose of Part II requires full immersion in the day-to-day activities of the men in uniform. The reader should feel, as much as is possible through the print media, what Brockport's Civil War soldiers felt. Because much of their experience was boring and tedious, some of their writing reflects this. Much of that material is included, for without it their ordeal cannot be understood fully. To leave it out would be to distort the record.

The principal correspondent to the *BR* from the 13th NYVI used the pen names "Sphinx" and "S." Sphinx was Lieutenant, later Captain, Eugene P. Fuller. The last letter from the 13th signed by Sphinx was dated April 21, 1862. Captain Fuller resigned from that regiment on April 27. Also, one of the *BR*'s correspondents, J.D. Barnes, was a member of Company G of the 13th. So, I will draw on his reports as well until, on August 23, 1861, Company G was transferred to the 3rd NY Cavalry as Company K. (Phisterer 1887)

Providing an account of the activities of the 13th through the letters by Brockport soldiers is complicated by the short duration of their tenure as correspondents and by the early dissolution of Company K. However, Company A received nine Brockporters after Company K disappeared and one of its members, Tyron J.M. Jewell, writing as Scorer, wrote for the *Rochester Union and Advertiser* (*U&A*). Because of the dispersal of Company K men throughout the regiment and the presence throughout the regiment of Brockporters who had not been in Company K, the regiment as a whole, rather than any company, really was the unit of experience for Brockporters.

After each section of the first-person accounts a brief summary of the action is added to provide an overview that should help the reader understand what has happened. These summaries are drawn verbatim from the "historical sketch" of the 13th in the 3rd Annual Report of the Bureau of Military Statistics of the NYS Division of Military and Naval Affairs on the DMNA website.

Recruitment

Recruitment for the first of the Brockport companies occurred during the initial phase of enthusiasm for the war effort as described in Chapter 1 above. By April 18, 1861, three days after Lincoln's first call for volunteers, "a paper has been circulated for volunteers, and last night about forty names had been obtained." Two days later, at the first Village War Meeting, the most eminent men in the community exhorted the young men among their neighbors to join the army. (*BR* 4/25/1861; see pages 20–22) By May 15, the regiment was sufficiently complete to be mustered into the service of the Union army.

The *BR* published two lists of names of the members of the company. (4/25/1861 and 5/16/1861) The first had 75 names, the second had 79 names and added that six Rochester residents had joined the company for a total of 85. Many of the names appear on only one of the lists. Eighty-nine members of Company K Brockporters appear in the American Civil War Research Database website (ACWRD). Other sources identify 13 Brockporters as members of the company whose names do not appear in the ACWRD for a total of 102. This number represents all the Brockporters who served in the 13th during its service, not just those who enlisted in April–May 1861. Seven joined at Rochester in August-November 1861, which was after the original company had been disbanded. Also, six of the 102 refused to take the oath and another six deserted at Elmira.

The residences of 11 recruits cannot be identified because the sources provide conflicting information. For instance, STCR and CTCR both claim some men and the *BR* gave one residence for some men on April 25 and another on May 16. Also, in one case, no residence was given. Using only the residences where no conflicting evidence exists, 39 men resided in Brockport, 20 in Hamlin, 13 in Sweden outside Brockport, 14 in Clarkson, and three in Rochester. (*BR* 5/16 says that there were four others, but I cannot identify them.) The Davis Report gives a figure of 43 for Town of Sweden men in Company K. Orleans County towns provided three, Ogden three, unknown one.

Besides those 102 men in Company K, at least 30 Brockporters joined other companies in the 13th. Six of them resided in Brockport, eight in Ogden, four in Clarkson, three in Hamlin, and one each in Kendall, Clarendon, and Parma, and one simply in "the vicinity." Five of them joined the regiment well after its initial organization, at dates from November 12, 1861, to September 8, 1862. Hardly had nine of the Brockporters settled in to Company G when they were transferred with it to become Company K of the 3rd NY Cavalry on September 1, 1861

Officers

The Brockporters who were officers in Company K had quite undistinguished careers. The company commander was Captain Horace J. Thomas, a village

A group of company officers of the 13th NYVI. *Courtesy of U.S. Army Military History Institute.*

lawyer. In 1860, he was 36, living with his 32-year-old wife in the house still standing on High Street at Park Avenue. The household included a 32-year-old "student-at-law" and the student's wife and 6-year-old child. Thomas had a very checkered military career, much of it recounted below, which led to his resignation on grounds of ill health on September 20, 1861. His military career was further clouded when, in September 1864, he hired a substitute to avoid being drafted. (STCR) Despite his apparent disgrace, he remained in Brockport after the war, continuing his law practice. In the 1870 census, besides his wife, a 28-year-old physician named Oscar Thomas and two housekeepers shared his household. Oscar's relationship to Horace is unclear.

The company's first lieutenant was Eugene P. Fuller, Fuller was a 25-year-old lawyer, who, in the 1860 census, resided with his parents in Brockport. His father, Jerome, was also a lawyer and his brother, Heber, 22, was a farm worker. The Fullers lived on Erie Street near Main, next door to Dr. Davis Carpenter and directly across the street from Elias B. Holmes. Holmes's stature is indicated by his reporting $239,000 in assets in the 1860 census, a handsome amount at that time.

After Thomas resigned, Fuller became captain and the company commander. However, his leadership, also, was quite brief, as he resigned on April 27, 1862, while the regiment was still training in Elmira. He was replaced by Alfred H. Hurlbert, not a Brockporter.

Fuller also served as captain and commander of Company H of the 108th NYVI from August 18, 1862, until June 6, 1863. In 1870, he lived in a rental house on State Street with his 27-year-old wife and two small sons and continued his law practice. By 1880, however, he was back in his parents' household with his two sons but no wife. No Eugene Fuller of his age is listed in the 1900 census.

Company K's second lieutenant at the time it was organized was Edwin A. Dayton, a 28-year-old clerk, residing in a Brockport hotel. He was cashiered October 15, 1861, shortly before the company was disbanded. Dayton, too, saw later service, first as second lieutenant in the 105th NYVI, then a captain when the 105th merged with the 94th NYVI. He was dismissed from that position on October 24, 1863, but reappeared in the 22nd NY Cavalry as a private. He was promoted to sergeant major, busted back to private, promoted again to sergeant-major, and finally commissioned a second lieutenant. Quite a career—enlisted, commissioned, promoted, demoted, cashiered, dismissed, and, finally, mustered out. I find no trace of him after the war. STCR says he "could not obtain any other facts" about his postwar residence. No Edwin Dayton of his age appears on any postwar census.

Another Brockporter who became an officer in Company K was John M. Richardson, who was promoted from private to sergeant on May 20, 1861, to second lieutenant a year later, and to first lieutenant on March 17, 1863. He resided in Sweden with his parents, John and Lucy. His father was a "mechanic." (STCR) In 1870 John was a miner in Montana Territory.

Five other Brockporters were enlisted men in Company K, but became commissioned officers later in other regiments. William Henry Joslyn, of Brockport, served in the 13th as a private, but was a captain in Company H, NY 21st Cavalry later; He was the brother of Mrs. Dayton S. Morgan, the reaper manufacturer's wife. Wesley W. Conner, of Brockport was a sergeant in the 13th, commissioned a second lieutenant in the 25th NYVI, promoted to first lieutenant and then captain. Edwin F. Clark, of Clarkson, was a corporal in the 13th and a second lieutenant in the 22nd NY Independent Battery of Light Artillery. John Beedle, in 1860 a single 32-year-old farmer living in the household of his father, a prosperous Sweden farmer, enlisted as a private in Company K, date unknown. Next, he was a private in Company D of the 33rd NYVI, enlisting on August 20, 1862. He became the first sergeant of Company I of the 49th NYVI on October 1, 1863, and a first lieutenant in Company G of the 108th NYVI on May 3, 1864. He became captain of that company on August 1, 1864, but was dismissed on November 21, 1864—quite a career. By 1870, he was living in the household of his father, still unmarried. By 1880, he was still a farmer in Sweden but had left his father's household and had a 41-year-old wife.

Six Brockporters in other companies of the 13th also saw service as commissioned officers in other regiments. The most interesting was Stephen Randall Stafford. He was born in Stafford, NY, and in 1860 was a 19-year-old student living in Brockport with his family on the southeast corner of the College/Utica Streets intersection. His father was a teacher. He was six feet, eight inches tall and weighed about 200 pounds, "in physique a model of classical proportions." (*BD* 7/9/1886) On April 30, 1861, he enlisted as a private in Company G, and went with it to Company K of the 3rd NY Cavalry on September 1, 1861. He was discharged from that unit "for minority" on September 18, 1861. Then, on August 17, 1862, he became a second lieutenant in Company I of the 129th NYVI, which became the 8th NY Heavy Artillery regiment. He was promoted to first lieutenant January 27, 1864, to captain, Company D, November 5, 1864, and "major by brevet, for faithful and meritorious services during the war" March 13, 1865. (Phisterer 424)

Stafford was wounded at North Anna, Virginia, in May 1864, but recovered sufficiently "to lead a desperate charge at Hatcher's Run (October 27, 1864), for which General Gibbon—his Division Commander—tendered him high praise and honor in the presence of the entire command." (*BR* 12/11/02) After the war, he became a career army officer. He served as a second lieutenant in the 38th U.S. Infantry from May 21, 1867, until November 11, 1869, and as a captain in the 15th Regular U.S. Infantry March 6, 1870, until he retired July 1, 1898, for physical disability.

In 1869, Stafford's regiment redeployed to the West, serving in Missouri, New Mexico, and Colorado. Among notable engagements, the regiment fought Apaches and Utes. From 1882 until 1890, it was stationed in the Dakotas and then was transferred to Fort Sheridan near Chicago where he commanded its garrison. The 15th helped contain the Chicago Railway Riots of 1894. (*BD* 8/1/1894) After retiring, Stafford returned to Brockport and entered the fire insurance business. He died at his office desk there on May 31, 1902. (*BR* 6/5/02)

A 28-year-old Hamlin farmer, Sumner Austin, enrolled in Company F of the 13th as a corporal, was promoted to sergeant and commissioned as a second lieutenant on February 15, 1862. He resigned October 9, 1862.

After the war he farmed in Kendall. John D. Barnes of Brockport enlisted in the same company as a private and became chaplain (a field officer rank) on January 6, 1862. He was "a licensed preacher of the Baptist Church and at the time of his enlistment was a student in the Brockport Collegiate Institute, preparing himself for ordination." (*BR* 6/27/1861) He resigned August 6, 1862. I cannot find him in the 1860 or 1870 censuses or the town clerks' reports.

Willard W. Bates of Kendall, age 25, had an extraordinary military career, ending in tragedy. He advanced from sergeant to full colonel in 37 months and was mortally wounded 19 days after his final promotion. He enlisted in Company F, April 30, 1861, as a sergeant and was transferred to Company C of the 25th NYVI as first lieutenant on November 7, 1861. He became captain of Company I on January 20, 1862, and was wounded in action at Chickahominy, Virginia, on June 27, 1862. Then he transferred to the 129th NYVI, which became the 8th NY Heavy Artillery, as lieutenant colonel on August 10, 1862. When the regimental commander, Colonel Peter Porter, was killed in action on June 3, 1864, Bates was promoted to colonel. He was himself mortally wounded leading the regiment in an attack at Petersburg and died June 25, 1864.

Swiss-born Jules F. Billard, formerly of Brockport, enlisted in Company F as a private April 30, 1861, was discharged for disability on June 16, 1861, enlisted in Company K of the 81st NYVI August 26, 1861, became first lieutenant September 14, 1861, and was discharged February 6, 1862. In 1870, he was an apothecary in New York City.

Oscar Sheldon was a 28-year-old thresher in Ogden in 1860. He mustered into Company G of the 13th and transferred with that company to the 3rd NY Cavalry September 1, 1861. He found a happy home in the cavalry, as he was promoted to corporal, October 31, 1861, to sergeant, October 31, 1862, to second lieutenant, December 27, 1862, and to first lieutenant of Company C on June 10, 1864. In 1870, he was a store clerk in Bloomington, Ill., with a wife and child.

FORMATION IN ROCHESTER

Brockport's involvement in the Civil War got off to a rather inauspicious start. Company K was organized April 22, 1861, the last of the companies to form that regiment. (DMNA website) It began its experience by a train ride to Rochester on the morning of May 3, 1861. As soon as it arrived in Rochester, its troubles began. It was supposed to join there the eight Rochester companies. (*BR* 5/9/1861) Rochester gave the first troops it was providing to the Union war effort a big send-off. A procession from Brown and State Streets was to escort the eight Rochester companies and Company K to the Central Railroad depot for their trip to their staging and training base at Elmira. Between 20,000 and 30,000 people lined the route. The soldiers were accompanied by "police, firemen, three bands, militia from Rochester's 54th regiment, veterans of the War of 1812," and Rochester's mayor and Common Council.

The Brockporters arrived at the Rochester station at 7:15 a.m. and, even though the show was long delayed in getting underway, never joined the festivities. Instead, the boys sat in the railroad carriages for hours, "as Capt. Thomas was not fully posted as to the arrangements made." Then, when the train finally pulled out, it left the Brockporters behind. "Unfortunately, Capt. Thomas had not understood an order directing him to transfer the men under his command from the cars in which they arrived, to those of the special train…The train went nearly to the city line before their absence was noticed by those on board, and it became necessary to return." (*RDD* 5/4/1861)

When the troops arrived in Canandaigua, no train was available to carry them onward. Six companies, including G and K remained overnight in whatever accommodations they could find. The situation was not improved by "some members of Capt. Tully's company," who "'cut up' a little, during their stay…and…no one wept when they went away." Fortunately, the hospitality of the residents eased the frustrations, and many soldiers found overnight lodgings with townspeople. (*RDD* 5/6/1861)

Training in Elmira

The experience of the troops when they finally reached Elmira the following day was not much better. The food was "sometimes miserable to the extreme; not only unpalatable, but most unclean…worse than convicts fare." (JDB in *BR* 5/16/1861) When the troops were mustered in, the federal government took over the victualling, but the hoped-for improvement did not come. The soldiers "don't like the fare as well as they did that provided by the State. There is more salt meat, and less vegetables." (*RDD* 5/25/1861) Two days later, however, "the grub is spoken of in none but complimentary terms. Supper last night, consisted of mush and milk…Breakfast this morning, boiled beef, fried potatoes, and fried pudding." (*RDD* 5/27/1861) The food, now, was "giving tolerable satisfaction." The daily ration for the regiment (nearly 800 men) was "184 lbs. pork, 614 lbs. beef, 827 lbs. bread or corn meal, 88 lbs. sugar, 2 bush. beans or peas or…75 lbs. rice, 50 lbs. coffee, 30 qts. vinegar, 15 qts. salt, 30 lbs. soap, 11 lbs. candles." (*RDD* 5/28/1861) That amounted to a pound of meat per soldier per day plus the side dishes.

The barracks for their housing were still under construction when the regiment arrived. To speed the work, General Van Valkenburgh, "goes down among the contractors and d—ns them" every morning. That "ceremony" was repeated by the general or one of his aides in "the course of the forenoon," "about the middle of the day," "at a later hour" and "toward night." As a direct result, no doubt, of those exertions, all the companies were housed adequately, though simply, by May 7. (*RDD* 5/8/1861) By May 13, the regiment was occupying twenty new barracks, 20 ft. x 80 ft., and "finely ventilated." The men slept in double-tiered bunks. "Each of us have a straw bed, two camp blankets, and an extra tick, unfilled, which we use for a sheet. Two of us occupy one bunk, and by spreading out our blankets, we make a covering of four thicknesses, affording warmth and comfort." (*BR* 5/16/1861) One Brockporter (JDB *BR* 5/9/1861) complained that: "Capt. Lewis' and Capt. Smith's companies have quartered together in Holden's Hall. Think of a bedroom containing nearly two hundred lively boys, and imagine how much sleep I get."

Uniforms and weapons were long in arriving. After nine days, "none of the troops have their 'soger' clothes or muskets, and the majority of the companies are entirely ignorant in regard to handling the latter article." (*RDD* 5/13/1861) Finally, 18 days after arriving at Elmira, each of the men received "a gray jacket and pants, and a heavy overcoat of mixed brown and gray, fitting the body closely, and having a high collar and large cape… The coats all have the large sized United States buttons, and they glitter in the sun like stars. Every one is in high glee." (*RDD* 5/25/1861)

The glee, however, did not last as long as the glitter. The overcoats were alleged to be "of some coarse material…The jackets and trowsers are made of a sort of satinet. The material is 'shoddy'…All the garments are cut and made in the most slip shod and disgraceful manner, and nobody expects they will last more than two months." Moreover, socks, underclothing, shirts, knapsacks, caps, and shoes had not yet arrived. (*RDD* 5/25/1861, 5/28/1861)

The State Military Board investigated the matter of the "shoddy" uniforms. It reported that Brooks Brothers had contracted with the Board to supply 12,000 uniforms of "all wool kersey" for $19.50 each. However, the contractor could not obtain enough of the right quality cloth. The Board permitted it to use a poorer quality cloth without changing the price. Brooks Brothers then produced the uniforms with cloth that cost less than half as much as the kersey. (*BR* 8/22/1861) The uniform material, a type of reconstituted cloth, was so notorious that shoddy became a synonym for poor quality.

The volunteers' weapons were also tardy and, when they finally arrived, they were 1840 muskets, "cumbersome and disagreeable" rather than the rifles that had been expected. (*RDD* 5/29/1861) On the eve of leaving Elmira, Sphinx wrote that, "Our uniforms and equipment are not what we expected…and…the 'Canal Board &c.,' at Albany, would be in danger of a coat of tar and feathers, should they venture in this direction." (*BR* 5/30/1861)

The weather was not conducive to preparing the troops for war, either. The first three weeks were "as trying, perhaps, as was ever known for the season." (*RDD* 5/29/1861) The week preceding May 25, had only two "really fine days…and those were regular scorchers." (*RDD* 5/27/1861)

Nor was the situation improved by the misbehavior of many soldiers. "There have been some fights and rows among the men…and…many men are armed with revolvers and Bowie knives." The problem was compounded by there being, "[s]omething like five thousand volunteers" in Elmira, but "only about fifteen hundred were organized into regiments…Over three thousand men, many of whom carried concealed weapons, have been wandering about at will, conducting themselves with a degree of license that was alarming…[T]here was no authority present sufficiently powerful to restrain the disorderly." (*RDD* 5/14/1861) Two soldiers were arrested for burglarizing a home in the city. (*RDD* 5/29/1861)

Some of the rowdiness was good-natured. For instance:

> *The men had a grand time last night, this morning, and to-night, in blanketing each other, or as they say, initiating them into the "Brown Jug Society." About twenty men take a blanket and place a man in it, and at the word, one, two, three, they throw the man some six or eight feet in the air. This process is repeated three times; then they cross fingers, and the man is a member. Some men as they are thrown up turn a complete sommersault, others come down upon their heads. The best feeling, however, is preserved. (*RDD *5/11/1861)*

The regiment was accepted by the State Military Board on May 7, (DMNA website) assigned the number 13 on May 8, and mustered into federal service for a three-month term on May 14. (Phisterer 1887) Six men in Company K refused to take the oath, six deserted, and two were medical rejects. (*BR* 5/16/1861) Those who refused the oath were treated roughly by their erstwhile comrades. They "were turned over to the 'knights of the black jug,' and after being divested of [their uniforms], were placed in the blanket, which knowing ones say has done service in another 'expedition,' and were most effectually tossed amid the cheers and groans of the faithful. In some cases a pail or two of water was thrown in to enable them to 'strike out.'" (*RDD* 5/18/1861)

As things settled down, the troops fell into a daily routine described by one correspondent this way: (*RDD* 5/16/1861)

5 a.m. Reveille and roll call
5:30 a.m. Surgeon's call
6 a.m. "Peas upon a Trencher" (breakfast)
7:30 a.m. Drill
8 a.m. Guard mounting
9–10 a.m. Commissioned officers drill
10–11:30 a.m. Drill of companies or squads
1:30–2:30 p.m. Non-commissioned officers drill
3–5 p.m. Drill of companies or squads
5:30 p.m. Evening parade
9:30 p.m. Tattoo and roll call
10 p.m. Taps and lights out

Given all the difficulties, it seems amazing that a well-ordered military formation could emerge from Elmira in barely three weeks. Company K was plagued by special problems. Captain Thomas fell ill shortly after arrival and did not recover during the stay, eventually resigning his commission on grounds of illness. Also, First Lieutenant E.P. Fuller was absent about a third of the time, traveling between Elmira and Brockport. Yet, a member of a Rochester company reported on May 15—11 days into their training—that Captain Thomas's company, with two others, is "also doing well, and will in time come up to the standard." He indicated, however, that they were not doing as well as the other companies in the regiment. (*RDD* 5/18/1861) Despite that brief period of training and the other obstacles to success, shortly before their departure for Washington, their drill "attracted a great crowd of people, and the regiment made a splendid appearance." (*RDD* 5/28/1861)

While stationed in Elmira, the Brockport soldiers enjoyed considerable communication with the home folks. Three Brockport area men visited their sons in camp and Lieutenant Fuller traveled twice to Brockport, first to bring four deserters and five new recruits to Elmira and secondly to receive a ceremonial sword. (*BR* 5/16/1861 5/23/1861) Six "heavily loaded" carloads of Rochesterians, including the Common Council, traveled to Elmira to visit their regiment shortly before its departure. No mention is made of Brockporters among them. (*RDD* 5/29/1861)

So began the service of Brockport's first troops. Their initiation did not go smoothly. The United States had not been at war since the Mexican War ended 12 years earlier. The mobilization effort was unprecedented in size and rapidity. Not surprisingly, mistakes were made and unexpected delays occurred. Nevertheless, however haltingly, Brockport's soldiers were on their way, though more frustrations lay ahead before they could play the role for which they had enlisted.

Chapter 6
Waiting for Action

Washington

The regiment left Elmira for Washington on May 29. Again, their departure was accompanied by much celebration, as reported in the *Rochester Daily Democrat*:

> *The greatest ovation that ever took place in this village, occurred to-day, upon the departure of our brave boys... The...regiments started for the depot, escorted by the several regiments now encamped here... The route from the barracks to the depot,...a good mile,...was crowded with a dense throng of spectators, who cheered the soldiers onward. A fine banner was strung across one of the streets, upon which was inscribed, in silken letters, "Onward to victory." The stars and stripes floated in every part of the place, and thousands gathered to witness the departure of the two regiments. As they moved onward amid the plaudits of the spectators..., tears were seen coursing down the cheeks of many of the fair ones..., the sight of which unmanned a number of our Rochester boys. As a general thing, however, the most of them were highly delighted in getting away to the scene of more active duty...All of the Rochester regiment appeared to feel highly elated, and amid the cheers of the citizens, and the remaining troops, the trains left. (*RDD *5/30/1861)*

The enthusiasm shown by the members of Companies G and K as they set off for war reflected the optimism that characterized the sentiment in the

North at the outset of the Civil War. Editor Beach expressed pride that they had "responded to the call of their country so cheerfully and with so much alacrity" and commented on "the brave spirit they exhibit." (*BR* 5/30/1861) One of his correspondents confirmed this, describing his comrades as "eager to get to Elmira," (*BR* 5/9/1861) and when orders came to move on to Washington, "unbounded enthusiasm prevailed through the regiment… Cheer upon cheer rent the air…Last night was the happiest one that our soldiers have passed." (*BR* 5/30/1861)

Still, their problems had not ended. They traveled to Washington in "freight cars, with rough board seats extemporized" that had no ventilation. So, the "Rochester boys were obliged to secure breathing holes…with a vigorous jab the muzzles of numberless muskets" pierced "their way through the stout boarded sides, and in very short order nearly every man had a separate window of his own." (*RDD* 5/31/1861)

The train took 21 hours from Elmira to Harrisburg, Pennsylvania. At York, the troops were introduced to the hostility of southern sympathizers:

> *Here three rounds of cartridges were dealt out to each man, guns ordered loaded. Within about five miles of the State Line, we passed picket guards, and the road is guarded from that point to Baltimore… When within a mile of the city, guns were ordered at half cock. The train stopped just outside the city limits and the regiments formed into line…Our colors were flying to the breeze, and to the tune of the "Star Spangled Banner," we entered the city.*
>
> *We marched through the principal streets, to the Washington depot, the band playing national airs. The avenues were lined with people, and the majority of the faces wore a gloomy, discontented aspect. The press may talk about the loyalty of Maryland, but it is rotten to the core. The batteries on the heights that command the city, are the opiates that quiet and for the time being put to sleep their secession sentiments and movements. As it was, they insulted and stoned the guard who were left behind to take charge of the baggage. (Sphinx* BR *6/6/1861)*

The regiment finally arrived in Washington at 11 p.m., a journey of 31 hours. However, their ordeal had not yet ended:

> *We were marched up and down the streets until nearly 3 A.M., in search of quarters, (none having been provided). We were finally put in an empty building, and our tired, worn out, supperless men, (without blankets, they being behind with the baggage,) found rest upon the hard floor. In the*

> *morning, they clamored loudly for breakfast. None came. Many were faint for want of food. At last, about 11 o'clock, the Quarter-master said the day's rations for each company would be on hand shortly—they came. What do you think they were?—remember, for a whole day—Three red herring, a piece of cheese, and six hard biscuits, to a man.(Sphinx* BR *6/6/1861)*

The third night since leaving Elmira (May 31), they slept in tents with no blankets, still hungry. The next day, finally, things improved. They pitched their tents, were fed "meat, bread, &c.,...in abundance, and a hearty breakfast and a hearty time we had, I assure you. We are now comfortably situated."

Nevertheless, the war was uncomfortably close. A picket of a Maine regiment, camped about a quarter mile from the 13th, was fired on at night, and the secessionist sniper was captured.

> *Just after this, another picket of the same regiment saw something approaching the lines. He called out "halt"—once—twice—three times—then fired, and killed—a stray cow that was unable to give the countersign. (*BR *6/6/1861)*

ARLINGTON HEIGHTS

The regiment camped on Meridian Hill in Washington until June 3, when it crossed the Potomac into Virginia, where it camped at Fort Corcoran on Arlington Heights. (JDB *BR* 6/13/1861) There, it was employed in constructing fortifications, mainly digging trenches, until the opening of the Manassas campaign. (DMNA) That they were present on enemy territory became plain to them very quickly. Their first night in Virginia "about midnight our advance picket guard was driven in, and a general alarm brought every man to his fighting post, but the enemy kept shady, and our troops rested on their arms for about two hours, when another general alarm caused us again to muster for fight—yet no fight." Two nights later they had two alarms, but "were really disappointed to return to camp without a single brush with the enemy." Rebels captured two men from another regiment, but a company of dragoons rescued them and captured the eight Rebels. (JDB *BR* 6/13/1861) This nighttime harassment by the rebels continued until the First Battle of Bull Run. (Sphinx *BR* 6/27/1861)

On Arlington Heights the Brockporters first encountered southern slavery:

> *When I was north I was told that the Virginia slaves loved their masters so well that they would be our worst enemies. But I find some strange infatuation is so possessing the Negroes; although promises of iron bracelets are made by their masters, yet the freedom-hating, chain-loving, whip-kissing slaves, are actually coming over to us, and offering themselves as our allies. I asked a slave the other day, why he could be so foolish as to run away from plenty and take up with scarsity? He replied that "Sambo get most starved by massa, 'cause massa could not get enough for himself to eat!" (JDB* BR *6/13/1861)*

Another serious problem that plagued the Brockport company on Arlington Heights was illness. The *BR* correspondent, JFB, suffered "a severe fit of illness" that required his resignation and the *BR* reported that 23 members of the company were "in the hospital—sick with measles and dysentery." A member of another company died of the measles, violent cramps induced by drinking too much "iced lemonade," and either "inhaling chloroform" or "a small dose of brandy and laudanum" for pain relief. (*BR* 6/20/1861, 6/27/1861)

On the positive side, JFB reported on June 15 that new uniforms had arrived. "[A]nd glad are our men to exchange the hateful grey 'duds' we got at Elmira, for this more agreeable, cool summer dress." (*BR* 6/20/1861) Nevertheless, they continued to complain that "our uniforms compare unfavorably with the other regiments." Also, in mid-July, they finally received the long-promised "rifles with sabre bayonets" and "Our men are delighted with them." (Sphinx *BR* 7/18/1861)

During the 18 days at Fort Corcoran, the routine was described this way: "Continued rounds of guard duty and labor in the trenches, does not give the boys too much idling time. Each term of fatigue duty lasts half a day, and about ten men from each company are detailed for the purpose." (JFB *BR* 6/20/1861)

Also, the brigade drilled several times a week and "Col. [William Tecumseh] Sherman [commander of the brigade that included the 13th] remarked that he had never seen a better drilled volunteer regiment than the thirteenth, taking into consideration the time it had been in the field." (Sphinx *BR* 7/18/1861)

CAMP UNION

On June 21, "we struck tents and marched some three miles to the south, and are now encamped near what is called 'Ball's Cross Roads.' We are far more exposed than...at Arlington Heights, and have to exercise the utmost caution. The enemy's lines are but a few miles distant and we are the most advanced regiment in this locality." The new encampment was called Camp Union. There, they continued to be engaged in "erecting earth works." (Sphinx *BR* 6/27/1861) "The same dull routine of camp life occur daily. The drill, guard duty, parade, &c., keeps us busy and the warm weather makes us long for the cool breezes of Lake Ontario." (*BR* 7/18/1861)

On July 15, the regiment moved again, this time leaving "for the interior via Fairfax Court House." Sphinx's account of Colonel Sherman's compliment seems confirmed by the fact that the regiment had "been assigned the post of honor, the right—front—of a brigade, in which are the famed sixty-ninth and seventy-ninth regiments of New York city." (*BR* 7/18/1861)

The morale of the regiment as it was about to go into battle for the first time is suggested by SRS in a July 15 dispatch: "I have noticed from the beginning that there has been a continued uneasiness to get forward into active service, to get into a 'big battle;' and whenever marching orders have come, they were greeted with a perfect uproar of cheering, and a perfect delirium of joy."

And by his boast:

> *Our regiment is the best that has been raised in the State, and one of the best in the nation. I have heard hundreds of people say in substance the same thing. Go through the different places and inquire which regiment is the best that has passed through. Echo answers, "The thirteenth," and you will hear the loudest encomiums, from all classes, upon the fine physical appearance of our men, the proficiency of their drill, and expression of the most perfect confidence in their courage and boldness. (*BR *7/25/1861)*

Besides his illness, Captain Thomas, the commander of the Brockport company, had other problems. His wife, Carrie, presumed to comment on her husband's troops in the public press in terms that caused her husband considerable embarrassment. About three weeks after they arrived in Washington, she wrote in the *U&A*: "We presume the majority of our half fed overworked volunteers have had star spangled banner to their heart's content and would say 'Give them anything, only let us go home.' We thought we detected a home sick look in most of their faces." (*BR* 6/27/1861)

At that time, she was boarding about a mile and half from the encampment with a "Southern right" man who had "seen about two weeks service in the guard house, but finally took the oath and obtained his freedom." (ibid.)

Three weeks later, she wrote to the *U&A* again: "A very large majority of the soldiers here are Democrats, with the exception of the north-western regiments. Republican principles are all right, but why do they make such cowardly men? Or is it only cowards who espouse Republican principles? Will any honest person tell us?" (*BR* 7/18/1861)

Editor Beach referred her to her husband for an answer. The lady returned to the fray with a third letter to the *U&A*, complaining that the *BR* and the *RDD* had seemed annoyed by her comment and saying, "We find a practical illustration that wounded birds flutter, and equally that 'birds of a feather flock together.'" (*BR* 8/1/1861)

Meanwhile, the affair had come to the attention of her husband, who wrote a long letter to the *RDD* denying any prior knowledge of his wife's missives. He "never saw, nor read, or heard of" his wife's letter "until I saw the portions of it you quote in your article." He denied that he was changing political parties and claimed that the only reason he had not gone into battle with his company was because "I was sick and unable to go on with the army, and...had been for ten days, before I ever heard of any movement of the army at all." (*BR* 8/1/1861)

The openness with which the Republic's correspondents described their activities and observations enhances greatly their value in gaining an understanding of the lives of the Union soldiers. However, it also underlines the casual attitude toward censorship and military intelligence. Southern sympathizers in the Brockport area and Confederate spies could read in the columns of the *BR*—and many other newspapers across the North—all sorts of valuable information about their enemy. For instance, in these early dispatches to the Republic, they could learn:

1. About the state of morale of the troops.
2. About their weaponry—that they were armed only with obsolescent muskets.
3. That "a grand attack will be made in a few days on Manassas Junction or some other point where an assailable blow can be struck." (*BR* 6/20/1861, a month before the battle)
4. That trenches were being dug around the fortifications at Fort Corcoran and "are being mounted with rifle cannon." (ibid.)

5. About the number of soldiers disabled by sickness.
6. About the vulnerability of Washington to a rebel attack. Arlington Heights was described as commanding "Washington as much as those large hills south from Brockport command the village." (*BR* 6/13/1861)
7. About the aggregate number of troops encamped around Washington (75,000) and the number on Arlington Heights (11,000). (*BR* 6/13/1861)

Chapter 7

Baptism of Fire

Blackburn's Ford

On July 16, 1861, the long-awaited battle orders finally came. The 13th "moved, in light marching order, with the 69th and 79th N.Y.S.M[ilitias] and the 2nd Wisconsin in the brigade," in the advance on Manassas. On July 18 it was present but not engaged in the battle at Blackburn's Ford. (DMNA website) The skirmish at Blackburn's Ford, a crossing of the stream known as Bull Run, near where the First Battle of Bull Run was fought, described in SRS's letter, was an unauthorized reconnaissance foray and a demoralizing defeat for the North. It ended in a disorderly retreat and resulted in 83 Union casualties, including one officer and 18 enlisted men killed, and 68 Confederate losses, including 15 killed. It was described in this letter of July 19, 1861, from Sphinx, written near Bull Run:

> *We left camp Tuesday, the 16th instant, about two o'clock, in the afternoon and marched to Vienna, a small village about ten miles to the southwest. There we halted for the night. The next morning orders were given that those who were unable to stand a long day's march might return. Seven of our company took advantage of this order; some of whom were really unable to stand the fatigues attending a long march. From Vienna our march was very slow, the road being obstructed by trees which had been felled by the rebels to cover their retreat. We passed Fairfax Court House to the left, and about a mile this side of Germantown, we discovered a*

breast work thrown up across the road. Sherman's battery opened with its rifled cannon upon it, cutting large holes through it at each shot. The guns not being responded to we rushed in, planted the stars and stripes, and to the music of cheers from ten thousand voices, marched into the deserted camp of the enemy. Here everything was in confusion. Meat lay upon the coals; clothing and food were strewed around; letters, and even miniatures, were found. In one house near by, were two secession soldiers sick with measles, who had been left behind in the hasty retreat. We were informed by the residents that fifteen hundred secession soldiers had left about two hours before our arrival.

On we marched, the roads still being obstructed by fallen trees. We halted about three miles north of Centreville, at a lately deserted camp. We learned from a pass dated July 16, and other papers, which we found, that we were in Camp Mason. We remained here over night, and the next morning again started forward. At Centreville was another deserted breastwork. Here we again halted. The artillery and first Brigade moved on; and the booming of cannon soon told us that an engagement had commenced.

We were formed in line and marched almost at a run, about two miles and a half, to Bulls Run. The balls here whistled past us, and the wounded upon the roadside, proved that they had not been sent upon a fruitless mission. We marched by the flank to the right and halted in a bunch of woods, awaiting further orders. The balls from the rifled Cannon, fell in fearful proximity all around, but fortunately no one of our regiment was injured. A splinter out from a tree by a passing ball struck one of our company in the face, making a slight scratch.

The second Wisconsin, although further from the enemy were less fortunate; a ball fell among them, severely wounding four of their men. We remained in this position with the balls falling hot and thick around us, for about an hour, with no opportunity to return the fire, and liable to be struck at any moment. I assure you it was a trying position; but our men stood it bravely, keeping in their places, and not showing the least sign of fear.— The firing upon both sides ceased simultaneously, and we were ordered to fall back. No company behaved more bravely than ours, notwithstanding our worthy Captain remained behind.

The enemy were behind strong breast-works, had heavier guns, and a considerable larger force than we. Our loss was considerable, several of the regiments being badly cut up. On our retreat we passed a member of the New York second, with his head all mashed in by a cannon ball—poor fellow, he never knew what hurt him.

It is impossible to give you, at this time, more particulars in regard to the battle, as we are ordered to fall in for the purpose of making another attempt to take their batter.

Saturday, July 20
No forward movement was made yesterday, and the men, therefore, had a day of rest, which was much needed....

I was able to get a more correct account of the engagement of the 18th instant. Our loss was not as great as at first reported; there were not to exceed twenty killed; and thirty or forty wounded. Bulls Run is only about two miles from Manassas Junction, and it is thought that we encountered the strongest opposition that the enemy can possibly bring against us. There were but three of our regiments engaged, and until the rebels retreated behind their breastworks, we had the best of it.

I forgot to mention that a prisoner was taken at Camp Mason. He was a fine looking man, armed with a Minnie rifle and sword bayonet. The idea that the rebels are poorly armed and have nothing to eat, has been dispelled by what we have seen at their camps; you may rest assured that in this vicinity, they are not only well armed, but have an abundance to eat.

We suffered on the march on account of water; what little we did get was poor, brackish stuff. Most of the men threw away their blankets and haversacks...and now have to sleep on the ground without covering. This is not very comfortable, especially when it rains, as it has the past two nights, still the men bear it without a murmur.

We have the utmost confidence in our Colonel, he exhibited great coolness and courage. There is no talk of going home now; all are eager to push forward.—Gen. McDowell complimented our regiment for the good order it preserved during the whole of the engagement.

We now occupy the advanced post on the turnpike, which is about half a mile to the right of the road where the battle was fought, and runs parallel with it.

Our scouts report it to be strongly fortified, and guarded by a large force. A darkey who was brought in yesterday by the picket, says that every white and black man has been forced to work upon the entrenchments for the last four or five weeks; that they are very strong and high, and that there is a "heap" of men there. We shall in all probability give the enemy a turn to-day; though, perhaps not until to-morrow. We are confident of victory, and if the Brockport company behave as gallantly as it did upon the previous occasion, the citizens will never regret its organization. (Sphinx BR *7/25/1861)*

FIRST BATTLE OF BULL RUN

Those expectations were correct, as this letter from Lieutenant Eugene Fuller to his parents reports. (*BR* 8/1/1861) Given Captain Thomas's resignation, Fuller was company commander. However, he, too, was ill, and had been since leaving Fort Corcoran a month before the battle, "and the fatigues and exertions of the march, battle and retreat, added to this have made me down sick." One can well imagine what thoughts and emotions went through the minds of the Brockporters who read the vivid, eloquent, and tragic account, fresh from the bloody battlefield. "On the 21st [of July] it [the 13th] crossed the Bull Run creek, about ten A.M., and was engaged with the enemy until five P.M., when it fell back with the whole line to the fortifications near Washington. In this action it sustained a loss of twelve killed, twenty-six wounded, and twenty-seven missing, out of six hundred engaged." (DMNA)

Bull Run was the first major engagement in the Civil War. The North had been supremely confident of winning a quick and easy victory. Lincoln's call for volunteers specified three-month enlistments. Those terms were nearing an end in mid-July 1861 and virtually nothing had been done. A battle was widely anticipated and everyone expected that it would be an attack on the Confederates stationed near Manassas Junction, Va., at a creek called Bull Run.

As word spread that the troops were moving out of their encampments across the Potomac from Washington, many civilians, including high government officials, poured out of the capital city in finery and carriages to witness the expected rout of the rebels. They mingled freely with the troops and caused much confusion, perhaps contributing to some delays that may have affected the outcome. When the battle ended in the way described by Sphinx in his July 26 letter below, written from Arlington, Va., the civilians were swept up in the general disorder. Most embarrassing was the capture by the Confederates of Rochester Congressman Alfred Ely.

> *On Saturday evening* [July 20] *orders were received to be ready to march at half past two the next morning. At that hour, the call sounded, and we were awakened from our half finished repose on the damp ground, to march to battle. We were soon on the move. It was a beautiful morning, and as the sun rose from behind the adjoining hills, its rays were reflected back from the thousands of glittering bayonets. I looked, and thought perhaps it might be the last sun rise I should ever witness, (alas, it proved to be the last to many in that moving multitude,) but I soon shook off all gloomy thoughts and*

passed on. About six o'clock our brigade was filed to the left, and marched by divisions into a piece of woods; the artillery were stationed in an open field near by and soon opened by sending a thirty pound ball up the road. This was not replied to. After a short interval, another shot was fired, but this like the first elicited no reply. Our attention was now called to a large body of troops on a road about three-fourths of a mile to the right of us, we knew that it could not be Col. Hunter's division, as it was moving in the wrong direction, and he, Hunter, had not had time to make the circuit. Our battery now opened fire upon them, sending shell and shot into their midst, and scattering them considerably. We soon heard a volley of musketry, and knew by this that they had been met by Col. Hunter. Volley after volley was fired, and the battle became general—on the right, on the left, and in front, the deep thunder of the artillery and the sharp report of the musketry was heard in frightful rapidity. We were ordered forward; and at double quick march, we rushed on to support the gallant Hunter; wading across Bulls Run, and climbing a steep bank, we found ourselves in close proximity to the enemy who were retreating; we opened fire upon them, and their falling bodies proved that our aim had not been in vain. They soon, however, gained the corner of the woods, and we were ordered to cease firing, and marched some three-fourths of a mile to a rise of ground, where we found a considerable portion of the "grand army" assembled; the battle for a time had ceased, and we were allowed a resting spell, during which General McDowell rode past the different columns, and was loudly cheered by the soldiers.

We were soon ordered forward again, and had marched about one-fourth of a mile, when a concealed battery opened upon us, the first shot taking effect upon two of Captain Nolte's company—they stood but a few feet from me when they fell. [The 13th was leading the brigade. Marcotte 28] *On we pressed almost running; we were ordered to the left to support a battery which was being raised to a slight elevation; we were here halted and ordered to lie down. The firing by this time had become terrific; the balls from rifled cannon passing over our heads in close proximity; several of our regiment were struck; Michael Toole, of our company was here wounded in the knee by a spent ball.* [Not reported in ACWRD]

We were ordered to charge forward and at a double quick pace, we moved towards the enemy's lines, and soon came in range of their musketry; it was there that many of our brave men fell dead or wounded. The firing was incessant; we replying with visible effect. Approaching a large piece of woods, between which and us was a log house we halted, but still continued firing. Here some one cried out, cease firing; that we were shooting our friends.

We stopped for a time; and during the interval a man came into our ranks, I asked him if he were a Union man? He replied, "No. I mistook you for a Baltimore regiment." I immediately took his sword and revolver, placed him under guard, and then firing was resumed. We evidently were getting the better of our opponents, when suddenly we observed the whole line of our forces to swing back like a gate, leaving our regiment unsupported. No order to retreat was given that I heard, and there was no occasion for it that I can learn. It was a stampede started on the hill by a cowardly regiment, aided by the civilians and teamsters who were near.—There was nothing now left for us to do but retreat, or be surrounded by overwhelming numbers, so we marched back up the road to a place where they were attempting to rally our forces, but the attempt was a vain one. The reserve had taken the alarm and scattered like chaff. Fearing I should lose my prisoner, I took him under my own charge; he proved to be Lieut. Dunalt of the twenty-seventh Virginia regiment; he belongs to General Johnston's division, and had come by forced march from Winchester to join Beauregard.

I walked slow to keep out of the jam, and had a good chance to view the field of battle. It was a terrible and sickening sight. Dead men and horses lay strewn in frightful profusion—here one poor fellow with his leg carried away by a cannon ball, was begging piteously for water—another prayed that I would take my sword and put an end to his misery, some were in the last agonies of death; others not so severely wounded were trying to escape dragging their mangled limbs after them. God forbid that I should ever be compelled to witness another scene like the one of Sunday last.

About a mile from the battle field a masked battery opened a terrific fire upon our retreating army—here they again scattered in all directions. I took a circuitous route along a stream, and just before sun down, found myself upon our camp ground of the night before.—Just below this was a remnant of our army drawn up in line of battle, I tried to join them but a volley of musketry opened upon us. (I forgot to mention that a few moments before I was joined by Ensign Gilbert;) [The 13th had three Gilberts, two in Company K, none identified as "Ensign"] *we held a council of war, and concluded that our only safety lay in staying where we were. So we lay down on the ground, the prisoner in the middle, and for all of me he could have escaped a hundred times; for I never slept more soundly in my life, and did not wake till long after daylight, and probably would not then had it not been for the rain.—The army had left during the night, and so we were obliged to start on alone.—Just by the fence we passed a dead man, he had crawled all the way from the battle field, some six miles—to die. We reached Centerville about six and a half in the forenoon. Here a church had been converted into a hospital. I went in and beheld another awful sight, but I will not sicken you with a description. On we went; just below Centerville Gilbert left me, being in something of a hurry to get back. I could not move faster on account of my prisoner, who was or pretended to be foot sore, and moved at a very slow pace. The road between Centerville and Fairfax was strewn with wagons and provisions, ammunition, horses, and all kinds and descriptions of property. I reached Alexandria safely about three in the afternoon, reported to General Bunyan who complimented me highly, put under my charge two Georgians who had been taken, and sent me by steamer to Washington.*

I could not get a bed for love nor money, all the hotels there being full to overflowing. I put the Georgians in the station hodie [?], *and happened luckily to meet Van Buskirk, he procured a bed for myself and prisoner at a private boarding house. In the morning I awoke sick all over, had the jumping tooth ache to boot. I had my tooth pulled, and took a [illegible] for camp, arriving at Jackson's* [where Captain and Mrs. Thomas were staying], *I found our camp had been moved. Most of our folks supposed me to be lost, and they gave me three hearty cheers upon my arrival. The men now say they will go any where with me, because I stood by them in the battle.*

[Almon] *Raymond,* [William] *Kelly, and* [William Henry] *Joslyn, of our company are among the missing. Raymond and Kelly I fear have been killed. Joslyn was last seen at a spring about a mile from the battle field. He may have been killed by the shot from the masked battery which opened upon our retreating forces, but I think if he did not go on toward home he got lost and was taken prisoner. Connery was shot in the arm; Thompson in the finger; Toole I have already mentioned. This sums up the disasters in our company, though from the regiment many are missing, twenty or twenty-five are supposed to be killed.* [ACWRD says Kelly, Raymond, and Joslyn were captured and later paroled. It lists no "Connery" in the 13th, and no man with a similar name was wounded at Bull Run. Charles and Joseph Thompson were in Company K. ACWRD has both of them wounded at 2nd Bull Run but neither at 1st Bull Run.]

I must not forget to mention the bravery of John Richardson and Charles Morgan of our company. When behind the battery, the artillery being nearly tired out, called for volunteers to carry cartridges; these two alone out of a whole regiment jumped up and worked for a long time carrying cartridges from the caissons to the guns right in face of the galling and well directed fire from the enemy's battery—providentially they escaped injury. Heber [Fuller's brother who died of disease later] *acted very bravely, as did all the company with one or two exceptions.*

I am so weak and confused, I fear I have given but a poor description of the day's proceedings—when I get stronger, I will try and be more particular. (Sphinx BR *7/26/1861)*

Your affectionate son,

Eugene

A letter a week later from Sphinx added a few details to the account in his letter to his parents:

A story is told of poor Kelly which will bear repeating. When behind the battery orders were given to advance in front and fire kneeling. Kelly insisted upon standing up, and when cautioned as to the danger of his position, remarked "Who's afraid." Took deliberate aim, fired, and said "I jayhawked the critter."

Private McIntyre is also entitled to great credit for his coolness and bravery; he voluntarily assisted at one of the cannon, during the whole of the time our regiment supported the battery.

*Without particularizing further, let me remark that every man in the company who was in the engagement showed great coolness and bravery. Our company taking six prisoners, and bringing them safely into camp, which was more than was taken by the rest of the regiment. (*BR *8/8/1861)*

Lieutenant Fuller commented, six weeks after the battle that "the federal forces drove the rebels about two miles in the Bulls Run battle, and had not the enemy received fresh troops, or had Col. Miles come up with the reserve federal force, the enemy would have been badly beaten." (*BR* 9/5/1861)

W.H. Joslyn, Almon Raymond and William Kelly had all been taken prisoner, so that no member of the Brockport company had been killed at Bull Run. (*BR* 8/15/1861) Joslyn, the company's orderly sergeant, was a 26-year-old farmer. He remained in prison for 10½ months. After his parole, he was commissioned a first lieutenant and, then, captain in the 21st NY Cavalry, but was not mustered because of a consolidation of units. He settled in Denver, Colo., in 1865. The STCR says that Raymond was a laborer and taken prisoner July 21, 1861. The CTCR says that Raymond enlisted for three years in the 105th NYVI as a private on December 12, 1861, and that he "has not returned." William Kelly had been born in Ireland in September 1844 and was a farmer. He was discharged in June 1863, re-enlisted in the 26th NY Battery in September 1864, and served until July 1865. He resided in Holley after the war. Also, John B. Nichols of the Town of Ogden, a member of Company G was captured and confined at Richmond, Va. He died of disease as a POW on September 1, 1861.

Joslyn and Kelly were released from prison by the Confederates in early June 1862. John Reando, "belonging to another company in the 13th regiment, well known in this village," was released at the same time. Joslyn returned home to a hero's welcome, vowing to return to his company [though it no longer existed]." (*BR* 6/5/1862) Besides the captives and the deserters mentioned on page 103, three Brockporters had been discharged for disability by the time of First Bull Run. In the next year, leading up to the battle at Gaines' Mill on June 27, 1862, another nine Brockporters were discharged for disability or hospitalized.

The official War Department records show that the Third Brigade that included the 13th NYVI was much the largest of the three brigades in its division at Bull Run and suffered much the heaviest casualties. It contained four infantry regiments and two artillery companies. The First Brigade had four infantry regiments and the Second Brigade had three. Also, one artillery company was unattached. The First Brigade suffered 223 casualties, including 19 enlisted men killed. The Second Brigade had 58 casualties, including three officers and 18 enlisted men killed. The Third Brigade had 581 casualties, including three officers and 106 enlisted men killed. The 13th suffered fewer casualties than any of the other infantry regiments in the Third Brigade, 11 enlisted men killed, 27 enlisted men wounded, and twenty enlisted men missing.

A possible identification of the "cowardly regiment" that started the "stampede" on the hill that precipitated the rout of the Union troops is offered by a footnote to the official "Return of casualties in the First Division" at Bull Run. It reads, with respect to the 2nd NYVI in the Second Brigade:

> *Colonel Tompkins reports 140 others missing, without giving names. As this regiment did not cross Bull Run, they must have been accurately informed as to their killed and wounded. This taken in connection with the fact that three of the officers are reported as deserters, known to be in New York City, leads to the belief that, their officers having set the example, the men were not slow to follow it.* (OR *351)*

Chapter 8

The End of Company K

Mutiny

The thoroughly demoralized men of the 13th straggled back to their original base, Fort Corcoran on Arlington Heights. By August 4, two weeks after the battle, the regiment was officially reorganized and ordered into federal service for completion of a two-year term of service. Originally, they had signed up for two years service to the state and were mustered into federal service for a three-month term. As late as July 15, six days before Bull Run, SRS could write: "There seems at least to be a prospect that the Rochester regiment will disband at the expiration of the three months enlistment; but I don't think that they will break up and then go home, but will immediately re-enlist again in some regiment where there is a vacancy, for the war or for three years, as the case may require." (*BR* 7/25/1861)

This seems to have been a general feeling, despite the hardships they had endured, the lack of proper food, uniforms, weapons, and housing. Bull Run changed all that. They knew now that war was not all fun and games. Its horrors had been brought home in very traumatic fashion. They might have suffered even that in victory, but in abject defeat, routed in a most humiliating way, army life was no longer fun.

The men believed, with good reason, that once their three-month term expired on August 14, they would be discharged and free to leave. On August 4, Sphinx wrote:

> *"Home, sweet home," has been the sole topic of conversation for the past few days. Rumors that the regiment was to be discharged have been circulated, and have produced a severe home fever among the men, that it will take a strong remedy to allay.—We are unable to ascertain the truth or falsity of these reports, but my opinion…is that you may expect to see the majority of us in Brockport within a few weeks. (*BR *8/8/1861)*

The words and actions of their superior officers in the days after Bull Run reinforced that belief:

> *These men were firstly sworn into the service of the government for but three months—which led them to believe that at the expiration of that period their service would expire. Immediately after the great battle at Bull Run they were ordered to Washington for discharge from service…The order was countermanded, and they were told that they were wanted for a short time until experienced men could be got to fill their places. (*BR *8/22/1861)*

However, on August 4, word reached the unit that Colonel Quinby had been directed by Special Orders 322, August 2d, 1861, "to report with his command to the Adjutant General of the United States army for duty, under the order of the United States Government, for the remainder of the term of enlistment of the regiment into the service of the State of New York." (DMNA) The federal government could not afford to permit their discharge and, at its request, Governor Morgan had transferred the regiment to the general government.

Understandably, many soldiers did not accept what they believed was the unilateral extension of their federal service. Moreover, they had been "infected by the contagion of mutiny" from the 79th NYVI, which shared their brigade and had been the scene of massive insubordination over the same complaint in the preceding days. (Jeffrey D. Wert, "Mutiny in the Army," *CWTI*, April 1985 per Brian Bennett) Therefore, when August 15 dawned many of them considered themselves to be civilians and refused to obey orders. Six of the ten companies, apparently including Company K, balked. The brigade commander, tough old veteran soldier William Tecumseh Sherman, would have none of that: "To-day Col. Sherman ordered a parade at 11 o'clock A.M., to tell the men just how things stood. He explained the general 'situation' of affairs, and concluded by informing them in a rather emphatic manner that he should hold them for the remainder of the two year term, and they must make the most of it." (*BR* 8/22/1861)

Sherman then invited those who were unwilling to serve to step forward. About eighty men did. He then informed them that they would be sent to Fort Jefferson on the Dry Tortugas islands in the Caribbean to do hard prison labor. About fifty men relented under that threat. The remaining recalcitrant 31 were marched off to spend six months at hard labor, along with 190 other mutineers from two other regiments. (Marcotte 35) An article in *CWTI* reports that most of the mutineers in the 79th went unpunished and that "The wrath of the army and government curiously fell most severely upon the anonymous members of the 2nd Maine and the 13th New York." (*CWTI* April 1985)

Only one member of Company K was among the prisoners. Ironically, he was Charles Morgan, one of the two heroes cited by Fuller in his account of Bull Run. Sphinx says that he "was not a resident of York State." The STCR lists him as born in the Town of Sweden, but has no further information about him. Also, the list included Fred Raymond, a Hamlin resident who was a member of Company F. (*BR* 8/22/1861)

Sphinx reported this incident thus:

> *After weeks of doubtful suspense, the question is at last finally settled. The thirteenth regiment is to remain in service two years; an order to this effect was published last week. The men took it hardly. At first some were disposed to rebel; but, as a general rule, better counsels prevailed and but few refused to perform duty. Those who did were disarmed, and sent to the Island of Tortugua. Company K lost but one man,...and as he behaved bravely upon the field of battle, I will withhold his name. Other companies were less fortunate—some losing fifteen and twenty men.* [In fact, no company in the 13th had more than thirteen men sent to Tortugas.]
>
> *We were informed that our regiment stood second to none in the service; that in consideration of arduous duties performed since its organization, and the bravery it displayed in the late contest, it would be allowed to join any brigade it might see fit to designate, select its own place of encampment, and that the men would be allowed to go home, upon furlough, in squads of eight or ten at a time. We are also to receive a full dress uniform from the government, and have already been furnished a pretty and substantial one from the State, consisting of light blue army cloth pants, and dark blue jacket. Their arrival was quite opportune for 'shoddy' was quite played out, causing numerous banners, not exactly up to regulation in size and color, to float to the breeze.*
>
> *Now that the suspense is over, a better feeling prevails in the regiment. It will probably be ordered to Fort Monroe,* [at Hampton, Virginia]

as a general desire is expressed in favor of that point, on account of the healthiness of the locality.

...I forgot to mention that the regiment was to be put on half duty, and recruited up to the full number now required. These things are...much needed, as the fatigues of the last six weeks have told fearfully upon some of the men...There have been some few desertions within the past week. If a deserter is caught, an example will be made of him, as a warning to others.

A gentleman from Rochester, accompanied by his daughter, rode up to the camp today, to visit his son. He was informed that he had deserted. The gentleman bowed his head and exclaimed "I had rather have heard that he was shot." The anticipated joy at meeting the son, and the brother, was by this intelligence changed to the deepest sorrow...

*Rumors of a forward movement to the part of the enemy are current, especially in the Rochester papers. If they do attack this locality, they must come with an over-whelming force, or their defeat is certain; and in any event if a battle is fought near Washington, the Union forces will stand a much better chance of success than they did at Bulls Run. (*BR *8/22/1861)*

The mutineers did not go directly to the Tortugas, according to two reports:

We arrived at Fortress Monroe, and landed the prisoners at the Rip Raps, opposite the fort. They were very quiet all the way down, and I think they wished themselves back again.

*The place where we landed them is the foundation of a very large fort to be built by them. It is in the middle of the Potomac. (*BR *8/29/1861, 9/19/1861)*

A letter to his father from Fred Raymond described life after the mutineers reached the Tortugas:

I do not complain of any treatment I have received since I left the regiment—but it has been hard. I suppose you saw the letter that was published, written from here about a man being tied up and left till he was insensible, and then taken down and to the hospital. It is so. I did not see him for three days. I am happy to say that the tieing up is done away with now, and times are better. As for me, I am getting along first rate, and if it was not for the name of prisoner I would rather stay here than be in Virginia. My health is good, and I have not seen a sick day since I left Washington, in fact I have gained seven pounds, and that you know is a good deal on a man's nose.

> *We have to work ten hours a day; but we have good food now, and a good appetite.*
>
> *I hear something about our going back to the regiment. Well I will go if they think my services will be better there than they are here; or will stay—it makes but little difference to me where I go; I can be contented; but they have me for only two years and then I shall be myself again; but till then I am a slave.*
>
> *I wish the government would pay us what was coming when we left the regiment so we could get tobacco and paper, and not have to beg all that we get, which is the hardest of all. If a man wants to write a letter, he has to beg a sheet of paper from one, an envelop from another, and a stamp from another. In fact it is all beg; not much give—and it is hard for me to beg; it goes against the grain. (*BR *11/28/1861)*

Seven months after their sentencing, 28 of the "insubordinate members of the Thirteenth Regiment" returned to Rochester on 30 days' furlough. One of the original 31 had been delayed by illness and one had died at Tortugas. Morgan's name is not on the list. (*U&A* 3/27/1862) Following their furlough, they returned to their units, and, reportedly, made excellent soldiers. (DMNA)

COMPANY K DISBANDED

In fact, the rebel attack that Sphinx feared did not take place. The rebel victors at Bull Run were as green and disorganized as the Union troops and quite incapable of following up on their victory. The 13th regiment now numbered about 500 men and Company K 55 men and had lost six soldiers by desertion. They were William C. Banta, George H. Williams, and Peter Meinhardt of Brockport; William J. Hack of Sweden; William H. Ransom of Hamlin; and Henry H. Nichols of Webster Mills, later Kendall Mills (Fuller in *BR* 9/5/1861, 9/12/1861).

The federal military leadership did to Company K what the rebels had failed to do. It abolished the company. Phisterer says that "October 29, 1861, Company K was consolidated with Company A." (Phisterer 1887) The ACWRD says otherwise. It has only nine of the Brockporters transferring from Company K to Company A on that date. The others went to seven other companies—ten to B, seven to E, six each to D and H, five to F, and one each to C and G. This was part of a general reorganization of the regiment in September–November 1861 and January 1862. Another part of the reorganization transfered Company G to Company K of the 3rd NY Cavalry. That included 15 Brockporters—six from Brockport, seven from Ogden and one each from Parma and Clarkson. Also, October 15, the regiment was transferred to the brigade of Brig. Gen. John Martindale, a distinguished attorney in Rochester before the war, in the division of Brigadier General Fitz-John Porter. (DMNA, Marcotte 16)

Lieutenant Fuller and Sphinx reported that Company K had performed well at Bull Run, so the change would not have been punishment. Certainly, the folks back home were proud of their boys at Bull Run. They received Lieutenant Fuller as a hero when he returned to Brockport on leave on September 3:

> *His return was not expected so soon, and the fact that he would arrive in the evening train was not known until in the afternoon, and then not widely. Still there was a great rush of citizens to the railroad depot to give a cordial welcome to one who had shed so much luster upon himself and upon his native village by his undaunted bravery. The village firemen, led by the martial band, were present in full force. By the time the train arrived the depot platform was full from one end to the other of people eager to take by the hand the heroic young Lieutenant. The train came, and upon the first appearance of the Lieutenant three hearty cheers were given him. As he descended from the cars to the platform he was seized by the hands and accorded such a welcome as is bestowed on those who faithfully perform their duty. (*BR *9/5/1861)*

Elias B. Holmes, Brockport's most distinguished citizen, delivered the welcoming speech. He referred to the ceremonial sword that the villagers had presented Fuller, remarking that it "has received, if reports be true, no dishonor at your hands. We hear that you waved it bravely on the battle field in the thickest of the fight at Bull Run." He complimented Fuller for capturing a rebel lieutenant and referred to "the brave boys composing company K,…sent from our firesides, and behaving with becoming—yes with patriotic loyalty and valor."

Fuller responded briefly and modestly, mainly taking advantage of the occasion to urge "these men I see around me [to] do their duty" by enlisting in the army. "The remarks of both speakers were loudly cheered." Then a "procession…marched down Main street to near the canal bridge; thence back up Main street to Erie Street to the residence of Lieut. Fuller's parents."

During the week that Fuller was home, he addressed an organizational meeting for a "Union Party," combining Republicans and War Democrats "In response to the vociferous calls of the audience." He denied any partisan interest, but urged defeat of the "peace party movement" and the election of "good men…who will not clog the affairs of government as some of them did prior to the Battle of Bull Run." Also, he called for "young men to go voluntarily and fight for their country," warning that otherwise they would be drafted and "there would be but little honor in serving their country because compelled to." Several days later, he returned to duty "taking along a number of recruits from Rochester." (*BR* 9/12/1861)

Colonel Quinby, the regimental commander, resigned because of the mutiny. Quinby had consulted Lieutenant General Winfield Scott on the status of the regiment and believed that his visit "has stimulated the discontent and insubordination of the regiment and it is now in a condition utterly beyond my control." He was replaced by Colonel John Pickell, "an aging Regular army colonel." (Marcotte 38)

Military and personal politics might have had something to do with the fate of Company K. Six weeks after John Pickell became regimental commander, "John H. Pickell, age 20" enrolled at Camp Pickell, Va., as a 2nd Lt., and was assigned to Company G of the 13th. Was the regiment reorganized to make room for the son of the regimental commander? (Phisterer 1898)

The men in companies I and K, which were dissolved, took the news badly. A member of a Rochester company reported:

> *Pickell's order was read at evening drill at his direction. Company I, with three or four exceptions, immediately threw down their arms, and refused to submit to it. At this, the Colonel, in a high state of excitement, declared, with an oath, he would shoot them, and ordered the guard to load; but changed his purpose, formed the rest of the regiment into a hollow square around them, took them prisoners, and marched them at once to Washington, where at last accounts they were lying in jail. The Brockport company were then informed they could remain together until further orders. The boys were feeling very badly over the prospect of their separation, and were quite low spirited—not being conscious of having done anything to merit such a disparagement. (*BR *11/7/1861)*

When the orders did come for disbanding the Brockport company, "the whole company have signed a protest and sent to General [Fitz-John]

Porter," apparently without effect. Their reaction to being disbanded is also indicated by this letter from "a young man formerly to work in one of the village furnaces": "I suppose that you have heard of the Brockport company being disbanded. I was assigned to company B. It is from Dansville; they are a fine lot of fellows, and the officers are as good as I want to serve under; but of course I would rather be in old company K after all. I do not want a braver or better captain than Fuller." (*BR* 1/6/1862)

Obviously, the reorganization altered Fuller's status. He had been made captain and commander of Company K when Thomas resigned on September 10. (Phisterer 1891, 1900) Thomas returned to Brockport on September 14, "in feeble health." (*BR* 9/19/1861) With the disbanding of Company K, the *BR* reported: "We learn that although Captain E.P. Fuller of company K had been assigned by Colonel Pickell to the Lieutenancy of company E, he will, by virtue of his appointment, take charge of the new company K, (Lieut Gilbert's,) unless old company K is restored to its former position. Matters in the Thirteenth appear to be somewhat mixed." (11/14/1861)

In fact, he became commander of the new Company K. (Phisterer 1891) At the same time that Fuller was promoted, another Brockporter was demoted. J.D. Barnes was removed as regimental chaplain, being "displaced by the Rev. Mr. Bowman, an Episcopal clergyman, formerly of Pittsford—Colonel Pickell being a member of the Episcopal church, and something of a stickler for its ritual." (*BR* 9/12/1861, quoting the *RDD*)

So, in five months, the first Brockport boys to march off to war had suffered from poor food, shoddy uniforms, obsolescent weapons, transportation snafus, inadequate training, and bad weather. They had slept in a train, on the ground with no padding or cover, on the floor in an empty building, and in tents. They had fought valiantly, been betrayed by a flanking regiment, and routed by the enemy. They had joined in a mutiny and in a protest. Their regimental commander had resigned in disgrace. Their captain had resigned under a cloud of illness and embarrassment. Their chaplain had been sacked. Their 2nd lieutenant (Edwin Dayton) had been cashiered. Their company had been disbanded in apparent punishment, for what they knew not, yet their 1st lieutenant had been promoted and given command of the company that replaced theirs. One of their comrades was in a Union prison on the Dry Tortugas, three others were in Confederate prisons, and six of them had deserted. None had been killed or were wounded at Bull Run. Yet, the home folks regarded them as "our brave boys" and heroes.

Chapter 9

The Peninsular Campaign

Afterlife of Company K

From the retreat from Bull Run on July 21 until the Peninsular campaign began on March 10, 1862, the 13th was stationed at Fort Corcoran under Colonel Pickell. The *BR* published no letters from the 13th during that period. However, one of its correspondents, who signed his name Yerrot, visited its quarters there, called Camp Stephan, at Editor Beach's request and submitted a lengthy, wordy report. (*BR* 3/20/1862). He praised the encampment extravagantly. It commands "the finest kind of a view of Washington and its vicinity, and also a magnificent panorama of the Potomac and the surround country." He called it "a glorious spot." He said that the camp "regularly laid out in streets, presents a well kept and ship shape appearance."

Yerrot gave a very unfavorable report on Colonel Pickell. He was told that the regimental commander "was hardly 'worth seeing'" and inferred "that the most pleasant relations do not exist between him and a part, at least, of his officers…I thought from the manner in which some of them spoke of him, that there was a 'screw loose somewhere.'" Captain Fuller, however, "did not seem inclined to say much either way." The only incident during the preceding 7½ months that Yerrot thought worth reporting was "an amusing though somewhat disastrous" windstorm that blew down many of the company's tents.

The following week, the *BR* (3/27/1862) published a long article by Yerrot, apparently based on his visit to Camp Stephan, in which he described at great length the transformation of "the gallant volunteer boys [who] paraded [on] the village greens…last spring" into "bronzed, stern visaged men…, distinguished from the 'sacred' mud through which they wade, only by their brass buttons." He described their manner of digging trenches, eating their chow, and sleeping on the ground, and noted that "the tactics and discipline of war have reduced their vocabulary to a few simple words, chief among which is the suggestive one, fight." The gist of the article was that the green troops of July 1861 had become hardened veterans.

Yerrot's conducted an informal interview of Lieutenant Fuller in Fuller's tent on March 8 through a haze of cigar smoke and champagne bubbles. Yerrot presented it as direct quotations, though the colorful language seems more Yerrot than Fuller. Nevertheless, it seems to convey Fuller's perceptions and reflections on his military experience. In any case, they are two Brockporters in the Union army attempting to convey to their families and friends what their experiences meant to them:

> *But Captain Fuller,…how do you like "soldiering"? The romance of the thing must have passed away long ago; what can you say for the reality? Do there not come times when you would gladly exchange war and its glories for Coke upon Littleton?* [a law book] *when all the gilded hopes of ambition melt away before the ever sacred memory of home?"*
>
> *As we lighted our cigars, the Captain answered, "That the habits, associations and memories of a man's former life should be cherished with a secret longing for their return, is not his fault; nor does it, I apprehend, militate against him.—we all have our 'spells,' you know; but, for the greater part, my experience as a soldier has not been unpleasant. Connected with the organization of our company and its departure for the seat of war, there may have been something of what you call 'romance,' but that quickly died out. There was none of it in the battle shout, the sabre stroke, the death throe and awful massacre at Manassas.—That day there was reality terrific, and men upon that field lived years in a single hour. Not unfrequently the people do the soldier great injustice by attributing the part he is acting more to a love of adventure than to any real sentiment of patriotism. No judgment could be more erroneous. The spirit of adventure does not prompt men to work for weary weeks in the intrenchments, or to perform the many laborious functions of a soldier's life. The lover of adventure for its own sake, may roam the prairie or the tangled forest, and find in them the kind of happiness he seeks, but the hum-drum duties of camp life are irksome and distasteful to him. No, sir!" continued the Captain, knocking the ashes from his Havana, and*

warming with his subject as he proceeded, "While I would be the last to seek to prolong a war of this kind, I do not wish to be exempted from doing my share of its work while a single rebel lifts a disloyal hand. Aside from the desire which I am sure animates every man in our regiment to serve his country, there is a determination on the part of each to retrieve Bull Run. We remember the wrongful victors of that day with a hatred almost sublime. We feel and know that we in common with all the brave Union fellows who fought in the battle, were entitled to carry off the palms of victory:—that they were wrested from us by a combination of unpropitious circumstances, beyond our control, rather than by the prowess of the enemy—and we have sworn to win them back again. Woe betide the rebel who comes within the range of the guns of the Thirteenth—particularly the Manassas rebel…"

And the Captain, having exhausted himself and his subject, ordered his orderly and a bottle of Heidsick. We "tarried long" over the sparkling nectar and eventually punished the entire bottle in the most condign manner.

"Do you know," said our hero, "that an occasional visitor was a God-send to us fellows of the camp? Social chit-chat and re-unions, if not positively contraband, are at least not encouraged here, the book of regulations is ominously silent on the subject of champagne and cigars, and therefore it is that we look upon the coming of a friend as a happy period when the rules of courtesy shall assuage the rigors of military discipline."

"And do you mean to tell me, oh, most amiable destroyer of Uncle Sam's enemies and rations, that the face of a friend is welcome only as the signal of a revel?" I exclaimed.

*"By no means! Nothing of the kind, sir. Friends are the bright cases of our soldier life. We think of them when, worn with the cares and perplexities of our monotonous duties, we rest upon our rude beds, which weariness has rendered soft as eider down, and when the long, fatiguing march come on, and patriotism and the hope of fame are our sole inspirers, does it surprise you that our minds sometimes stray away from the hard realities of the situation, to wonder if our friends still think of us? Believe me, sir, as I before remarked, friends are a God-send to the soldier; and now I think of it, here's to our friends!" We drank the toast—the volunteer Captain and I, in his canvas soldier home—together, and save the music of the west wind, as it murmured among the tent ropes, not a sound or voice responded! (*BR *4/3/1862)*

Colonel Pickell was a commissioned officer in the regular army from 1822 until 1838 and returned to service only when Quinby resigned. He was only 60, but was aged and feeble and died in 1865. He "could command the regiment in camp, but was too infirm to follow it into battle." (Marcotte 38) Therefore, as General McClellan was launching his long-awaited offensive to capture the rebel capital at Richmond, the so-called Peninsular campaign, he replaced Pickell with Colonel Elisha G. Marshall, effective April 20, 1862. (Phisterer 1888)

PENINSULAR CAMPAIGN BEGINS

Nearly a month after Yerrot's interview and 8½ months after Bull Run, the 13th went off to war again, in McClellan's Peninsular campaign. This involved shipping an army of 105,000 by boat from the Washington area to the tip of the Virginia peninsula to launch a drive to capture the Confederate capital, Richmond. This was enormously expensive and ultimately futile. As usual, McClellan grossly over-estimated the numbers of his enemies (in fact, 17,000). Instead of attacking when he first met resistance at Yorktown, he settled down for a month-long siege. Historians agree that he should have attacked at once.

Midway through the siege, Sphinx wrote this letter to the *BR*:

> *Two weeks in sight of the enemy's fortifications, a fortnight within range of their guns, two immense armies so near to each other and no battle!*
>
> *You at home are getting impatient, we are not. Some of us were taught at Bull Run that there was at least a little truth in the adage, "the more haste the less speed." We have got to do the fighting, you have not; if we are content you should be, for although you have much depending upon the issue, we have more. You may fear the result, we do not.—The newspapers may have shaken your confidence in our leader* [McClellan]. *Ours grows stronger day by the day…Our opinions are not based upon articles written by unprincipled and designing politicians, but upon what we have seen and know of the man. Our confidence is not misplaced, for as sure as the sun rises in the east, Yorktown is doomed, and ere thirty days shall have passed, the stars and stripes will wave from the dome of the Capitol at Richmond. This is no idle conjecture, and were I permitted to disclose what is daily taking place at this point, you would coincide with my opinion. Upon the twentieth day of May next, just think of what I have written, and perchance your correspondent was not wholly a false prophet…*

> *The 13th…occupies its time in ball playing, picqueting, eating and sleeping, about three times a day—by way of variety—a huge shell passes over or bursts in close proximity to our bivouac, which is located…about one and a half miles from the enemy's fortifications…*
>
> *Our orders are not to fire unless attacked, but it is pretty hard to remain twenty-four hours under a constant fire from the enemy and not be allowed to reply, but it is for the best as we could do little if any damage to the enemy and would thereby discover our position. Artillery duels are of constant occurrence, and during the past week there has been some sharp skirmishing. This place might be taken by a charge, but the loss of life would be terrible and our object would be partly accomplished, we not only want to vanquish but to "bag the game."*
>
> *The fortifications in front of us are strong and numerous. They are built upon the arc of two circles, are connected by rifle pits and extend from river to river.*
>
> *The old rifle pits built during the revolution are still visible, and now serve as a cover for our sharp shooters.*
>
> *Our boys are in good spirits, and "anxious for the fray." There is considerable sickness in the regiment and we can now turn out hardly four hundred and fifty men for duty.*
>
> *The day of the battle draws near.*
>
> *The siege of Yorktown in 1781 established our independence; the siege of Yorktown of 1862 will secure its perpetuity. (4/20/1861)*

Fuller resigned from the army April 27, 1862, a week after writing the above letter. He returned to Brockport, organized Company H for the 108th New York Volunteer Infantry regiment, and was mustered in as a captain on August 18, 1862.

Therefore, his dispatches from the 13th ceased. Fuller's place as correspondent for the *BR* was taken by a writer who used the pen name Yerrot. However, except for the above interview with Fuller, Yerrot gave no special attention to the Brockport soldiers, or even the 13th regiment. Rather, he acted as a war correspondent, reporting a broad overview of the campaign he observed. Later, Sphinx filed a few dispatches from his new regiment.

Sphinx's place in reporting on the 13th regiment was taken by Tyron J.M. Jewell, using the pen name "Scorer," presumably because he was the scorekeeper for his regiment's "Base Ball games." He was a member of Company A with its nine Brockporters. The *U&A*, for which he wrote, circulated in Brockport. So, he wrote about Brockporters for Brockporters, even though he was not a Brockporter and his paper was not published in Brockport. Early in the siege of Yorktown, "Scorer" described the activities of the 13th:

> *Chaplain* [Brockporter J.D.] *Barnes arrived in camp from Washington Saturday evening, where he has been looking to the welfare of the sick belonging to the regiment, who we left behind at Fort Corcoran. Several of them have returned to the regiment, looking well, but their faces are not bronzed as are those who have been with the regiment since we left Fairfax.*
>
> *Our camp is on a piece of ground last used as a corn-field, near a splendid peach orchard (very near the spot where Lord Cornwallis surrendered), within range of the enemy's guns, and in sight of York River, where we can see the gunboats.*
>
> *On Sunday, a rebel balloon made its appearance above the trees, but went down again immediately; it was a singular shaped affair. It was not up long enough for them to get any idea of our force, for our army lay in the woods and in ponchos…*
>
> *On Monday morning at daylight 200 of our regiment and a part of the 22d Massachusetts started out on picket. Companies A, F, D, G, E, and a part of I, were on the reserve, with about the same proportion of the 22d Massachusetts—the rest were on the outposts. The reserve lay in sight of the rebel fortifications, and the pickets were posted almost (you may say) under their guns. Two pieces of the 5th Massachusetts Battery were on picket with us.*
>
> *At about half-past 10 o'clock some one proposed a game of Base Ball. Sides were chosen and it commenced. While we are on picket reserve our guns are stacked, but we must keep on our traps; so you see we played with a load about equal to two overcoats on our backs. It was decidedly "cool" to play a game of Base Ball in sight of the enemy's breastworks mounted with heavy 64's and 32's…*
>
> *The game was finished before dinner time, and we pitched into our rations of hard bread and "salt horse" with a will. That devoured, some lay down for a nap and rest, others to play euchre or "sixty-six." Meanwhile the ball was getting a new cover made from the leg of a fine calf boot found there on the ground…*
>
> *At about half-past 12 o'clock we were suddenly called to our feet by the report that the rebels were throwing up a fort to the left of our line of pickets, about half a mile away, and Capt. Griffin took his Battery over and commenced on them with shell, which they replied, but without any damage.*

At about 3 o'clock another game of Ball was proposed and we fell in with our traps on, (by the way, they were not taken off after we left camp,)…During the game Capt. Griffin's battery was giving the rebels "balls on the fly," which I think they would have preferred to "muff." Nothing disturbed the game until suddenly the cry of "Coffee!" was raised, and time was called about five minutes, when it was again resumed.

While the game was going on Gen. McClelland and Gen. Porter passed by, with three aids, on their way to the outpost pickets. The rebel balloon again made its appearance. It is a hot air balloon, and does not stay up long enough to get any information of account. The game was finished just as the cry of "Coffee from camp for Company A," was raised and away we went for our cups, took a dip and cut again…

*Yesterday afternoon there was very sharp and heavy firing out on the river till near sundown; to-day we hear an occasional shot in that direction. I must close, for it is nearly time for evening inspection, and I must rub up a little, as we came in from picket this morning, and it rained just enough last night to make us scour our guns and brasses. (*U&A *4/24/1862)*

At least two of the "Base Ball" team were Brockporters. Samuel Brower, first baseman on the losing team in the second game, who had two hits and one of the 12 runs (the other team had 14 runs); and Joseph Parker, shortstop on the same team, who had four hits and no runs.

A dispatch from Scorer reports the role of the 13th in the conclusion of the siege:

Last Sunday morning 200 of the 13th and a part of the 22d Mass. were detailed for picket duty, under command of the Colonel of the 22d. They went out before daylight, and when they arrived at the picket lines a flag of truce, with three men, had just come across from the rebel fort. They said the fort was evacuated, the rebels having left the night before. The 22d and 13th were immediately deployed as skirmishers, the 22d on the right. They mounted the works and entered Payton's Battery. Not a soul was to be seen. The guns on Payton's battery all remain mounted except those that were dismounted by our shots, and two that had burst by an overcharge of powder in their efforts to shell our camps. As soon as Col. Gove, of the 22d Mass., arrived in the fort, he sent back to camp for a flag, which was sent to him in a bag, for fear our Regiment would get the start of him. When the flag was unfurled to the breeze the cheers which arose from the men (already searching for torpedoes) awoke us who were back in camp. The

22d Reg't Mass. Vols. was the first inside the rebel works, which was at about 5 o'clock—no later.

At about 4 o'clock in the afternoon the boys returned loaded with trophies and tobacco, which they had gathered in Yorktown and the forts around. Tobacco was cheap for a few days. All the trophies worthy of notice here will be sent to Rochester to be placed on exhibition. Among the trophies is a flag which floated in the city of Yorktown. It was taken down by Wm. S. Foster, of Co. A. who will retain it after it has been exhibited.

At about 6 o'clock the gunboats ran up the river and shelled the woods above Yorktown. At about 9 o'clock we received orders to be ready to march at a moment's notice. We were under marching orders till 8 o'clock Monday evening, when we were called into line and marched to Yorktown Heights, about three miles, through a drizzling rain and mud over shoes. We went away without blankets or knapsacks—consequently we lay without covering all night in the rain. At daylight I took a look around Payton's Battery, most of the guns of which are spiked with twisted wire. The tents inside the forts are mostly cut so as to be useless; the barracks were left in a very filthy condition; flour, bacon, straw and old clothes were strewed around and mixed up without regard to looks, comfort or cleanliness. I returned to where the Regiment lay, after being gone about two hours. At 9 o'clock Tuesday morning we went back to camp, struck our tents and packed our knapsacks, and inside of two hours our whole brigade was on the way back to where we lay the night before, just outside of Fort Magruder. Here we pitched our tents and stayed until about 2 o'clock Wednesday afternoon. Tents were then struck and we started for the landing, to embark for West Point, [Virginia]. *At about 6 o'clock we went aboard the "Hero," the same boat which took a part of the 13th from Alexandria to Fortress Monroe…The 2d Maine were stowed on the Hero with us "Regulars," making it uncomfortably close quarters. As soon as we were loaded, the Hero went to the center of the stream and anchored. At about midnight a squall of wind came up which caused her to drag anchor and come down stern first on to the bowsprit of a schooner which lay at anchor. The bowsprit of the schooner tore off a part of the upper deck and the stern flag-staff of the Hero, and a member of Company A had a very narrow escape.—It tore his knapsack to pieces, on which his head lay, and carried his haversack overboard…*

We steamed up at daylight and arrived off West Point at 8 o'clock Thursday morning and were taken ashore in pontoon bridge boats. We camped about five hundred yards from the banks of the York river on the field which Gen. Franklin's division drove the rebels from after landing.

Our gunboats ran up the Pamunkey river and destroyed the railroad bridge and a train of cars which stood in the track. All day long the dead and wounded were brought in. [Presumably from the Battle of Fair Oaks, which was in progress upriver.] *Some of the dead had their throats cut, some had their faces smashed in with either the boot heels or butts of the Rebel's muskets. Troops who were in the engagement say that it was a regiment of Negroes and the Texas and Alabama troops who committed these brutalities…*

We moved our camp yesterday about one mile west of the river. We now lay with the rest of our brigade, near the swamp where several of our men lost their lives on Wednesday last…Today is…very warm…but a light breeze is blowing, making it a little easier for us, for we are to have a brigade drill this afternoon…The order to report at New Kent Court House is expected every day.

I forgot to tell you of the infernal machines [land mines] *which were found all around Fort Magruder and "Payton's Battery," as the fort is called, which surrounds Yorktown itself…They were laid around and buried so as to leave the cap exposed to anything that passed over it. Several lost their lives by them. I am glad to see General M'Clellan come out and say that Rebel prisoners must remove them at their own peril. When we left Yorktown 40 Rebel prisoners were at work removing them. They were marked by our men with a stake driven in the ground and a white rag on it…*

*Orders have come for us to be ready to march to-morrow morning so I must close. (*U&A *5/16/1862)*

Another member of Company A wrote:

Yesterday it was my detail to go on picket again. As we proceeded to the line established for our pickets, we heard several shell bursts near our works. We had no sooner arrived than the right wing of the 22d Massachusetts were ordered to the front, as skirmishers—the remaining five companies, and one hundred and fifty men of the 13th to follow in the rear as reserve. No accident happened until we had proceeded about half way between our works and those of the enemy, when one of the 22d stepped on one of the rebels' concealed torpedos, which bursted, wounding six men. I have since learned that three of them are dead. The accident happened not thirty feet in front of our company. This unexpected event threw us into confusion for a moment, but we again closed up, and marched on. The skirmishers at this time entered the fort, and their loud cheers announced the evacuation. We

> *did not pass into the fort through the main entrance, but scaled the wall, and marched to the town, of which we took possession. We succeeded in securing many trophies. I was fortunate enough to obtain a piece of the Merrimac that was sent to Gen. Magruder for inspection. It was a piece taken from her where a ball from the Monitor struck, doing much damage... We found one man, and made him a prisoner, that was brought up in Dansville, and was acquainted with a good many men in our regiment. (*RDA *5/17/1862)*

Yerrot described Yorktown about a month after its capture:

> *I have seen Yorktown, and am disappointed. From the various newspaper reports and the assertions to persons who had been on the spot, I was prepared to see fortifications on a scale of unparalleled strength and ability. What I did see was this: a few miserable houses forming the village of Yorktown, compared to which Redman's Corners is a large and flourishing city; surrounded by long lines of earth works, from four to eight feet high, in which to make a breach, it seems to me, would not be very difficult; 50 to 100 dumbled guns; plenty of the debris of a retreating army... Of course my estimate of the place is all wrong, for we are assured by all our most skillful warriors that it was protected by the strongest earth works ever erected, but of one thing I am sure, I would far rather have been safe at home, than behind any of those banks of dirt when a hundred pound dahlgreen ball came whizzing that way. (*BR *6/5/1862)*

The official account of the role of the 13th in the Yorktown siege follows:

> *On the 5th of April the regiment arrived in front of Yorktown and was immediately ordered in the advance, three companies as skirmishers and the remainder in support of batteries, and on the 7th the whole regiment was ordered on picket in a cold and severe storm. During the thirty days of the siege it furnished over twenty details for picket and several for fatigue duty—was frequently engaged in light skirmishes with the enemy and almost constantly under fire, its camp...being within easy range of the enemy's guns. All its duties, however, were performed cheerfully, and with intelligence, promptness and courage. In this respect the siege was a most excellent school, and prepared the entire army for the severe trials and the unflinching courage of its subsequent campaigns. The last approach before Yorktown was dug within fifty yards of the enemy's outposts by a detail of two hundred of the men and officers of this regiment, and one hundred and*

fifty of its men and officers were on picket the morning of the evacuation and were among the first to enter the enemy's works. (DMNA)

The Union forces took chase and caught up with the Confederates at Williamsburg on May 5. A pitched battle occurred in which the Union lost some 2,100 men and the rebels at least 1,700. Although the campaign never reached Richmond, it did clear eastern Virginia of the rebels. Sphinx's prediction about entering Richmond was wildly optimistic. Not until April 4, 1865, nearly three years later, did that happen. McClellan's massive army, including the 13th, inched its ponderous way up the peninsula toward the rebel capital for some two months.

HANOVER COURT HOUSE

The 13th did not take part in the next two major engagements of McClellan's Peninsular campaign, at Williamsburg, May 5, and Fair Oaks or Seven Pines, May 31–June 1. However, it was in the Battle of Hanover Court House, May 27, as reported by Scorer:

The 13th, together with Griffin's battery, have the honor of ending the fight on the left of the line at the Battle of Hanover Court House, by driving two regiments of rebel infantry—the 2d and 18th North Carolina—from the field. They were compelled to leave so precipitately that they left their haversacks and knapsacks, and our boys had the pleasure of putting on airs to complete suits of rebel underclothes, shawls and blankets, and in some cases sported watches and other jewelry left by the flying fugitives. They were completely routed and demoralized…

On the morning of the 22d May, Gen. Martindale's brigade struck tents…, but an order came that the 13th were to remain where we were. We were all at a loss to understand what it meant. Various rumors flew around camp, and among others that we were to be discharged; but there is no such luck. At about 4 o'clock a heavy thunder shower came up, and in this we were ordered to strike our tents again and move our camp. We marched to our new camp, about three-fourths of a mile. I never saw it rain harder, but soon after we reached our camp the rain stopped, and it cleared off beautifully. It took us till after tattoo to dry our clothes. At about 8 o'clock on the morning of the 23d we struck our tents and took a road to the right…to the town of "Old Church." Here we camped in a splendid clover field. We were followed by the 1st Connecticut regiment, who camped by the side of us. A regiment of Lancers arrived the same night. In front of the "Old Church Hotel" stood a pole from which the stars and bars floated first. This was cut down, and the beautiful Stars and Stripes (belonging to Co. A) raised upon it for the first time. There they floated until the 31st, in rain and shine…

We lay there at "Old Church" in quiet until next morning at about two o'clock, when we were called into line and marched off about eight miles. We rested a while, and marched back to camp in the rain, after destroying a ferry boat, and the Lancers driving in the rebel pickets.

Next day the 5th New York (Duryee's Zouaves) and a battery of light artillery belonging to the 4th Rhode Island regiment arrived as reinforcements. Now the formerly quiet village of "Old Church" looked right lively, as an old darkey said, "I never seen so much business done here before." Hoecakes, milk and sweet potatoes are brought into camp by the darkeys in any quantity, and as long as specie lasts we can live. Strawberries and green peas, too, we get for cash. The 26th…we spent in getting ready for something, but we did not know what…May 27th we had reveille at daylight and our brigade marched off in a drenching rain at light marching orders, carrying our rations, rubber blankets, and some of us took overcoats. We marched about twelve miles, when we were obliged to build a bridge for the lancers and artillery to cross, when we again took up the line of march. Two hours after we arrived at the place where the battle of Hanover Court House was fought. We arrived after the first fight, but did not stop, as they are fighting further to the right. We pass Charley Cady's house, and go about one and a half miles further towards the Court House, for our brigade was sent out to burn the bridge, and Col. Duryee, our acting General, accomplished his object, when we were faced about by General Porter and marched back near where the first fight took place. Here the rebels were trying to turn our left flank. As we came up behind the 44th, who lay along behind a fence, Gen. Martindale rode up and welcomed us. We gave three cheers and a tiger and on we went under orders from Gen. Porter. We formed in line of battle behind the 44th N.Y. Gen. Marshall sent out skirmishers, and the regiment followed after, crossing a plowed lot and through a small piece of woods, then into a corn field. When about half way across the officer in command of the skirmishers gave notice of two regiments advancing. He had hardly spoken when they fired. We all dropped, then gave them a volley and loaded again. After the first volley

> *we rose and commenced to "load and fire at will." All this time, Capt. Griffin was giving the rebels shell as fast as two pieces could be worked, which I can assure you was not slow. We fired in this way for fifteen or twenty minutes, when the enemy started on a double quick, leaving their knapsacks, haversacks, &c., to the woods. We then advanced into the wheat field, where Col. M. gave us a rest, which we needed, for we had marched between twenty-two and twenty-five miles and had had no rest until now. We lay here about fifteen minutes and then advanced across the Virginia Central Railroad track into the road and moved by the right flank to the hospital, where we encamped or rather, slept. As soon as we broke ranks we looked through the knapsacks which lined the road towards the woods, and many a letter and private wardrobe (if a soldier's knapsack may be so-called) was ransacked by us. Our ambulances were at work all night bringing in the wounded and squads of prisoners were brought in during the night. In the morning squads went out on tours of observation, bringing in various trophies, and up to the time we left the hospital ninety-two prisoners had been brought in by the 13th. During the action only one man was mortally wounded..., He has since died. (*U&A *6/13/1862)*
>
> *The official record lists seven wounded of whom one died. (Phisterer, 1888)*

An anonymous member of the 13th summarized the role of the regiment at Hanover Court House this way:

> *We arrived upon the field late—for we had had from fifteen to twenty miles of marching since morning, and therefore did not bear the brunt of the battle as other regiments had done; but we did all that we were ordered to do, and in such a manner as to win the thanks of our commanding officer... We took about one hundred prisoners... They described our fire as being very severe upon their ranks. (*RDA *6/17/1862)*

Brigadier-General John Martindale, the commander of the brigade in which the 13th served, confirmed Scorer's account of the regiment's role in the Battle of Hanover Court House:

> [T]*he 13th Regiment at the Battle of Hanover, following the lead of their Colonel, who there bore himself with signal gallantry, pass*[ed] *me with wild cheers as they pressed forward to relieve the regiments which had withstood the shock of four times their number for more than an hour,* [in]

> *eager pursuit of the rebels, who retired for a time fighting in order, but at length broke and fled.* (U&A *6/20/1862)*

Another correspondent of the *U&A* said that the 13th performed "nobly" at Hanover. (*U&A* 6/19/1862)

The DMNA said:

> *On the 8th of May the regiment embarked at Yorktown, and on the 9th reached West Point. It then marched to Cumberland, White House, Tunstall's Station, and several miles beyond the latter place, where it was detached (May 22) for special duty at Old Church, on the road to Hanover. Its duty as explained in Gen. Porter's order, was "to secure the army from attacks, in rear or flank, by parties of the enemy passing down this branch of the river, and to patrol the country between the turnpike and river." In the discharge of this duty it moved to Old Church on the 23d, and pushed its reconnoissance to Hanover on the 26th, where it discovered the enemy in heavy force under General Branch. It then returned and destroyed the communications with the country beyond the Chickahominy. On the 27th it moved forward in the advance on Hanover Court House, was assigned to position on the left of Griffin's battery, assisted materially in driving the enemy from their line, and captured ninety-one prisoners, eighty-four stands of arms, fifty-five sets of accoutrements, and three chests of medical stores, with a loss of only seven wounded (one mortally).*

The only Brockporter wounded at Hanover Court House was Chester W. Vantine of Clarkson. He was shot in the neck by a bullet that killed a soldier behind him. (*BR* 7/3/1862) This led to his discharge for disability on October 11, 1862. He was a carpenter's apprentice and the son of carpenter Joseph Vantine. After the war, he was an agent for an oil company in Elmira.

After the travails of training, the debacle of First Bull Run, the mutiny, and the dissolution of Company K, the 13th, with its Brockport contingent had finally become an effective fighting force, battle-tested, having tasted the bitterness of defeat and the tragedy of comrades killed in action, as well as the sweet taste of victory. They had witnessed acts of great courage and the shame of cowardice. Much more of the same lay ahead.

Chapter 10

The Seven Days' Battle

Prelude to the Seven Days' Battle

From the Hanover Court House encounter on May 27 until the Seven Days' Battle of June 25 to July 2, the 13th was engaged in picket duty and building bridges.

Scorer's June 4 letter (pages 117–19) continued with this description of the regiment's activities after the Hanover Court House battle:

> *At about ten o'clock a.m. the next day we took up our line of march back towards* [Maj.] *Gen.* [Fitz-John] *Porter's headquarters and encamped directly opposite the hospital. Here we made ourselves as comfortable as possible by building "bough shades." At about three o'clock p.m.* [Maj.] *Gen.* [George B.] *McClellan made his appearance at Gen. Porter's headquarters opposite our camp. The regiment turned out en masse and gave him three cheers.*
>
> *Charley Cady came down to see the regiment, many of the men being well acquainted with him—some being school mates in Rochester, from him we get some valuable information.*
>
> *May 29th we lay in camp until about 6 o'clock p.m., when we take up and march back to camp, which place we reach about two hours after midnight. We go to rest and have reveille at 8 o'clock a.m., and prepare to march again, but it is a false alarm…May 31st we have reveille at 2 a.m.*

We fall in and march a little after daylight on awful roads (as it rained hard all night before.) We arrive at Gaines Mills, eight miles from Old Church, at about 10 o'clock, and join [Brevet Major] *General* [John H.] *Martindale's brigade again. We lay on a hill near a brook, within sight of the Chickahominy River.*

Sunday morning [June 1] *we are called into line and march down to near the river and stay there till half-past 1 o'clock, when we return to camp again in a scorching hot sun. At 5 o'clock p.m. we have Sunday inspection.*

All day long the artillery kept up a heavy fire across the river to protect our men, who are building a pontoon bridge over the river. Monday we lay in camp all day…

Wednesday [June 4] [Major] *General* [George B.] *McClellan's general order is read that we may expect a day of excitement to-day or to-morrow. Last night and nearly all day it has rained very hard, drenching us all. We lay in water last night an inch deep. It is very disagreeable to be wet and no chance to get dry. (*U&A *6/13/1862)*

Two days later, June 6, Scorer reported on some more of those activities from near Gaines' Mill:

My last came to rather a sudden close. I had left it and was getting my bed ready for a shower that was coming up, and was then suddenly called away, and did not return until after "lights out." I then made up my mind to wait until morning. But when morning came we were ordered to get ready for picket duty; so you see that I had no time to finish. That night it rained all night, and almost floated us out of our tents before morning.

At 8 o'clock a.m. we were marched away from camp, and each man got an axe or shovel at the Engineer Department, after which we started for the Chickahominy Creek. We arrived at the Creek and had unloaded several wagons loaded with logs cut for the bridge, when our batteries suddenly opened on something across the Creek, which were replied to "right smart." One of our batteries wanting to shift position, we were marched back to where [Major] *Gen.* [Winfield S.] *Hancock's brigade lay the day before. We lay there about half an hour, when we were marched farther to the right, where another pontoon bridge was being thrown across by the 50th N.Y.V. Here the six companies on the right went into the woods to cut logs, and Companies H, C, D and A were put to work building the bridge across the swamp. Before they went to work five men from each of these four companies were sent out into the swamp as skirmishers. The moment they got in sight of the rebel pickets, which are on the opposite side of the river, a shot from one of them struck about fifty yards in front of us, and the picket who fired it was seen going over the hill at double quick, and was soon out of sight. The skirmishers were then deployed through a swamp up to their waist belts in water. There they had to stay while the rest of the men laid the sleepers for the bridge through the swamp. Just before we left the swamp the rebels showed themselves in small force. We returned to camp about 6 p.m., got a full ration of whisky, dried our clothes, and went to bed.*

We had more rain last night…

The wounded are getting along finely, but the health of the regiment was never poorer. Never were so few reported for duty as at present…

This and my last letter are written on paper from a North Carolinian's knapsack. I don't see that it is any better than what we get in the North. I must close to get ready for guard. (U&A *6/14/1862)*

Another letter from Scorer describes more of the company's activities before the Seven Days' Battle, which effectively ended the Union effort to capture Richmond in 1862:

Since I last wrote you…, we have moved our camp to a healthier location, about half a mile nearer the Chickahominy.

The regiment went out on picket on…the 7th, and returned about noon the next day, nothing very exciting having occurred. Chaplain [Brockporter J.D.] *Barnes preached in the afternoon, but to a small audience…*

On Monday we moved our camp, after the review by Gen. Prim, the Spanish General…From our present camp we can plainly see the camp of [Brevet Brigadier] *Gen.* [Edwin V.] *Sumner* [Jr.] *across the Chickahominy, and further to the right we can see the rebel pickets with the naked eye, they do not trouble us, but from appearances I should think that our batteries (which occasionally send over a shell or two) disturb them not a little. The…view from our camp reminds me very much of the Genesee Flats…*

The oats on the flats look as if they needed cutting. This farm belongs to Dr. Gaines, a strong "secesh." He is now under arrest for saying, "that if any Union soldiers were buried on his place he would dig them up and burn them after the army moved away." He has a splendid residence, behind which is a beautiful grove. A little to the left of it, across the road, is where fifteen North

Carolinians who were wounded at Hanover Court House, are buried, having died of their wounds. In this grove is the building that was used as a hospital for the rebel wounded brought from Hanover Court House.

On the opposite side of the road from Dr. Gaines's house, is a distillery, now used as a hospital; also a barn used for the same purpose for our sick and wounded.

On Tuesday morning [June 10], *at about two o'clock it commenced raining and continued to do so until nearly noon, drenching all of us. In the afternoon, while we were forming for evening parade, the battery which stands about 1150 yards to our right, opened on "secesh," and gave them about a dozen rounds in quick succession. The officers who had glasses, say it caused considerable of a stir among them.*

I understand from good authority that Lieut. Cooper will soon return to Rochester to recruit for the 13th. [2nd/1st Lt. Albert G. Cooper served with Co. D, 1/31–10/31/1862.] *This surely does not look like discharging us before our time is up, as we earnestly hoped. But if we must stay, the "milksops" won't grumble but grin and bear it; although reduced to almost the smallest regiment in the brigade by sickness, I can see no other cause for the decrease in our numbers, for we have lost very few by the rebels.—It is often remarked by others how fortunate the 13th is in not losing any more when they go into action or on picket. I do not remember of one being killed on picket duty since we have been in the service, while there is hardly another regiment in the division which has not lost more.*

Yesterday our regiment had their first company drill since we returned to the brigade. Last evening Gen. Martindale rode over to our camp to look around, inquiring into the health of the regiment and how they liked their present location…

This is a beautiful day, a light breeze blowing, making the heat of the sun, which would otherwise be almost insupportable, quite agreeable. Professor Lowe's balloon "Intrepid" makes daily observations from the brow of the hill behind us.

Gen. McClellan passed our camp last evening on his way to headquarters after a visit to Gen. Sumner's camp, and the regiment turned out en masse and gave him three rousing cheers, at the time the boys were just going after their coffee and had their tin cups in hand. The General asked them: "Boys, are you dry?"…

We are all patiently waiting for the decisive battle which is to take place before Richmond. (U&A *6/23/1862)*

A week later, June 17, the "decisive battle" was still pending. Scorer's long letter reads much like a diary:

> *On Friday, June 13th, everything was quiet, until about 4 p.m., when the order came to strike tents, pack knapsacks, and prepare for a march. The Regiment then fell in and marched off, leaving their knapsacks, with the sick men to guard them. The Regiment marched over the hill about a mile and a half, and then marched back again, (they were gone about three hours,) tents were pitched again as before, and pants were dealt out to those who needed.*
>
> *Early Saturday morning,…two companies (D and C) were sent down to the Chickahominy on picket. At about noon the Regiment was all ordered out on picket, Co.'s D and C having just returned, but this time they took back track to Cold Harbor, five miles from camp, toward Old Church, where the rebels were said to be advancing to cut off our supplies…At 11 a.m., Sunday, the Regiment returned from picket, but they hardly got their rations swallowed when it commenced to rain, accompanied by thunder and lightning. While the Regiment were out they ate an abundance of strawberries and cherries, which they found plenty.*
>
> *On Monday nothing of consequence happened until night, when the rebels opened a battery in the woods, on the bridge builders, but the 20-pounders to the right of our camp soon silenced them.*
>
> *Tuesday was a beautiful but quiet day, nothing happened of any consequence until about 11 at night, when we were called up, struck tents, packed knapsacks, and again prepared for a march. About half past twelve we marched for Mechanicsville, a distance of about five miles, where we laid down to rest until daylight.*
>
> *All the houses and buildings bear marks of the rebel artillery, for I did not see a building in this village but had one or more ball holes in it. In some, shells had burst inside the house, tearing chimneys, plaster, floors, and everything in their way. Soon after daylight we were called to attention, and marched about three quarters of a mile farther, toward "Ashland." Here we rested in a field, with a battery of brass 20-pounders, the 18th Massachusetts and 2d Maine. This march was performed without knapsacks, and in the cool morning air, so that everybody felt almost as fresh when we rested as at the start—Almost as soon as we arrived here, orders came for us to go on picket, but Col. Marshall protested, as it is not our turn. Our knapsacks, &c., were left at camp, near New Bridge, to be brought by the wagons…From the top of the hill in front of us,…we could plainly see the rebel camps and hear their drums. Soon after we had got*

> *our tents pitched an order came for us…to return to our camp near New Bridge. We started at about five p.m. and reached camp about nine o'clock in a heavy rain, and everything in the shape of tent poles was scattered so that companies hardly got the same one they left. Whisky and quinine were again dealt out. While we were in Mechanicsville several large snakes were killed in the field where we camped. One of the 18th Massachusetts boys was bitten by a copper head while on picket. The snake was killed. It was about eight feet long.*
>
> *To-day everything was quiet until noon, when the battery of six pieces, which lays to our right, commenced shelling a rebel earthwork, which they had thrown up (in sight) behind the house of Mrs. Price, on the hill opposite. Our battery had hardly stopped when the rebels drew a battery down behind their earthworks and threw several shells into our camp. One struck directly in front of the musicians tent and bounded over the Colonel's tent and over the camp of the First Michigan into the woods. On examination they were found to be percussion shells (none of them exploded) from a Parrot gun; one of them which we picked up was not loaded. At the time the rebels commenced our boys were crowded on the brow of the hill behind our battery and when the first shot struck before them there was scattering, and but few remained to see them fire the second or third shot. No one was hurt.* (U&A *6/30/1862)*

The next day, June 18, Scorer continued:

> *Gens. Porter and* [Major General Charles] *Griffin directed our battery to open fire on "secesh" yesterday. Soon after the firing ceased Gen. M'Clellan rode up with his staff and took a look at "secesh" and rode off towards where our balloon lay. Soon after the balloon went up and the rebels fired a couple of shots at it, but did no damage. This morning we were awoke at three o'clock and ordered to pack knapsacks, strike tents and prepare to move, and at five a.m. we left camp without breakfast. Some coffee which was hastily made was poured into our canteens; we marched about two miles and camped about one mile to the right of where our old camp was and farther back from the river.*
>
> *Several shot and shell have struck about one-fourth of a mile to our left, some of them struck near other regiments of our brigade, since which, all but our regiment have moved further to the right, out of range.*
>
> *For three or four days back our ears have been annoyed by some miserable "secesh" who is practicing his hand (perhaps both hands) on an old bass*

> *drum; it seems to come from some point...on the opposite side of the Chickahominy; perhaps it is some decoy to draw the fire of our batteries so that they can find out our position. (*U&A *6/30/1862)*

The DMNA summarized those activities, preliminary to the Seven Days' Battle, as follows: "The regiment returned to Old Church on the 29th [of May], and thence moved to the army on the 31st where it took up camp near Dr. Gaines' house. Picket and fatigue duty followed, until the 26th of June, when the battle of Mechanicsville was fought."

MECHANICSVILLE AND GAINES' MILL

Finally, on June 25, the climactic Seven Days' Battle of the Peninsular campaign began. The battle consisted of principal engagements at Mechanicsville, Gaines' Mill, and Malvern Hill. The 13th was involved in all three. At Mechanicsville, June 26, it helped repulse a poorly coordinated rebel assault. At Gaines' Mill, June 27, it formed the first line of defense against an attack that eventually broke through, though at awesome cost to the rebels. That defeat led McClellan to give up his attempt to capture Richmond. During their retreat, the Union forces occupied a virtually impregnable redoubt at Malvern Hill, with the 13th holding the extreme left of the line. An unsuccessful rebel assault there on July 1 cost the attackers some 5,650 casualties to 3,000 Union losses, but the withdrawal continued and the Peninsular campaign ended in failure. (Marcotte 56–61)

Scorer was wounded at Malvern Hill (*RDA* 7/15/1862) and filed no dispatches to the *U&A* until he described the hospital where his wounds were treated. (9/2/1862) However, an account of the role of the 13th in the battle was supplied to the RDA by Lieutenant Charles Curtis Brown of Company A. Brown had enrolled as a private at age 33. He became sergeant later that year and 2nd lieutenant on January 9, 1862. He became a captain and company commander on October 16, 1862. Later, he served as major, brevet lieutenant-colonel, and, briefly, acting commander of the 22nd New York Cavalry regiment. (Phisterer 1071, 1893) Brown described the beginning of the battle in a July 7th letter at the end of the retreat: "Our regiment was ordered to 'fall in' about noon [on June 26], and marched towards Mechanicsville, where they halted in line of battle about two miles this side of it. Two or three of the companies were sent out on picket that night, after being under fire of shells for five hours—the fire not ending till 9 p.m." (*RDA* 7/15/1862)

John Cawthra, a member of the 13th's Company E, to which seven Brockporters had been transferred, described the Mechanicsville engagement:

> *The fighting commenced on Thursday* [June 26]. *Our right under* [Brigadier] *Gen.* [George A.] *McCall was attacked by Stonewall Jackson's forces. Our brigade was ordered to Gen. McCall's support, but we were not brought into action, though we were under a severe fire from stray shells. The fighting was desperate on both sides, but we could not gain on the rebels who had overwhelming numbers, so we were ordered back. (*U&A *7/12/1862)*

Brown reported on the Battle of Gaines' Mill, which he heard only from a distance: "Being officer of the guard that day, I was sent with the wagon train to cross the Chickahominy…At early morn the battle recommenced. All that day we who were with the train listened with aching ears to the terrific explosions of cannon and musketry." (*RDA* 7/15/1862)

Because Brown remained with the retreating wagon train he did not witness the Mechanicsville or Gaines' Mill engagements. Another member of his company, John G. Wensel, described the Battle of Gaines' Mill in a June 28 letter. Wensel died in an army hospital on September 14:

> *We had one of the hottest battles yesterday that the 13th has ever been in, and repulsed the enemy twice with great slaughter. The third attack they made they came upon us with three lines of battle, one after the other. Of the first line scarcely a man came out; when the second and third came forward and forced us back. Most of the time we were only twenty-five yards from them. We killed and wounded over twice the number of our regiment, and took one of their battle flags. I cannot say whether we can claim a victory or not; we have crossed the river and what will come next I cannot state—time only can tell. I do not know the exact number of killed and wounded in our regiment; it will perhaps reach fifty or more. I think our company has suffered most…I received a spent ball in my head which knocked me senseless for some five minutes, but did me no serious injury. It pained me much last night, but I am all right this morning and ready again…We are all in good spirits.*
>
> *Stonewall Jackson attacked us with very superior numbers. We lost all our knapsacks and clothing. All I saved was my portfolio and ink, which I*

put into my haversack in the morning…There are fifteen killed, wounded and missing in our company. (U&A *7/7/1862, 10/1/1862)*

Cawthra also reported on Gaines' Mill:

> *The fighting was resumed the next morning. McCall fighting on the retreat with his shattered forces, and fell back across the Chickahominy. The brunt of the fight now came on our division and* [Major General William B.] *Franklin's. The rebels came upon us in overwhelming numbers, expecting to drive us into the swamp.*
>
> *Our brigade was stationed in a ravine. We felled the trees and with rails made a barricade which we got behind. The first rebel regiment which went for us we cut to pieces, drove them off, took their colors and a number of prisoners. A brigade of rebels came upon our little regiment, numbering 350 men. The enemy also came upon our left by tens of thousands. We fought until dark, but they were too much for us and cut us up badly, but we piled the ground with their dead. The right and left gave way, when we retired. The enemy were closing upon our right and left flanks and our regiment came near being taken prisoners. Here the 13th lost 101 in killed, wounded and missing…A few of us stuck by the colors and tried to rally the men but was of no use and we fell back to the flats, where the artillery and cavalry held the scattered brigades in check…*
>
> *We lost all of our knapsacks, tents, clothes, and everything but our accoutrements, wagons and baggage…We got to the James river and they attacked our right, our gunboats helping us. It was a desperate struggle, but we gained the day and drove them back two miles. We then retreated further down the river and took up a good position on high land* [Malvern Hill]. (U&A *7/12/1862)*

Henry H. Cusick of Hamlin, a member of Company B, provided another, brief account of Gaines' Mill:

> *We took a rebel flag from the 5th Tennessee…I know that every time old Remington spoke, some poor rebel fell. I shot away most all of my cartridges that day in less than three hours time. The barrel of my rifle got so hot, that I couldn't hold my hand on it. I gave them five rounds, when the rebels were not over twelve rods off and every shot counted, I will warrant you. But still they pressed down upon us, but so drunk, they could hardly stand up; so we had to leave our breastwork of logs. We lost some over one hundred men that day.* (BR *8/14/1862)*

Henry Cusick, Hamlin farm boy, wounded twice in the 13th NYVI; later in the 18th and 25th Light Artillery and the 7th Heavy Artillery regiments. *Photo provided by Mary Smith.*

Brockporters seem to have been in the thick of the Gaines' Mill battle. Gifford Freeman of Clarkson and Fred Raymond of Hamlin were killed. In 1860, Freeman had been a farm laborer living with a 27-year old Daniel Freeman, perhaps a brother. Raymond, one of the mutineers, had been a Hamlin farm boy, living with his farmer father, dressmaker mother, and two younger siblings. Seven Brockporters were wounded. Charles Morgan, of Brockport, who was cited for bravery at First Bull Run and imprisoned for mutiny, was reported missing. In fact, he had been wounded and, later, was discharged for disability. The other wounded were Charles O'Dell of Hamlin; John Ball, a Rochesterian who enlisted in Brockport; James H. Snyder of Clarkson; and William McIntyre, George H. Soles, and George W. Coon, all of Brockport. John G. Beadle, a 23-year-old farm laborer from Ogden, was captured. Later, he was released and served in the 22nd NY Cavalry.

The DMNA account of the role of the 13th in the Battles of Mechanicsville and Gaines' Mill follows:

> *In this action* [the Battle of Mechanicsville] *it occupied a position on the extreme right. Three of its companies, deployed as skirmishers on the Ashland road under Capt. Hyland, were exposed to a severe fire of canister and musketry until withdrawn at midnight, with a loss of two in prisoners. The remaining companies were moved from the right to the center, and were for some time under a heavy artillery fire.*
>
> *On the 27th the battle of Gaines' Mill was fought. In this action the regiment was on the left of the line (the brigade being placed to the right of* [Major] *Gen.* [Daniel] *Butterfield's), where it shared in the repeated and desperate assaults of the enemy. It did not fall back, however, until the*

line on both sides of its position was broken and its ammunition exhausted, and then it carried with it the colors of the seventh Tennessee battalion, which had been captured by the gallantry of Sergt. John Marks. The loss of the regiment was ninety-seven killed, wounded and taken prisoners, out of about four hundred engaged.

MALVERN HILL

The 13th next fought in the Battle of Malvern Hill. Brown rejoined his regiment on June 30 and resumed his report with an account of a skirmish at Malvern Cliff (Phisterer 1888) and then the Battle of Malvern Hill on July 1:

Just as we arrived near Turkey Bend,... Companies A and D were sent to guard a side road, which road afterwards was the scene of a most terrific conflict. We stayed there till a large portion of the troops of our corps passed, and then were relieved by some other corps...

About 4 o'clock p.m. we were ordered to "fall in." The whole division was up and the bands played "Hail Columbia," "Star Spangled Banner," &c. We gave three cheers for the Old Flag, the Union and McClellan, and moved back to the field just behind that same side road...

Soon there commenced a fierce cannonading between ours and the enemy's batteries. It was tremendous on our part, and continued till nearly dark... Our regiment was moved with others forward to the hill, just by the guns. We lay here all night, everything being quiet.

About 9 a.m. the next day (Tuesday [July 17]*), the cannonading began again. It lasted till noon. We were told by Capt. Powers, Gen. Martindale's A.A.G., to rest till 4 o'clock, when we expected the attack. But about 2 o'clock he came again and told us to get ready, that an attack of the enemy was expected immediately.—We moved still nearer, and brought up our position on the side of a hill, just behind the batteries. Soon it commenced, and the shot and shell flew over our heads at a fearful rate. We were obliged to lie close to the ground, for as yet it was artillery only. The bullets from a shell that burst just in front of us, struck one of Co. A's boys—Jewell* ["Scorer"], *of Franklin street—in the head, making a severe but not dangerous wound...*

About 4 o'clock Gen. Martindale came to us and addressed us a few words, saying that now we were to prove the sincerity of our promises when we left Rochester. That we were not to yield to the foe however great the pressure. In a few minutes he came and said he would lead us himself to the conflict. He was on foot, and alone, and telling us to be as cool as on evening parade, we followed him to a new position.—The musketry had now commenced to add fury to the scene. The bullets flew like hail over and around us. One of my men was hit just by my side…I have not seen or heard of the man since.

It now grew dark. The firing increased in fierceness as troops kept coming up on both sides. The enemy would move brigade after brigade, each behind the other, and our fire made fearful havoc.

It being dark, and the guns somewhat foul, the flames of fire that leaped from the guns was greatly increased in appearance, and every discharge of musket or cannon lighted up the darkness. And now those who were there witnessed a scene, awful, grand, terrific and sublime, yet infernal in its character. Our lines of troops were ranged around the brow of a hill, very abrupt and high on our left but less so in front, and sloping on the right. In front, at the foot of the hill commenced a flat, or swale, which was bounded by a wood in which the enemy's forces were held, and from which they issued to advance on us. Between every two brigades was a battery of guns, from the six pound light artillery to the thirty-two pound brass howitzer. Behind us a half mile were twenty pound Parrott guns throwing shell. All the guns with us on the hill threw grape and canister, and only an initiated one knows the effect of canister thrown from a thirty-two pound howitzer. I never saw such working of guns as on that night. The incessant firing of musketry, and nearly as much so of the artillery, was a scene never to be forgotten. The grape and canister, as they left on their messages of destruction, seemed to be living demons, who shrieked and yelled with delight as they hurled themselves against the shrinking bodies of the rebels. The enemy could not answer. We drove them out of the field entirely. [Marcotte 60 comments, "It was one of the few engagements of the war when artillery probably inflicted most of the casualties."]

About 9 o'clock the firing ceased, only an occasional shot breaking the silence. We lay down on the field…About 1 o'clock we were aroused from our sleep and started for this point. The road was, as before, crowded with troops of all kinds moving the same way. It began to rain about 6 a.m., which made the roads very bad indeed. We had had nothing to eat since the day before, at noon, and it was 3 p.m. before we got anything, and then nothing but dry crackers. I have learned lately to eat raw pork, and I

> *assure you I prefer it to pork that is cooked. A hard cracker with a slice of raw pork, and a cup of coffee, is no meal to be despised by a soldier on the march or battle field.*
>
> *Just after getting here a couple of guns began to shell us from a hill some distance to our rear, which was soon stopped by the capture of the battery. Since that time we have been pretty quiet here...Our brigade is fearfully reduced. We have lost one hundred and ten men the last two weeks. We have only three hundred for duty in the regiment, officers and all....*
>
> *I think that General Martindale values the regiment pretty highly now. General W.F. Sherman, our old brigadier, used to say that we were good for nothing but fighting. Since we have been in action under General M.'s own eye he can appreciate the merits of the regiment in a battle field.*
>
> *It was really amusing to see the way he has hung around the regiment ever since we left Gaines' Mills, and the climax was to be led on the field of battle by himself. (*RDA *7/15/1862)*

Cawthra also provided an account of the Battle of Malvern Hill:

> *The enemy attacked us again in the morning* [July 1] *with all their might. They threw their masses, crazed with whisky, upon our right, our left, our centre, rushed to our cannon mouths to be mowed down like grass. Our men were invincible. They knew there was no retreat—we had to fight or die. We charged them with bayonet time after time, but still they closed up. They were like the leaves in number, but as the night came they began to waver and fall back, and by nine o'clock we drove them from the field. Our artillery kept up the most terrible fire imaginable until half past ten o'clock...*
>
> *During the six days' fight we had scarcely anything to eat, nor had we much sleep. (*U&A *7/12/1862)*

Some idea of the intensity of the involvement of the 13th in the Seven Days Battle is provided by the casualty figures. Brown mentions seven wounded, including two former members of "Co. K—the Brockport company," Sergeant George H. Soles wounded "in the arm" and "Bell...shot in the face." The official casualty figures for the 13th were 15 enlisted men killed in the Battle of Gaines' Mill and one officer and three enlisted men died from their wounds. In the Seven Days' Battle as a whole, 51 enlisted men were wounded but recovered and two officers and 54 enlisted men were missing for a total of 126 casualties for a regiment that numbered only 300 officers and men at the conclusion of the battle. (*RDA* 7/15/1862, Phisterer 1888) Also, 69 desertions were reported. (*U&A* 10/4/1862)

The soldiers in the regiment were proud of their performance and believed that they had been lucky. Two Rochesterians reported that some recruiting officers in Boston had said of the 13th that "there was no braver soldiers or better fighting men in the army of the Potomac" and "None stood higher for bravery and skill as fighting men." (*U&A* 8/30/1862) A soldier in another unit said in a letter to a Rochester newspaper, "We saw that veteran regiment, 'the bloody 13th'…and though diminished in numbers, there was no diminution in their courage and bravery." (*U&A* 9/11/1862) One of its officers "writes home that the regiment is composed of the most fortunate set of men he ever saw. In the hardest of the seven days' fighting before Richmond, regiments with whom they fought side by side were cut up badly—the 13th escaped with only four or five killed, about forty slightly wounded and a few taken prisoners." (*U&A* 7/14/1862 [The official figures do not agree.])

Scorer, home on furlough after being wounded, expressed a similar opinion: (*U&A* 7/17/1862) "He describes the fighting as very severe, and explains why it was that the 13th lost so few killed while many were wounded. A part of the time they fought behind breastworks of trees, and their arms and heads were exposed. The rebels poured their fire into the logs, and glancing balls struck the arms and sometimes the scalps of the men [including Scorer]. Few of the balls entered their bodies."

The DMNA account of the 13th in the Battle of Malvern Hill follows:

> *The regiment…moved with the corps to James River, and arrived at Scotch's Neck on the afternoon of the 30th* [of June]. *It was in the reserve at Turkey Bend and stood to arms all night. On the morning of the 1st of July it fell back and took position on the heights of Malvern Hill in support of the batteries, where it remained for about three hours, and was then moved to the extreme left of the line, and came under a hot musketry fire from the enemy. A few minutes later it was moved to the right and center to support the batteries against a desperate charge, and throughout the entire engagement was in active duty.*

The army continued its retreat to Harrison's Landing on the James River. The army remained there, more or less under siege by the Confederates, until they were evacuated on foot to northern Virginia (Kilmer 2: 428)

The DMNA reported on the 13th between Malvern Hill and the Second Battle of Bull Run as follows:

> *On the 2d it reached Harrison's Landing and rested with the army in security. The regiment remained at Harrison's Landing until the 14th of August, when it moved with the corps towards Newport News; embarked at that place and disembarked at Aquia creek; from thence by forced marches to Falmouth, Crittenden's Mills and Kelly's Ford, at which latter place it picketed on the 26th with a section of artillery and squadron of cavalry; on the 27th burned baggage and moved to Warrenton Junction; from thence at 3 A.M. of the 28th to Bristow Station; 29th reached Manassas Junction and passed towards Gainesville.*

Though the Peninsular campaign was a costly failure, it made the 13th a battle-toughened veteran regiment. More than any other experience, it earned for them the affectionate nickname of "the old 13th." However, while they were engaged in one combat after another, a controversy regarding their commander was raging on the homefront, a quarrel that was facilitated by the transparency and open communications that typified the Civil War.

Chapter 11

The Colonel Marshall Controversy

Despite Scorer's positive reports, all was not well in the 13th through the Peninsular campaign. It had the reputation that "no volunteer regiment in the service has experienced so many real misfortunes as" it. (*REE* 6/5/1862) The regiment had had a succession of commanders. Colonel Isaac F. Quinby had recruited it and led it through the First Battle of Bull Run when he resigned on August 5, 1862. He was succeeded by Colonel John Pickell from August 20, 1861, until March 31, 1862, when he was removed due to his inability to serve in the field. After three weeks under the interim leadership of Lieutenant Colonel Carl Stephan, Colonel Elisha G. Marshall took command on April 20. (Phisterer 1888, *REE* 6/5/1862)

Marshall was a career West Pointer, class of 1850, and had served with distinction in the Indian wars. He was a rough, tough, no nonsense disciplinarian. (Marcotte 65) This soon led to trouble. The *REE* reported of Marshall:

> *We have it upon unquestioned authority, that his behavior from the start has been characterized by the utmost arrogance and brutality, and that it is chiefly in consequence of such conduct that so many of the officers of the regiment have resigned, and others only await the result of operations at Richmond, before following their example.* [In fact, five officers resigned—one for ill health—and one was mustered out for a promotion in another unit between May 17 and June 5, 1862.] *(Phisterer 1888,* U&A *6/19/1862)*

> *If it is true that private soldiers, in ill health, have been strung up by the thumbs, as a punishment for falling out of the ranks, and this against the remonstrances of a physician, if it is true that similar punishment has been decreed against others who were unable to leave their tents, and escaped by the intervention of their Captain, who said he would protect them at the risk of his own life, if it is true that Col. Marshall is accustomed to curse both officers and men on parade, and ornament his official discourse with the most obscene and threatening language,...the offender should be ousted with just as little ceremony as he was imposed upon the regiment. (6/5/1862)*

Two weeks later, the Rochester *U&A* published a defense of Marshall, quoting "a member of the regiment":

> *When Col. Marshall took command things were in a bad way; the best officers and men were discouraged. Now it is different. Both officers and men feel that they are superior as soldiers to most of the regiments about them and the Generals feel and say so too...The poor and inefficient officers who could not bear the thought of doing their duty resigned before Col. Marshall came...None of the...resignations were accepted until the Colonel reported them inefficient. One of those resigning officers allowed a man in his company to die without even going to see him once...Another... left some of the names of his company off the rolls and therefore they could not be paid....*
>
> *Col. M. has punished men, but not sick ones...Men have been tied, but none by the thumbs, or in any other cruel way. (6/19/1862)*

Another member wrote of Marshall: "Since he has taken command of the 13th Regiment,...he has made wonderful improvements in it, in every respect—in discipline, in drill and in appearance, and he has gained the respect of both officers and privates...He is not the man that he is represented in the Express as being; far from it." (*U&A* 6/19/1862)

The *RDA* (6/20/1862) responded the next day by alleging that "There are scores of letters in this city and vicinity" that charge Marshall with "[c]ruelty to soldiers, arrests for trivial causes, ungentlemanly demeanor towards inferior officers, and the grossest profanity when addressing his officers and men" and that "make the matter a good deal worse than we shall undertake to represent it."

Marshall's immediate superior, General Martindale, the brigade commander, entered the fray with a long letter (*U&A* 6/20/1862) that was mostly a discourse on the importance of discipline in military organization, but also defended Marshall and reported that, "This morning I have instituted an inquiry into the discipline of the 13th Regiment, and the alleged matter of complaint against Col. Marshall." He said, "It is unquestionably true, that since the assumption of the command of the Regiment by Colonel Marshall, the discipline has been more stringent than ever before; but it is equally true, that the improvement of the regiment has been marked. Indeed, Marshall's discipline "has already exalted the 13th Regiment to rank with the foremost in the Brigade."

One of Marshall's subordinates also came to his defense, saying that, "The 13th is to-day what it never was before—a body of soldiery—all owing to the Marshall administration." He quotes a corporal's remarks that "now the officers have to attend to their business." (*U&A* 7/1/1862)

The most damning account of misconduct and indiscipline in the 13th before Marshall came from 36-year-old Albert G. Cooper. He had been a correspondent to the *Rochester Daily Democrat* until he defected to the *Rochester Daily Union and Advertiser*, apparently over the Marshall controversy. He had entered the service as a private in Company A, became 2nd lieutenant in Company D on January 31, 1862, first lieutenant on May 13, 1862, and captain of Company I on October 31, 1862. He wrote a letter to "a gentleman in this city," who passed it on to the *U&A*, which published it:

> *When Colonel Pickell took command...our regiment was in a terrible condition, the greatest dissatisfaction prevailed, and the regiment soon became badly demoralized...*[S]*ome of the officers grossly neglected their duty; were constantly visiting Washington rum shops and houses of prostitution; some were arrested and lodged in the Central Guard House; officers were seen almost daily drunk in camp; were receiving visits in camp from noted prostitutes. In one case a member of Col. P.'s staff introduced one of the most noted prostitutes of the City of Washington to Col. P. as a sister-in-law; prostitutes were present in carriages at dress parades; in one instance there was one of these noted women seen in the tent of a Captain in broad day light; officers would go to Washington on spurious passes; on several occasions one half of the officers were absent at dress parade, and I have known as many as twenty-seven privates to be absent also. Of course, while this state of affairs was in vogue, the companies to which these officers were attached were shamefully neglected, as also was their study of tactics, so essential to all volunteer officers. Why was it that Gen. Martindale, at the review near Munson's Hill, said in the presence of*

> *about 75,000 troops, "that if he could have the handling of this, the 13th regiment, for two weeks, it would not be the laughing stock of this great body of troops?"...Of course, the privates were allowed to "run wild" when and where ever they chose and thereby became as demoralized as their officers. Under Colonel Marshall, things were vastly improved. The regiment was never in as good discipline as at present, and Col. M. is as popular with the officers and men...as any Colonel in the army. (7/8/1862)*

When the "Rumors and complaints" about Marshal reached Scorer, he weighed in:

> *Col. Marshall does not allow wire-pulling for favoritism about him. In consequence of which, an officer resigned. Shot and shell too are unpleasant, so they are "on the fly"—so another resigned. If an officer does not do his duty, does not attend to his men when sick or dying, he is reminded of it by Col. M., and if the offense is repeated, Col. M. is not very particular about using kid gloves. Col. M...also requires that company commanders account for all government property they receive. Fault is found with this and another one resigns...One thing is certain, Col. M. is just the man for the regiment on the field. Certainly nothing can be said against his conduct at Hanover Court House. Any regiment might well be proud of such an officer. (*U&A *6/30/1862)*

A Dansville editor, A.O. Bunnell, who visited the 13th after the Second Battle of Bull Run, added his voice to Marshall's defense with this comment: "No officer in the army takes better care of his men, by whom he is devotedly loved, and none are more highly esteemed by their superiors than Col. Marshall." (*U&A* 9/12/1862)

In the midst of the controversy, the *U&A* (7/10/1862) reported that Colonel Marshall "arrived here this morning in quite feeble health, suffering from an attack of fever contracted on the Peninsula before Richmond" and was to be confined to his hotel room for "a day or two." Marshall returned to the regiment and remained its commander until May 13, 1863, when it was mustered out. He had been wounded at Fredericksburg on December 14, 1862. Subsequently, he reorganized the 13th as the 14th New York Heavy Artillery Regiment, which was recruited in Rochester and mustered in during the autumn of 1863. According to the REE, "The old men [of the 13th] will go with him almost to a man." (*BR* 5/28/1863) It served in 13 engagements before being mustered out on August 26, 1865. Marshall was wounded again at Petersburg on June 17, 1864, and captured in action on July 30, 1864. (Phisterer 1476–77, 1491, 1897) He was released from prison in December 1864, and returned to Rochester. He remained in the regular army after the war, but received a disability discharge in 1867, retired to western Pennsylvania, and died in Canandaigua (presumably at the veterans hospital there) in 1883, still suffering from his war wounds. (Marcotte 66)

One wonders how the 13th could have been the object of such glowing reports before Marshall took over, and yet described during the controversy as having been so poorly run pre-Marshall. The bottom line is that Marshall remained in his command until the regiment mustered out and was regarded as sufficiently able to be given command of its successor. Given Colonel Pickell's infirmities, it seems likely that the misconduct of his subordinate officers was reported accurately. In any case, as the following chapter shows, he commanded an effective fighting force in the battles that ensued after the controversy.

Chapter 12

Second Bull Run to Fredericksburg

Second Battle of Bull Run

After the retreat from the Peninsula on July 1, 1862, the 13th was not engaged again until the Second Battle of Bull Run on August 30. William Lakeman, assistant surgeon, provided this account of the regiment's travails after they left Harrison's Landing:

> *We have had a rough time since we marched from Harrison's Landing, August 14th, and from the date of this you can judge of the distance we have travelled. Of the hardships and fatigue endured none can know but those who have endured.*
>
> *We disembarked at Aquia creek, but I cannot describe all that occurred on the march of a large army. Suffice it for the present to state that from the 14th to the 30th we averaged about 20 miles per day, besides picket duty, short rations, hot sun, bad water and dusty roads. We fought on the 30th—oh! a hard day for the 13th—were severely cut up, repulsed and fell back. There have been several days fighting about Manassas. We were in the battle field on the 29th and deployed as advance skirmishers, were on picket all night, and marched to the battle field on the 30th, which was very destructive in every respect. Tell the Lieutenant Colonel that the 13th has added new laurels to those originally earned, and has elicited the praise of even* [Major] *Gen.* [Daniel G.] *Butterfield.*

Corporal Theodore H. Jameson of Brockport, 20, killed in action at the Second Battle of Bull Run, August 30, 1862, while serving in the 13th NYVI. *Courtesy of the U.S. Army Military History Institute.*

Oh! Had all done as we did the brigade would not now number only 650, not sufficient for one good regiment....

I have slept on the ground without a blanket ever since I left Harrison's Landing, but, thank God, I am well and ready for work. I was on the field with my regiment having been ordered there. I never saw such a fire as our boys faced from three sides. Still on they went. I felt cool and self-possessed. That is the best way to feel. Thank God, he has preserved me... We have now been in thirteen engagements...

We have now and then some fun, even though so much used up. This morning a fellow came peddling cigars. The Colonel don't allow smoking, but he turned around and said, "Why the h-ll don't you smoke, boys?" So Company B all had cigars. Another boy came peddling papers. The Colonel said, "Boys, go and get your papers." Colonel Marshall is a bully fellow in the field.

Our regimental colors were not with us in the field, but the Stars and Stripes which we carry have fifty holes in them, and the flag is in ribbons.

> *All the Color Guard were wounded, and Parmely brought the colors in. (*U&A *9/6/1862)*

Lakeman appended his notes. Some of them were:

> *Thursday, 28th. Reveille at 2 A.M., to march at 3:30, fell in at* [?], *no breakfast, and feel tired. Halted for night within one mile of Manassas Junction. We passed Bristow's Station and the battle field of the 26th. Saw many wounded and dead of both sides. Much railway property destroyed by rebels.*
>
> *Friday, 29th. Started at 7:30. Severe and continued cannonading till a late hour last night. Resumed this morning and seems in the direction of the Gap. Marched as far as Manassas Junction and went on the Battle Field. Regiment was pushed forward as skirmishers and remained all night on picket duty. The Rebels driven back. Hard fighting on both sides.*
>
> *Saturday, 30th.* [2nd Bull Run] *Spent a miserable night. Cold and hungry. Pickets called in. Marched toward Centreville. Passed over Bull Run field. Battle is opened and we are now awaiting a severe contest. God knows how it will end. This day many will bite the dust. In the field all day—fighting hard…A very severe fight took place. Many of our boys were killed and wounded…We were exposed to a galling fire from three points as we charged. The Rebels came out in good style. Our left wing gave way, but I shall never forget the 13th going up the hill. Our flag is literally perforated. We fell back in some confusion. (*U&A *9/6/1862)*

Charles Curtis Brown also provided a description of the 13th at Second Bull Run:

> *We never stopped marching till we got to Bristow's station, two miles from Manassas Junction where we lay till next day, when* [we] *passed through the Junction and moved to the left of the line of battle on the plains of Manassas.*
>
> *There we were thrown out as skirmishers and remain so all night. A fierce battle was raging until long after dark. We only exchanged a few shots with them. Next morning* [September 30] *we marched to the old battle ground of Bull Run. We were stationed at a point near the left of the line. After driving the skirmishers out of a piece of woods in front of us, we double quicked across an open field under a tremendous fire of canister*

Sergeant George H. Hill of Brockport, 20, killed in action at the Second Battle of Bull Run, August 30, 1862, while serving in the 13th NYVI. *Courtesy of the U.S. Army Military History Institute.*

> *which caused many a poor fellow to bite the dust. At last we got to the hill top where we opened a sharp fire on the foe. The rebels were doing their best to shell us, but did not do much injury. A battery of ours was throwing shell over our head, adding to the horror of the scene and once in a while hurting our men. Our men were falling fast. A second line that came out of the woods to support us either dared not advance or were ordered not to, for they went back. Our boys saw it and finding there was no use to stay any longer so our brigade took a run to the woods again. Across the field the canister of two batteries and the musket balls of the line in front of us swept a perfect hail storm of lead and iron. Man after man went down before it. I never expected to reach the woods unharmed, yet not a scratch did I get. It was a badly fought battle as ever I saw. At least thirty thousand men never fired a shot, and that behind our own lines. (Brown 64)*

The DMNA account of the role of the 13th at the Second Battle of Bull Run follows:

> *Here* [near Manassas Junction on August 29] *it deployed and engaged the skirmishers of the enemy until dark, and remained on picket during the night. On the 30th it moved to Bull Run, and, although worn out with fatigue and hunger, engaged the enemy. It was first assigned to positions under a cover of timber, and there with the 18th Massachusetts*

> *and 1st Michigan, charged across an open field in the face of a heavy fire of musketry, shell and canister from three sides and reached a point within thirty yards of the enemy. Here it fought desperately. During the day, out of two hundred and forty men it lost three officers and twenty-six privates killed, four officers and seventy-three privates wounded, and ten missing* [a 48.3% casualty rate].

Marcotte says of the 13th at Second Bull Run that "none suffered as much as the 13th, in a doomed but heroic charge moments before the Confederates' trap was sprung." (67) The official statistics bear him out. They report that those engagements at Manassas Junction and Bull Run cost the 13th three officers and 38 enlisted men killed or died of their wounds, four officers and 62 enlisted men wounded but recovered, and eight enlisted men missing. (Phisterer 1888)

The casualties at Second Bull Run included six Brockporters. Corp. Jacob Spaul of Brockport was killed and John J. Leonard of Sweden, William C. Webb and Joseph Thompson of Brockport, and Charles Thompson and Henry Cusick of Hamlin were wounded. Cusick, who is quoted above (page 129) on Gaines' Mill, was also wounded at Fredericksburg, December 13, 1862.

ANTIETAM AND SHEPHERDSTOWN

Before and after Second Bull Run, the 13th was on the march almost constantly until it reached Sharpsburg, Maryland, where it served as a reserve regiment during the Battle of Antietam. This did not mean, however, that the regiment saw no action, as the letters below disclose. Charles Curtis Brown recounts that experience (with some confusion on the days):

> *After the fatigue of our march to Fredericksburg, we left that place Friday night* [August 23?], *marched all night except two hours. Marched about the country till Monday night, when we had one night's sleep. Tuesday morning we commenced to march. That night on picket, no sleep of consequence. Marched all next day, slept all night till half past one next morning. Marched all day, slept all night. Marched all next day, picket all night, no sleep, marched part of the day, fought the rest of the day* [August 30?], *marched all night, stopped all day,* [August 31?] *marched all night and the next day* [September 1?] *till ten o'clock at night, slept that night,*

> *marched next day* [September 2?] *till 10 o'clock a.m. when we arrived at Hall's hill. Slept two nights and marched the third night* [September 4?] *and part of the day* [September 5?] *till we stopped here. Last night at 12 M. we were called up in arms to prepare for a cavalry raid and slept on our arms in line all night but no raid. Do you wonder that we are fatigued after undergoing all of that, on top of the march from Harrison's Landing to Fredericksburg? I think we will remain about here for some time. (Brown 65)*

In fact, four days later, as Scorer reported in this letter:

> *At 7 A.M., Friday, Sept. 12th, we were ordered to pack up ready for a march; three days rations were given out and everything got in trim. At 8 o'clock we started with knapsacks, &c., passed over the Aqueduct, through Georgetown and Washington to the Baltimore & Ohio RR. Depot, where we lay down and rested about a quarter of an hour. We then started and counter-marched as far as 7th street, out of which we march towards Rockville; we camped for the night about one mile outside the District of Columbia.*
>
> *At 6 o'clock next morning…we started again…, passed through Rockville. Sunday we passed through Clarksville and Hyattstown… We passed through Urbana, crossed the Monocacy river. Here the rebels destroyed the railroad bridge, four miles from Frederick, we camped… Monday we passed through Middletown, passing on the way several squads of rebel prisoners.*
>
> *With a few others I passed over South Mountain where Sunday's battle was fought, and what a sight! I witnessed there dead rebels laying in heaps all over the mountain. Our men were burying our dead and gathering up arms, &c…We arrived at Boonsville Tuesday night, Sept. 16. Next morning we marched over the hill (Morrell's division* [including the 13th] *was the reserve* [for Antietam]*) and lay in the valley all day but were not called on. Nothing could be heard but cannon and musketry all day long. Nothing happened to our brigade except that two of the 25th N.Y. lost their legs by a shell from the rebs.*
>
> *Thursday morning we had orders to be ready to march at daylight, but did not start till after 1 P.M…At about 1 o'clock we marched off to the left, crossed the Antietam river where the hardest fighting of Wednesday was done. On top of the hills we were deployed as pickets, relieving the 36th Ohio. As we were deploying, the balls flew around lively enough; one of the 36th was shot dead just as he was relieved. There was very little*

firing through the night. At daylight not a reb was to be seen. All night long the rattling of wagons and artillery was heard moving towards the river.

At about 6 a.m. some of our wounded commenced hallooing to us to come and bring them in—that the rebels had gone—and, sure enough, they had gone. Our brigade was then deployed as skirmishers towards Sharpsburg. We crossed through the town, took several prisoners, but met no enemy armed...

At about 10 a.m. we started towards the Potomac, three miles from Sharpsburg. We camped within half a mile of the river and stayed there all night. Our batteries were playing into the rebels all the afternoon and evening and succeeded in driving the Rebs. from their guns, when 100 men from our Brigade forded the river and rolled the abandoned pieces off the bank. Our folks captured 17 pieces of artillery, a battle flag and several prisoners on Saturday morning.

At a quarter past 9 a.m. we started to cross the river...We got about one mile from the ford when we heard skirmishers firing. The citizens reported the rebels in force about one mile from the river and drawn up in line-of-battle. The Col. (Barnes) commanding Brigade ordered out skirmishers and the 118th Pennsylvania Volunteers to take the position on the bluff. They had hardly got out when the rebels were seen advancing in force. They advanced so as to cut off a part of our skirmishers, who they took prisoners...

As soon as Col. Marshall saw there was danger of being cut off he gave the order to retreat in good order, which was done. We got across the river completely tired out and rallied in the woods...As soon as the Rebs were seen advancing on us our batteries on the opposite side threw their shells over into them with a will.

*Several regiments of our troops were formed in the canal on the Maryland shore, who acted as sharpshooters, picking off the Rebs who ventured down the bank in sight. Soon after we had formed in the woods Sergt. Martin and the new recruits joined us and we were ordered to our old camp, where we now remain. (*U&A *10/1/1862)*

Brown also reported on the Shepherdstown engagement:

About nine o'clock yesterday morning...our brigade crossed the river...We moved up the bank of the river toward Shepardstown...An aide rode up and found the rebels drawn up in line of battle about three quarters of a mile from us and in considerable force. We were deployed in line of battle on the heights above. The banks along here are bluffs about fifty or sixty

> *feet high. They are nearly perpendicular. The 25th NYV and our regiment, each about one hundred men, were on the right of the road…, the 118th P*[ennsylvania]*. vols. numbering about nine hundred men were on the left of the road. After a short time of skirmish firing, the 118th opened fire, the rebels returning it fiercely…We found that the rebels were bringing down upon us five times our force and that we must fall back and recross the river. This would expose us to a murderous fire from the rebels unless our artillery could keep them away from the bank. The artillery on the Maryland side were working famously, throwing shell fiercely among the foe. The order came to fall back. We had come down from our position on the right and gone up to support the 118th but before we could open fire, "fall back in good order" was the word. We got down the bank and moving to the crossing place plunged in, not being nearly as particular as we were in going over. The 25th and our being ahead got over comparatively unharmed, having only seventeen wounded and taken prisoner, but the poor 118th in their first battle only numbered three hundred, wounded and all, that were here out of nine hundred yester morning. More than half the regiment, I think, was taken prisoner…* [T]*hey sent over some cavalry who went about a quarter of a mile from the bank, found some of the enemy but did not ascertain their strength and position, but came back after exchanging a shot or two. (Brown 69)*

The next day, September 22, Brown wrote again:

> *Our brigade has been in another precarious position. After I wrote of my safety that same evening our brigade was sent out as skirmishers and for the night as pickets in front of Burnside's line. We were just in front of the village of Sharpsburg on a range of hills, the rebels being on another range, and two stone walls held by the enemy between us. All night long we could hear artillery and wagons moving to the left and backwards toward the river. We immediately divined that the rebels were leaving. The morning proved the surmise to be true, for not a sign of a rebel could be seen…We found that the rebels had all crossed the river into Virginia. They had several batteries planted to dispute our passage, but soon our batteries got into position and opened such a fire that they were forced to leave, abandoning four pieces of artillery which I saw our artillery bring over next morning. (Brown 70)*

The regiment suffered no casualties at Antietam, and one officer and five enlisted men wounded but recovered at Shepherdstown. Also, 12 enlisted men were reported missing at Shepherdstown. (Phisterer 1888) One of the wounded was Jacob Fertig of Clarkson.

The DMNA account of the role of the 13th at Antietam and Shepherdstown follows:

> *On the 12th of September the regiment moved on the Maryland campaign; crossed the Potomac at Georgetown; marched through Rockville, Frederick, and Keedysville, and joined the main army before Sharpsburg on the 16th. During the battle of Antietam (September 17th) it was in the reserve under Gen. Porter. On the night of the 18th it was deployed as pickets in front of* [Major] *Gen.* [Ambrose E.] *Burnside's position, opposite the bridge, and the next morning advanced as skirmishers through Sharpsburg and captured some prisoners from the rear guard of the enemy. On the 20th it crossed the Potomac with the brigade, at Sheperdstown, was met by superior force of the enemy and compelled to re-cross the river under sharp fire from the enemy on the bluffs. Here the regiment lost eighteen in wounded and prisoners.*

FREDERICKSBURG

After Shepherdstown, the 13th spent nearly six weeks camped near Sharpsburg. Then, on October 30, they began marching again, ending up on December 11 becoming heavily engaged in the Battle of Fredericksburg. Nine days after Shepherdstown (September 29), Scorer described a week's life in the camp of a veteran regiment between marches and battles:

> *Camp and picket guard, and two drills per day of an hour each, is the extent of our laborious duties at present. They are laborious indeed, for we never get more than one day's rest between guard and picket…*
>
> *Sunday, Sept. 21st. At 4 P.M. on that day we were suddenly called upon to go on picket. All were ready in less than twenty minutes, and we were posted on the Maryland side of the Potomac. Not a reb was to be seen, except a lookout on the church steeple at Shepardstown, and now and then a cavalryman clear out of range. Some of our men were over the river, burying the dead who were killed the Saturday before. We were relieved Monday night by the 32d and 9th Massachusetts regiments. Tuesday morning we moved our camp to a cleaner place, about 50 yards east of a straw stack. At about 3 P.M. on the same day we were called into line as a support for*

Griffin's Brigade, who crossed the river for the purpose of getting a couple of caissons and a dismounted piece left by the rebs. They returned in about an hour, with what they went after, and we marched back to quarters.

About 10 o'clock, just as almost all were asleep, we were called on to give three cheers for the fall of Richmond. No details were given, and it proved to be a "sell"; but it served for a topic of conversation and argument for quite a number till nearly morning.

Wednesday forenoon it rained. We drew clothing, &c., and short rations. Every thing was quiet all day and night.

Thursday we got orders to drill two hours each day, morning and evening…At 4 P.M., 60 men were detailed from the 13th for picket duty… Everything was quiet that night.

Friday…noon two rebel officers and nine privates, paroled prisoners, were escorted over the river, under a flag of truce. The escort returned about 5 o'clock. Some friends of a soldier of the 118th crossed over, under flag of truce, to obtain his body…

Saturday morning, at 9 A.M., we were relieved, after being on picket about forty hours. Most of the men were without rations—not even a cracker; but by begging around we made out to stay our appetites until we reached camp. Then the rest of the day was spent in cooking rations, which were drawn for three days…

Sunday morning, at 10 o'clock, we had the usual Sunday inspection…

*Last night fourteen men were detached for Division Guard…This morning seventy-five men of the regiment were detailed for picket again. There are also eighteen men for camp guard. This will give you some idea of what duty our regiment of less than 200 men, has to do. (*U&A *10/13/1862)*

In fact, a month later, Scorer wrote: "At inspection Friday morning there were 139 guns out and 21 on guard duty, which embraces all that are in the regiment." (*U&A* 11/1/1862). Note: a regiment at full strength contained 1,000 men.

Early in their stay at Shepherdstown, the tedium was relieved by a special event, as described in this unsigned letter (probably from Scorer):

We still remain in camp here, with little variation of duty beside picket and camp guard, but since I last wrote we (our corps) have been reviewed by President Lincoln and Gen. McClellan. Friday, Oct. 3d, "Old Abe" arrived at Gen. Porter's headquarters at 9 A.M. [Major General

> George W.] *Morell's Division was formed and lay waiting till 12 o'clock, when "Old Abe" and Gen. Mcclellan and staff made their appearances, passing by Morell's division toward where* [Major General George] *Sykes' Division lay, to our left. When they made their appearance on top of the hill in front of them, a salute of twenty-one guns was fired by one of Sykes' batteries. After they had reviewed Sykes' Division, they rode back to where "the fighting Brigade" (Martindale's) lay, which consists of the 18th Massachusetts, 25th and 13th N.Y.V., 1st Michigan, 118th Pa. V., 22d Massachusetts, 2d Maine, and (for the occasion) Berdan's Sharp-Shooters and a battery. The President noticed particularly the 25th and 13th N Y.V., for he stopped between them—only for an instant, though. Gen. Morell rode with the president while passing through the Division, and Gens. McClellan and Porter rode together. Martindale's Brigade was at least half smaller than either Butterfield's or* [Major General Charles] *Griffin's, and why? Echo answers, why! (*U&A *10/11/1862)*

Even when the troops were not engaged in fighting (which was most of the time), the fear of enemy action was nearly always present:

> *This morning, 42 men from the regiment go on picket. It is rumored in camp that the rebs have planted some batteries on the opposite side of the river, back of Shepardstown, and that their cavalry and infantry were seen moving towards the river last evening. If it is so, we think it is to cover some other move they are making in some other point. (*U&A *10/11/1862)*

> *On Thursday morning early, Griffin's and part of Sykes', and three regiments of* [Brigadier General Daniel] *Tyler's brigade, crossed the Potomac on a reconnoissance. Heavy firing was heard in the direction of Harper's Ferry, and it gradually worked westward until it sounded as if directly opposite.—They returned on Friday night, closely followed by the rebs. "Nobody hurt." (*U&A *10/27/1862)*

On October 30, the regiment finally moved out of Shepherdstown, though the soldiers knew not where they were bound. Brown reported from a camp near White Plains, Virginia:

> *Last Thursday evening we broke camp and left Sharpsburg sleeping that night near Harpers Ferry. Next day moved across the river and encamped four miles beyond Ferry…Nov. 2nd we marched to Snicker Gap, about*

nineteen miles. Yesterday morning we started for this place, resting about five miles from here. Today we came on. It began to snow this morning and does so still, but very slightly so that not more than half an inch is on the ground. It is cold and deadly wintry. We are in the woods. We probably march tomorrow, but where I cannot tell. (74)

Scorer's accounts provide a better sense of the life the soldiers were leading on that march:

On Thursday afternoon [October 30]*...everybody in camp began to prepare for a move and at five o'clock we got the order to strike tents. At six o'clock we started off towards Harper's Ferry. The first three miles of the road was rather rough, but when we got along side of the canal the road improved considerable.*

At half past ten we turned into a field, about three miles from Harper's Ferry, where we prepared for a sleep, without pitching tents. A clear sky was our tent for the night and a couple of blankets our covering...

Yesterday morning we started at about ten o'clock and got about two miles before we had to halt to let troops pass coming from the other way...

At about three o'clock we crossed the river to Harper's Ferry on the Pontoon bridge. We passed the famous engine house where John Brown held his own so long...Passing through the town,...we turned to the left and crossed another Pontoon bridge over the Shenandoah river...We went but a short distance when we passed several ambulance loads of sick from the 140th...

*We camped about five miles from Harper's Ferry, in a large field. It seems as if the owner of it anticipated soldiers, for he had stone fences instead of rails along the road, but we found all the rails that were necessary for cooking purposes. (*U&A *11/7/1862)*

Four days later, he resumed his account with the march:

We drew two days' rations to be ready to march at 7 a.m...We had reveille at 5 a.m., but did not march till half-past eight. We marched six miles towards Leesburg, when we turned off to the right towards Snickers Gap...At 6 p.m. we camped about one-fourth of a mile from Snickersville, making our day's march about 18 miles. During the march the new recruits lightened their knapsacks of considerable extra stuff...

Very few of the men put up their shelter tents, as there was a stack of straw handy by and something to lay on, with no other cover than the blanket...But before morning they wished they had the tents up, for about midnight a high west wind came up, and, to add to our discomfort, it rained enough to wet our blankets through.

Monday... [we] *heard heavy firing through the Gap at 2 p.m., but we were not disturbed by any orders to move...Monday afternoon most of us put up our tents, as there was a fair prospect of spending another day in camp. We went to bed, making up our minds to rest. But at about twelve o'clock the Sergeant Major came around with the order that we move at daylight.*

We had reveille at 4 o'clock and breakfast as soon as possible after, but did not move at daylight. Col. Marshall ordered that the tents be left up until further orders, and they have not been taken down since. At 3 p.m. we had regimental inspection and evening parade...

*We had an hour and a half skirmish drill this morning. The new recruits are now being drilled in the manual two hours at a time. (*U&A *11/13/1862,)*

Scorer's letter of November 13 continues his account:

Thursday morning, Nov. 5th, we had reveille at 4 o'clock and started at daylight—marched about 17 miles—passing through Middleburg. Every house almost was used as a hospital for secesh wounded. Not a pleasant face or welcome look met us on the road, nor in the town...

We bivouacked about four miles from Middleburg on a side hill. Rail fences and dead sheep made their way into camp in quantities, the one administered to the comfort of the outer and the other to the inner man. A very cold wind blew all night, which added much to the discomfort of those who slept on the ground without tents.

Friday morning we again started at daylight towards White Plains. We marched about four miles when we were overtaken by a snow storm. [About nine in the morning a snow storm set in and continued till the next day. A regular old nor-easter....Ltr of 11/11/1862] *We camped about one-fourth of a mile from the railroad station at White Plains, in the woods. Somebody's haystack added much to our comfort...I am inclined to think if the kind ladies of Rochester and vicinity could have seen the new style of mits used by the boys on this occasion, they would have taken pity and have some sent to the regiment. Government socks are made to answer for mits. (*U&A *11/20/1862)*

Camp life was rudely interrupted at this time by an event that sent shock waves through the regiment—President Lincoln's removal of General McClellan. Though McClellan was immensely popular with the troops because of his evident solicitude for their welfare, he drove Lincoln crazy with his excessive caution and indecision. Actually, the solicitude and caution were two faces of the same coin. By this time, however, Lincoln had decided that it was more important to defeat the South than to spare the lives of his troops. In his letter, dated Dec. 23, Scorer reports on the men's reaction:

> *Soon after we arrived at the camp a lot of mittens came for the regiment, and among them one package of five pairs of nice yarn mittens for the "veterans" of Co. A...The ladies of the Relief Association will please accept our sincere thanks for the mittens sent to the regiment, and the ladies of the Second Ward Association will also accept the thanks of the "nobs" for their kind consideration in sending them the above mentioned five pairs of yarn mittens.*

> *Reveille as usual at 4 a.m., Saturday morning, Nov. 8th, and we started at 7, passing through White Plains over a slippery road, made so by the snow the day before. We followed the Railroad about four miles.... We camped about three miles from Warrenton...after a march of about 12 miles. We find lots of fence rails and good water near at hand, which are the most essential to comfort in camp...*
>
> *Sunday morning six companies of our regiment were detailed to guard wagon and ammunition trains. This beats everything in the way of marching we have had—to be obliged to follow a mule train—halt as often as they do, start up, stop and start again. Oh, Ceasar, ain't it tedious! (11/11/1862)*

> *Monday morning...the Adjutant read Gen. McClellan's farewell to the Army of the Potomac, after which we were marched out where the Brigade were formed along side of the road where Gen. McClellan was to pass. We waited some time before the General made his appearance.*
>
> *We were called to attention by the first gun of the battery on our right when they commenced firing the salute. Soon after, Gen. McClellan made his appearance, followed by Gen. Burnside with his staff and escort of cavalry. He was received with three rousing cheers and a "tiger." As he passed by any regiment with the old torn and dirty stand of colors, he took particular notice of them—gave them an extra wave of adieu. Many a*

> *cheek was moistened by tears that has not known such a thing for more than eighteen months.*
>
> *After he had passed we were marched back to camp. The Colonel was in no pleasant humor, for he then ordered the officers to drill their companies two hours, but after drilling about an hour we were called in, by reason of an order from headquarters for the officers to go and bid Gen. McClellan farewell…In the afternoon we are ordered to drill another hour. We also got orders to be ready to move at a moment's notice.*
>
> *Tuesday all day, except while drilling, was occupied discussing the removal of Gen. McClellan. (*U&A *12/29/1862)*

In another letter Scorer says: "Warrenton is rather a pretty village, about the size of Brockport, with one Catholic and four Protestant churches… There is about 250 rebel prisoners confined now in these churches, among which are 150 wounded. The village before the war, contained 2,000 inhabitants." (*U&A* 11/20/1862)

From November 9th until the 17th, the 13th was camped near Warrenton. Then they moved on again, as this letter from near Falmouth, Va., dated Nov. 24 reports:

> *On Friday, Nov. 14th, after our usual morning drill, we received a mail… In the afternoon Col. Barnes gave us a turn at brigade drill, which completely tired out the new recruits as well as the old companies. After which we had evening parade…*
>
> *Saturday we had grand review by* [Major] *Gen.* [Joseph] *Hooker* [who later became commander of the Army of the Potomac]…*The 13th never appeared better. Sunday we prepared for a march, drew rations, &c.*
>
> *Monday morning, the 17th, we started before daylight, passing through Warrenton at daylight. We went direct to Warrenton Junction…and camped…near Elk Run, marching a march of 18 miles thro' woods and across fields….*
>
> *Tuesday morning at 4 o'clock reveille sounded, but we did not get started till near 10 o'clock. We passed through Elk Run and camped about twelve miles from where we started. Water was very scarce all along the road, which made the march seem five miles longer…All complained of sore feet that night, and every one was short of rations. Hard bread very scarce. The 118th Pennsylvania came to our boys and begged crackers.*
>
> *Wednesday morning we struck tents at nine o'clock but did not start till noon. We went only five miles, towards Fredericksburg, when we*

encamped…All day Thursday we had showers of a few minutes duration. In the afternoon the bugle blew for drill. All looked astonished at such orders, but we went out and drilled in the mud, &c., till the rain drove us in…All night long it rained like fury. Our shelter tents were of no more use than paper houses, and Friday morning found a great part of the boys drying their blankets and clothing by large fires of rails which had to be carried nearly three-fourths of a mile.

Saturday morning we got orders to move at 8½ a.m. The tents were all struck and all were ready when the order was countermanded. Tents were pitched again, and all was going on as usual when, at about noon, the bugle again blew to "strike tents," and again all packed ready for a start. The wagons all went, and after waiting until 5 p.m. the order came to camp again for the night. The Colonel sent for headquarter wagon and it soon returned and tents were pitched again.

Sunday morning we struck tents at daylight, but did not get started till about 9 a.m., when we struck through the woods and marched about nine miles where we have since remained…Since we have been camped here,…the boys have been very short of rations…Those who had money bought from two to three days rations of the Brigade Commissary, but to do so they must get an order from a commissioned officer…

*Since we have been here the weather has been very cold, especially nights, and shelter tents are not good for much to keep out cold or rain either, and if they get wet they are not a very comfortable thing to carry over one's shoulder. (*U&A *12/1/1862)*

After the Battle of Fredericksburg, Scorer wrote:

Thanksgiving Day dawned upon us very short of rations. To the soldiers it was a day of fasting instead of a feast. The officers had a dinner of "hard tack" cooked in all the different styles imaginable, while most of the privates had only one or two "Hard Tacks" for all day, and some were without any. [Nine pieces were considered a day's ration.] *Never since we have been in the service have we been so short of rations…*

Monday, December 1st, the whole brigade are ordered out for picket. We marched to within a mile of our last camp, nearly 12 miles, where we stacked our arms and rested for the night. Early next morning we marched back to camp…

Thursday, December 4th, we had a general clearing up around camp, companies were assigned new places…and streets were made…and almost everybody built fireplaces.

> *Wednesday night, December 10th, the officers had a big time, and kept us awake till near midnight. Next morning we had roll call at four o'clock. We then struck tents, packed up, and prepared for a march. At daylight we started towards Fredericksburg. Before daylight we heard the distant firing of heavy guns, which continued all day. All day we lay within sight of the spires of Fredericksburg...Just before dark, we moved into a piece of woods for the night, made our coffee, etc., put up our tents, and had a good night's sleep.*
>
> *Next morning we had roll call at daylight, and after getting one day's rations, we moved down near the bank of the river. "all was quiet on the Rappahannock" till nine a.m.; when the heavy guns opened once more. We lay that night in the position we were all day.*
>
> *At daylight December 13th we had reveille; and were all ready for a start at short notice. The balloon "Eagle" made an ascension. At 10 a.m. we were called to attention, started for the river, crossed the pontoon bridge, and passed up through town...Passing through the town out towards the railroad, a shell from the rebel battery struck in our regiment, wounding one of Co. G and one of Co. C. The railroad was cut down about six feet below the level flat in front of the hill where their batteries were, and about 500 yards across this flat is where the 1st brigade* [including the 13th]...*made the charge. Behind the bank we formed and fixed bayonets, then charge across the flat under a perfect shower of rifle balls, shot and shell. For thirty-five hours the regiment lay there, pouring into the rebs (who were in rifle pits) the ounce pills whenever one showed his head.*
>
> *Sunday, December 14th, at nearly midnight, the first brigade was relieved, and marched down to the street near the river, stacked arms, and rested...All day the 15th we lay in the same position. Just at dark, as all were preparing to take a sleep, the order was given, "Fall in, 13th." We fell in, and marched up to the main street and lay down with our arms by our side. In this position we remained until about two a.m., when we were again called into line and marched back towards the bridge where we lay the day before. For the first time we became aware that we were evacuating the town...From there we marched back to camp where we are now. (*U&A *12/26/1862)*

Captain Albert G. Cooper, of Company I, wrote to his wife: "Saturday our regiment was engaged, and, if possible, has won new honor for Old Monroe...All day Sunday we were obliged to lie close upon the ground, as the enemy's sharpshooters had a fine opportunity to pick us off. It was almost sure death for a man to even get up on his knees." (*U&A* 12/20/1862)

So, the 13th had fought and suffered another defeat. The official statistics show that five enlisted men in the regiment were killed and five died of wounds. One of those killed was 25-year-old Joel H. Soles of Sweden outside the village, who had been transferred from Company K to Company B and then to Company D. Six officers and 52 enlisted men were wounded but recovered and seven enlisted men were missing. (Phisterer 1888) Michael Tool[e], 19, of Clarkson was among the wounded who recovered. Earlier he had been wounded in the knee by a spent bullet at First Bull Run. The *U&A* reported that, "Of the 780 forming the regiment originally, but forty-two are still in the ranks. Some have left to serve elsewhere in the army, many having been given commissions, others have resigned through ill health, many bear honorable wounds which disqualify them for the field, and, alas! many more sleep in the soldier's grave." (1/3/1862) Scorer claimed on January 12 that, "There are now present in the regiment doing duty 175 of the 'old originals.'" (*U&A* 1/23/1863) On March 3, he revised his figure to 188, including "only two of the original line officers who still remain line officers. But there are 13 line officers now present, who were privates of the original regiment" (*U&A* 3/10/1863)

The DMNA account of the 13th in the Battle of Fredericksburg follows:

> *The regiment remained at Sharpsburg until the 30th of October, when it crossed the Potomac at Harper's Ferry and passed successively through Snicker's Gap, Middleburgh, White Plains, New Baltimore, Warrenton, Warrenton Junction, Elktown, and Hartwood, and arrived opposite Fredericksburg on the 19th November. It remained in camp without special duty, except a reconnaissance to Hartwood Church (December 1st), until the 11th December, when it moved on the Fredericksburg campaign. It crossed the river on the 13th, and came immediately under the fire of the enemy; advanced through the north end of the town across the open ground beyond the railroad, and took position in the extreme front, facing the stone wall and rifle-pits occupied by the enemy and within close range of their artillery on the immediate heights beyond and to the right and left. In this exposed position the men were obliged to fire lying down, taking advantage of a slight rise of ground running parallel with the front of our line. Here it remained, receiving and returning fire until nightfall, and was not relieved until 10 P.M. of the 14th. Its loss in this engagement, out of 298 officers and men, was five killed, sixty-three wounded, and seven prisoners.*

During the second half of 1862, four more Brockporters were discharged for disabilities.

This account of the 3½ months from Second Bull Run to Fredericksburg documents the lives of typical Union soldiers—the marching back and forth, the camping in miserable circumstances, the false alarms, the inconclusive skirmishes, the food and supply shortages, the endless uncertainty, and, finally, the two pitched battles and humiliating defeats. By this time, of course, the regiment had become well tested in battle, and had acquired its respectful nickname of the "Old 13th," by which its veterans insisted on being called for the rest of their lives.

Chapter 13

The End of the Old 13th

After Fredericksburg

After Fredericksburg the 13th went into winter quarters in camp near Falmouth, Virginia. The 13th did not see battle again that winter, except that two companies, composed of soldiers who were not part of the original regiment "formed the left of a brigade" and "were in the midst of danger" in the Battle of Chancellorsville, May 1–3, 1863. (*U&A* 5/16/1863) At Chancellorsville four enlisted men in those companies were wounded and recovered and one was missing. (Phisterer 1888)

The regiment, however, remained in an area where combat was possible at anytime and, therefore, continued in a state of more-or-less constant alert for some time. This included some skirmishing and picket duty. For instance, Scorer wrote that on December 30 they:

> *were suddenly ordered to pack up, draw two days' rations, and be ready to move at 12 o'clock. Everything was bustle till that hour—some tearing down their tents and packing up their drygoods, others cooking, etc. At 12 o'clock the order came to leave tents standing, as a guard would be left in camp; so those who tore down their tents put them up again, taking only their blankets, rubbers, haversacks and canteens. We left camp at half past 12 and marched till midnight, (taking only a few short rests,) when we*

reached Harwood Church…We camped about one mile from the church in an open field. Next morning we marched to the Rappahannock and crossed the ford. Our skirmishers surprised the rebel pickets who were around a house, and in their firing at them a stray ball struck a Miss Richards, who was in the house, wounding her severely.

About one mile from the river we came to a deserted cavalry camp, which had all the appearance of being left suddenly. We pass on through a dense wood for about six miles or more, recrossed the river at Ellis' Ford, and camped that night about one mile from the river. Next day we returned to camp, marching about twenty miles…. All were completely tired out. (U&A *1/23/1863)*

A similar expedition was aborted three weeks later:

The next day (Saturday) [January 17] *came rations of onions, potatoes, dried apples, &c., another sign of a move, for never do rations come so plentifully unless they want to clean out the Commissary Department… They load down the men and empty the wagons…*

Tuesday morning, Jan. 20.—Tents were ordered to be struck and 'pack up' sounded. The Regiment started at one p.m. towards the ford above on the Rappahannock. Night over took the Brigade only about five miles from camp, and they camped in the woods. Next morning they start again, and move about one mile and a half. The rain of the night before made it impossible to move the artillery through the mud. Again the Brigade… camped in the woods. All day long, it rained or drizzled, and all night.

Thursday, Jan. 22d.—All prospects for a forward move seemed to vanish, for squads were sent back for axes to build corduroy roads, so as to be able to get the artillery back to camp…

Saturday afternoon (Jan 24th) the 5th corps started on their way back to camp which was reached about four p.m., a tired lot. (U&A *2/3/1863)*

The DMNA describes the activities of the regiment after Fredericksburg as follows:

On being relieved it returned to the streets of the city, and remained until the 15th; then moved to the upper part of the town and supported the pickets during the evacuation; at 8 A.M., on the 10th, recrossed the river, but was immediately ordered back and remained until daylight, acting as rear-guard while the pickets were withdrawn. On the 17th of December the regiment

> *reached its old camp opposite Fredericksburg and remained there until the 30th, when it joined in a reconnaissance, crossed the Rappahannock at Richards' Ford; moved up the river about seven miles, captured a few cavalry pickets; recrossed the river at Ellis', or Barnett's Ford, on the 31st; encamped for the night, and returned to its old quarters on the 1st of January. On the 20th of January it joined in the second advance on Fredericksburg, moved about three miles and encamped; 21st advanced about two miles and there remained mud-bound; built ordinary road for the artillery, and reached camp on the return on the 24th.*

That maneuver on January 20–21, 1863, was the infamous and ill-fated "mud march," a doomed attempt by Major General Ambrose B. Burnside to recover the initiative after the disaster at Fredericksburg. He attempted to move his army up the Rappahannock River a few miles above Fredericksburg, re-cross the river, and catch Lee unprepared. However, the weather was so abominable that his troops became completely bogged down in the mud and could not travel.

THE FINAL FOUR MONTHS

During its final four months, the regiment was camped near Falmouth, Virginia, increasingly preoccupied with the impending termination of its two-year service commitment. Scorer mentioned this topic in nearly every letter in 1863. Especially, he speculated on the mustering-out date and on the likelihood that many men would re-enlist.

He described the daily routine of the regiment during this period: "We have our usual quantity of drill each day. At 6 a.m. we have reveille, at 7 squad drill of one hour, at 9 company drill of one hour and a half, at 1:30 p.m. battalion drill of one hour and a half, at 4 evening parade, at half past 4 guard mounting, at 8 we have tattoo, at half past 8 taps or lights out." (*U&A* 1/30/1863)

That routine was interrupted for picket duty, For instance, on "January 8th, fifty men were detailed for picket" and on "January 11th, our pickets returned." (*U&A* 1/23/1863) And on January 27,

> *At 7½ a.m.,...a detail was made from the regiment for picket guard, leaving only the camp guard and forty men for brigade headquarter guard in camp.*

> *All day and all night it snowed, the wind blowing an accompaniment...It was truly awful, walking through this Virginia mud and snow the distance of five miles, to where we were posted on picket; and then, after being completely wet through, to have to stand post...Many of the brigade (for it was a detail of 1,500 from our brigade) did not have a chance to dry their feet even until noon Jan. 29th." (*U&A *2/6/1863)*

Later, Scorer describes the picket duty more fully, "But fortunately for us all picket duty is not an every day duty or even a weekly duty, but only about once in fifteen or twenty days, but when it comes four days are used up, for we have to stand post three days and a quarter part of the fourth day is occupied going out, and coming back to camp."

Scorer also described a somewhat related activity: "Several of our regiment (myself among them) were detailed as a guard at the houses of the inhabitants inside the lines to prevent the soldiers from robbing and insulting the women; for you must know there are very few men around in these parts. All who were not exempted by disease have been forced to join the S.C. army." (*U&A* 2/6/1863)

Also, some time was spent on construction work. "The Brigade are now building a corduroy road to Division headquarters" (*U&A* 3/17/1863) and it built three "redoubts...near the railroad...intended to protect the railroad bridge across Potomac Creek. The rebels made an attempt to destroy it, but got no further than to drive in our cavalry pickets." (*U&A* 3/26/1863)

Another activity during this period were the regular Sunday inspections and occasional "inspections of the camp and quarters." (*U&A* 3/17/1863) One of the inspections included "President Lincoln..., accompanied by [his two sons,] General Hooker and a numerous escort of officers, cavalry, and company of lancers. The President looked rather care-worn and anxious. He rode a bay horse after a style peculiar to himself. I should think the stirrups were rather short for his knees were nearly as high as the pommel of his saddle." Scorer complained that the troops were "standing in a cold wind without overcoats for two hours or more before the President arrived... Then, after waiting an hour or more, and going through several changes of front and base, we commenced to march in review. We marched nearly a mile around to pass by the President just in the right shape...After passing through several mud holes, &c., we started home, and arrived at camp about four o'clock, pretty well tired out, and hungry too." (*U&A* 4/14/1863)

One incident that caused much agitation in the regiment was the return of its regimental colors and Stars and Stripes to Rochester. Colonel

Marshall had sent them via Major George Hyland, Jr. to be presented to Mayor Bradstreet. In a letter to the mayor, Marshall explained that they had "become so tattered and worn as to be no longer of service." They were displayed in the Reynolds Arcade for a week and, then, moved to City Hall, in accordance with "the wish of the regiment." (*U&A* 1/3/1863) The *REE* reported that the national flag had "forty-seven bullet holes" and the regimental colors had a "faded fringe and tattered edge." (*BR* 1/8/1863)

When word of this action reached the regiment,

> *our usually quiet camp was thrown into a state of excitement...We are to be deprived of* [the flags] *for the remainder of our four months...As soon as it became known..., a protest was put in by all the officers. All but one were in favor of their remaining with the regiment...But, sirs, the officers and men of the 13th would rather part with almost anything now rather than those colors...But it is the hope of the old members of the regiment... to carry those flags with them, and show the ladies who presented them that they had not reposed their confidence in vain. (*U&A *1/5/1863)*

Despite the protests, the flags remained in Rochester and were returned to the regiment only when they reached Elmira on their way home.

Despite their continuing duties and some discomforts from the weather and inspections, the men of the 13th enjoyed a pleasant final four months in the service with much time out for recreation, including snowball fights. (*U&A* 2/26/1863, 3/3/1863) Some soldiers took advantage of the extra free time to visit other Rochester regiments camped nearby. On January 16, Scorer visited the 33rd New York Cavalry (*U&A* 2/3/1863) and in March he spent a couple of days with the 108th NYVI. (*U&A* 3/17/1863) The 13th also entertained visitors from other units. (*U&A* 2/6/1863, 3/3/1863, 3/25/1863) Those visits sometimes took the form of inter-regiment "base ball" games. On April 1, the 13th beat the 140th, 28–11, in the latter's camp. A return contest in the 13th's camp gave the home team its second win, 23–22. After the first game, "The players all adjourned to the Quartermaster's tent, where original package and commissary and segars were discussed for an hour or more." The 13th provided similar hospitality after their second victory. A third scheduled game was not played because of bad weather. (*U&A* 4/8/1863, 4/9/1863, 4/14/1863)

A big reason for the improvement in the lot of the 13th was the better food, clothing, and shelter in their Falmouth camp: "Never...was this or any other army better fed or clothed than we are at present...Our habitations here are of all sorts and sizes to suit the occupants; they are built up of logs and the roofs are covered with shelter tents; almost all have fireplaces which make them quite comfortable." (*U&A* 3/10/1863) Also, they built ovens for a bakery that "supplies us with fresh bread every day." (*U&A* 3/25/1863)

MUSTERING OUT

Finally, the long-awaited day arrived. The regiment, minus the two companies of later recruits, left Washington by train at about 5 p.m., April 29, and reached Elmira about 5 a.m., May 1. It left Elmira by train at about 3:30 a.m., Saturday, May 2, (*U&A* 5/4/1863) and arrived in Rochester at about 5:30 p.m., May 4, where it "was received with the most enthusiastic demonstrations by the citizens of Rochester and towns about...During the day flags were waving from every staff and many private buildings were decorated." No doubt, the enthusiasm of the celebration was fueled in part by the fact that the 13th was the first Monroe County regiment to return from the war. The *U&A* chronicled the celebration:

> *Tens of thousands, including all sexes and ages, gathered about the Valley Depot, and lined the streets and the buildings facing the same throughout the route designated for the procession to pass.*
>
> *The 54th Regiment, the Union Blues, Col. Barnes' 11th Artillery, Gen. Williams and staff, the Fire Department, two Bands, the Mayor and Common Council, and other organized bodies, were in line at the Depot half an hour before the train arrived.*
>
> *The Union Grays were stationed up the track, and as soon as the train came in sight of the city they fired the salute. The first gun set the multitude in motion, and it was impossible for the Police to keep any considerable space open near the cars for the regiment to form upon for reception. As the train approached the Depot, cheer upon cheer went up, and people rushed at the moving cars to grasp a friendly hand, and many of the soldiers jumped off to embrace fathers, mothers, wives, brothers, sisters. The meeting was a most animating one...*
>
> *After a little unavoidable delay, Lieut. Col. Schœffel formed his regiment and Mayor Bradstreet made an address of welcome...*
>
> *The procession then moved down Exchange street and through the streets laid down in the programme under Col. Amaden, as Marshal, assisted by Capts. Updike and Preston.*

The 13th carried the colors they had sustained upon so many fields, and their appearance at all points was the signal for enthusiastic cheers from the men, while from every roof, balcony and window upon the route the ladies waved their white handkerchiefs in token of welcome and approval. The passage of the regiment was the grandest thing in its way ever seen in Rochester.

On arriving at the Square in front of City Hall, the 13th formed close up to the steps, with the other military as a guard, and outside those was a mass of citizens seen as far as the eye could reach in either direction. The Mayor introduced Rev. Dr. Pease, who made an appropriate prayer…

Judge Chumasero then addressed the Regiment…

Col. Amaden, Marshal of the Day, then thanked those who had responded to the invitation to join the procession and dismissed the companies.

The 13th then went into City Hall and partook of a dinner which had been prepared by the city…The soldiers were hungry, having fasted most of the day, but many of them were so eager to see their friends they did not remain long at the tables. Before separating, however, the boys gave hearty cheers for the citizens of Rochester, the Mayor and Marshal, Committee of Arrangements, General McClellan and Fitz-John Porter. The deafening cheers given for the Generals were evidence conclusive of the attachment of the regiment to the gallant commanders.

The men were dismissed to go to their homes or among their friends…

Since the regiment arrived the soldiers have been the lions of the city, and attract a good deal of attention wherever they go. City Hall is a sort of headquarters to-day, and thousands have called upon the boys there. (5/4/1863)

The speeches by the dignitaries heaped effusive praise on the soldiers, but perhaps their sentiments were best expressed by their brigade commander during the Peninsular campaign, Major General Fitz-John Porter:

I am indeed very glad to know the 13th has reached home to be welcomed as it has been and as it deserved. There has been no regiment from the State whose fortunes have varied as frequently or which has borne more for the sake of our country. There has been none whose comfort and success have excited so much anxiety to those in command, or whose prosperity and glories have been more gratifying. I doubt if any regiment has suffered more from all causes pertaining to the battle field, nor do I believe there is one which can point to a brighter record than its services in its old division

> *and in the 5th army corps. The welcome by its friends is a reward for its sufferings.* (U&A *5/?/1863)*

The regiment received its final pay and was mustered out on May 12, 13, and 14. (Phisterer 1888) According to the *U&A*, "the eight companies which returned brought 316 men, including the sick from hospitals. About 190 were said to be original members of the 13th. In all over 1100 men had been enrolled in the Regiment." (5/4/1863) The official casualty list includes two officers and 61 enlisted men killed, two officers and 20 enlisted men died of wounds, 11 officers and 205 enlisted men recovered from wounds, and two officers and 102 enlisted men missing for a total number of casualties of 405. Also, 44 enlisted men died of disease and other causes. (Phisterer 1888) The *BR* commented that two Brockport members of the regiment had died of wounds and one had died from disease while in the service of the 13th. (5/28/1863) However, Editor Beach apparently had a short memory for on 11/7/1861 he had reported that Private Joseph C. Thompson of the Brockport company in the 13th had died of typhoid fever and on 12/11/1862 he announced the death from "congestion of the bowels" of Private Henry J. Hunt of Clarkson, a member of the same company.

Colonel Elisha G. Marshall, the regimental commander, was detained in Washington on court-martial duty, but when he did return to Rochester on May 29, he was accorded a similar, though more modest, greeting:

> *Col. E.G. Marshall...was met on his arrival by a large throng of citizens and an escort of military. The Union Blues, Capt. Hill, turned out in response to an invitation from the members of the Old Thirteenth as an escort. The officers and men of the Thirteenth, or so many as were in the city, were present, drawn up in line in Railroad Avenue, with Newman's Band.*
>
> *When Colonel Marshall left the train he was warmly greeted by a host of old friends and citizens generally. Gen. Williams, ex-Mayor Clark and Colonel Amaden, conducted him from the cars to the carriage...The appearance of the Colonel before the soldiers of the Old Thirteenth brought from the boys three hearty cheers, given with a will. The band played "Hail to the Chief," and Col. Marshall, with his attendants, entered a carriage drawn by four bays, and followed the Blues, the boys of the Thirteenth, under Capt. Sullivan, marching after the carriage.*
>
> *The colors and battle flags of the 13th—soiled but never dishonored—were carried by members of the regiment, some of whom had borne them on the battle field—in the centre of the column of the Union Blues. The*

> *procession was a very pleasing one and of the triumphal sort. As it moved to City hall the streets were thronged, and the Colonel received all along the way evidences of a hearty welcome.*
>
> *On reaching the square in front of the Court House, the escort formed, the Colonel left the carriage and proceeded to the steps of the building... Here he was received by the Common Council and city officers...Ald. Rowley...addressed Col. Marshall with a long, laudatory speech to which the colonel responded in kind.*
>
> *At the close of his address the men of the 13th gave three cheers for Colonel Marshall, in which the multitude heartily joined...The soldiers and the crowd gave cheers for McClellan and Fitz-John Porter also... The ceremonies of the reception being at an end, Col. Marshall went down into the crowd and shook hands with the boys of the 13th, who appeared delighted to greet him. (*U&A *5/30/1863)*

Surprisingly, given its earlier intense interest in the 13th, the *BR* was silent about the arrival of the Brockporters of the 13th in their hometown. It did publish a short report on the reception in Rochester and added this information with respect to the Brockport contingent:

> *Of the seventy-nine persons who composed company K when it left this village, four refused to take the required oath at Elmira, but three have died—two from wounds, nineteen have deserted, two have resigned, twenty have been discharged, a few have been transferred to other regiments, and the following named twenty returned home on Saturday last, and were received by a large concourse of our citizens and the martial band with great enthusiasm, Hon. Jerome Fuller welcoming them in behalf of the citizens in an eloquent and stirring address, which was heartily applauded.* [The names followed.]
>
> *With two or three exceptions the above named twenty have on all occasions proved themselves valiant soldiers and sterling patriots—ever ready and willing to perform with alacrity their whole duty to their country.—They are entitled to the highest respect of their fellow citizens, and posterity will with gratitude recount their deeds of valor. (5/7/1863)*

The *BR* includes Wallace E. Hughson among the returnees, though the ACWRD calls him a deserter. All of the men listed had enrolled in Company K. Among the Brockport area men who enlisted in companies of the 13th other than K, only Stephen Osborn and Warren Rowland, both of Clarkson, were mustered out with the regiment.

The statistics for the 139 men from the Brockport area who served in the 13th (in all companies) for whom I have documentation are: killed in action (4), wounded (10), wounded twice (2), wounded and captured (1), captured and died in prison (1), other POWs (5), discharged for disabilities (22), discharged for promotions (3), other early discharges (6), deserted (14), refused to take the oath (2), resigned (3), cashiered (1), died of disease (3), died of wounds (1), transferred to another regiment (13), unknown disposition (28), and mustered out with the regiment (18) (not counting those who were wounded or prisoners and survived). So, total battle casualties (killed, wounded, and captured) were 24. Of the 109 men whose fate is known, only 18 survived the war in the regiment unscathed, a shrinkage rate of 84.4 percent.

A Rochester newspaper reported this: "Several members of the Regiment belonged in Brockport, and when they reached the town, they were escorted by music and banners. No heroes ever received a more hearty welcome, and none ever more deserved it." (5/?/1863)

The DMNA account of the mustering out follows:

> *The regiment remained opposite Fredericksburg until the 27th of April, when it left camp and stacked its arms at Stoneman's Station. It reached Washington on the 28th, Elmira, May 1st, and Rochester, May 4th. During its term it had 1,300 men on its rolls, including the new company raised for it in the fall of 1861, and two companies recruited in the fall of 1862. It returned with eighty-two of its original members, 130 who had enlisted for its unexpired term, and 126 of its three years' men. The last named were assigned to duty as provost guard, the former were mustered out at Rochester on the 14th of May, and formed the nucleus of a new regiment—the Fourteenth Artillery, N.Y.S.V.*

Thus ended the career of Brockport's first company, two years of ups and downs, experiences that were probably pretty typical for all those who responded to Lincoln's first call. Through the columns of the *BR* and the letters and oral reports of the soldiers, the entire Brockport area community was closely involved in those experiences. They formed a very substantial part of Brockport's involvement in the Civil War. Probably, the lives of the seven Brockport companies that followed Company K of the Old 13th did not receive the same degree of attention. Nevertheless, they were an integral and important part of Civil War Brockport. Their experiences cannot be examined here in the same detail as the treatment of the 13th. Their day-to-day lives replicated in large part those of the 13th. Therefore, the chapters that follow will deal mostly with the highlights of their experiences.

Chapter 14

Some Special Topics

Leadership

As might be expected, a major preoccupation of the soldiers concerned the quality of their leaders. Their lives depended on it. They got most excited over the fate of General McClellan. He was virtually worshipped by the boys in blue. During the Peninsular campaign, Sphinx wrote that, "there is not a man in the vast army of the peninsula but would willingly lay down his life for McClellan" and Yerrot said that his men, "will go with him to the death." (*BR* 5/1/1862, 6/19/1862) When he was removed, they were in despair.

McClellan's popularity was based largely on the perception of the troops that he was devoted to their welfare. For instance, Sphinx wrote that "We...believe that he will take care of the private, not only on the field of battle but in camp and will see that many wants hitherto neglected, are supplied." (*BR* 8/8/1861) However, too often that led to excessive caution in his exercise of command. He consistently grossly over-estimated the strength of the enemy and refused to act unless he felt certain of success. Several times, at crucial moments, he failed to follow through a success to clinch a victory. Lincoln finally lost patience and removed him from the command of the Army of the Potomac.

Scorer reported the reaction of his comrades when they received the news of McClellan's removal:

> *Tuesday all day, except while drilling, was occupied discussing the removal of McClellan. Opinions are formed and expressed not very flattering to the*

> *Union cause. Some went so far as to hope that we would be driven back to Washington in the next fight; some that the Government would have to recognize the Southern Confederacy, &c....*
>
> *Hundreds of officers have or will offer their resignations on account of these recent removals.*
>
> *Monday...we bid adieu to our loved Gen. Geo. B. McClellan. He passed through the lines with uncovered head, amid the roar of cannon and the deafening hurrahs of the troops. Old troops shed tears and new ones wanted to; it was the saddest scene I have witnessed since we bid adieu to our friends at Rochester. (*U&A *11/20/1862)*

On the other hand, if McClellan "were to return to the Army of Potomac as commander" his reception "would make secession tremble in his boots and be sure victory for our army." (*U&A* 2/9/1863) "McCLELLAN and VICTORY would be the cry of this badly demoralized army...Strict discipline is all that prevents this army from becoming a perfect mob, and that discipline was brought about by General McClellan." McClellan was so popular that the soldiers "will buy anything which is written by their former able leader." (*U&A* 2/26/1863)

Scorer alleged that, "In less than a week after Burnside took command, we saw a difference in rations, etc. We were never short before." At a review for McClellan's replacement, "When Gen. Burnside rode by we simply presented arms. Had it been Gen. McClellan there would have been loud cheering, but not one greeted Burnside." (*U&A* 1/30/1863) "Ask a soldier of the army of the Potomac his opinion of General McClelland, and his reply will be 'He is my man!' Ask their opinion of McDowell and Pope—all express the same one, and that is that McDowell is a traitor and Pope is incapable of commanding a large force." (*U&A* 10/13/1862)

Similar protests greeted the court-martial of General Fitz-John Porter, which "has justly caused great indignation in the Fifth (formerly Porter's) Army Corps. On the same kind of evidence every General in the army might be dismissed from the service." He "was, like Gen. McClellan, too popular with the army." (*U&A* 2/6/1863)

In a complaint about the incompetence of a high-ranking officer, one of the *BR*'s correspondents reported that an unnamed, politically appointed general had allowed a rebel force to escape a trap that McClellan had set because, "The gorge which he should have guarded was left open and they [the rebels] slipped through it and were 'o-p-h' before Gen. —— comprehended what was going on."

Of course, the quality of the leadership of the regimental commander received much attention from his men. Colonel Quinby seems to have had the esteem of his troops. The correspondent for the *RDD* said that he "is on hand early and late, quiet, but efficient, and has already proven to all who have watched him, that he was born to command" (5/18/1861) Sphinx wrote after 1st Bull Run, "We have the utmost confidence in our Colonel, he exhibited great coolness and courage" and "there was no more brave or efficient officer than he on the field." (*BR* 7/25/1861, 8/8/1861) Also, Quinby's officers presented him with a set of silver service and his wife with a large silver goblet at a ceremony in Rochester six months after his resignation, "as testimony of their love and respect for you as a man, and their admiration for you as a soldier." (*U&A* 2/24/1862) His successor received less respect. The *U&A* called Colonel John Pickell, "a superannuated old fogy" (3/13/1862) and the *BR* reported that "One or two private letters received during the past week from the thirteenth regiment" said that, "there is a great amount of growling about the incapacity of the Colonel [Pickell]." (11/28/1861)

On the other hand, Colonel Marshall, the regimental commander from April 20, 1862, until the unit was disbanded, was very popular with his men, At the time of the controversy described above (pages 136–40), one of his men wrote that "Col. M. is as popular with the officers and men at present under his command, as any Colonel in the army. There is no Colonel that looks after the interest of his men more than Col. M." (*U&A* 7/8/1862) "Beloved by all" (except, of course, the *REE*, see pages 136–37), said the *U&A*. (5/23/1863) After the second Battle of Bull Run, a newspaper editor who visited the camp of the 13th wrote that, "No officer in the army takes better care of his men, by whom he is devotedly loved and none are more highly esteemed by their superiors," (*U&A* 9/12/1862) Scorer called him "gallant," (*U&A* 9/11/1862) and the regimental assistant surgeon said that he "led them bravely to the fight" and called him a "bully fellow." (*U&A* 9/6/1862)

The soldiers, also, of course, expressed opinions about the lower regimental officers. When a list of promotions was announced, Scorer had this to report: "Considerable dissatisfaction was felt at some appointments, and the disappointed aspirants to office vented their spite by sending in their names to the Adjutant as wishing to join the Regular service, (cavalry service seemed to be the favorite)." (*U&A* 11/13/1862)

On the other hand, one soldier wrote of Eugene P. Fuller, "I do not want a braver or better captain." (*BR* 1/6/1862)

AFRICAN AMERICANS

If Scorer is to be believed, the soldiers displayed harsh prejudice toward the African Americans they encountered. They expressed strong dislike for the institution of slavery, but had little sympathy for its victims. They were critical of Lincoln's Emancipation Proclamation, believing it would prolong the war. Here are a couple of examples from his dispatches:

> *"Niggers" (gentlemen of color they are called in Massachusetts) or "Massachusetts men" as we call them are getting quite scarce in our brigade; in fact, they are not as plenty anywhere in the army as they were before that famous proclamation was issued. They have gradually disappeared. The new regiments and the Massachusetts officers are the last to part with them, but they get so saucy to the men, (and some of the officers uphold the niggers,) that it is dangerous for them to show themselves around some camps after dark. In fact, Negro stock is far below par, and still falling.*
>
> *We have only two in our regiment and they are comparatively civil, know their places and keep them too. They are cooks or servants for officers. It will not be a safe place anywhere North for negroes, after the army returns.* (U&A *2/11/1863)*

> *We wonder if the Government will expect a white soldier to salute a Negro officer when the Negro regiments come into the service? If so, we think they will be disappointed in their expectations.* (U&A *3/10/1863)*

Yerrot visited a plantation that had been abandoned by its owners and wrote an account of the behavior of the released slaves that reflects the patronizing attitude of the northern soldiers:

> *About fifty slaves of all ages were frolicking on the grass plot or holding high wassails in the parlor and drawing rooms... The darkies are living in clover now on the production of last year, and will continue to do so until winter, for there will be an abundance of fruits—but they have not plowed a furrow or raised a hoe—and they will be like sheep without a fold when the cold winds of winter come on. Many of them reflect the sentiments of their owner... Poor creatures! from having looked upon their master all their lives as the highest authority known to their simple minds, is it any wonder that they should believe him now, in their ignorance of his true condition?* (BR *6/12/1862)*

SUTLERS

Personal items for Civil War soldiers were provided by "sutlers," peddlers who were assigned to regiments and whose prices were supposed to be overseen by officers of the regiments. In practice, that supervision was often lax and they were widely regarded by the soldiers as profiteers and cheats, exploiting their captive customers. Also, some soldiers engaged in that commerce and were similarly disliked, as were profiteers among the local residents. This explains the incidents described by Scorer in four of his letters:

> *Just before evening parade a sutler with a load of bread, which he was selling out at 25 cents per loaf, passed camp, and just arrived at the corner of the road, when over went his wagon, (with a little help of course,) and the bread disappeared quicker than he ever sold a load before. Men could be seen walking off in every direction three, four, and even ten loaves under their arms. This is the way sutlers who overcharge, are induced to lower their prices. (*U&A *10/11/1862)*

> *Gen. McClellan issued an order some three months or more ago that no soldier should act as peddler in any camps in the U. S. army, but the order is frequently broken, even by men in uniform pedling segars, letter paper and the like.—One of these persons made his appearance in camp, selling segars. A crowd of the boys gathered around, each taking a segar. He asked who pays? "Go to the Colonel," said the boys. He did not go, but suffered the penalty for pedling. He had his stock confiscated. (*U&A *10/27/1862)*

> *The sutler of the 91st Pennsylvania moved his shop further away from our camp, perhaps the reason was that his neighbors borrowed his wagon without his consent. (*U&A *11/1/1862)*

> *We saw a bread peddler closed up the other day in just the style this war should be. He began selling his bread for 10 cents per loaf, found ready sales, raised it to 15 cents, when some hundreds of hungry soldiers closed upon him and before he could say Jack Robinson, some 1,800 loaves were distributed free gratis. (*U&A *11/20/1862)*

MAIL SERVICE

Another common complaint of the soldiers is expressed by Scorer in these excerpts from three of his letters:

> *We do not get our mail regularly, consequently do not get the Union regularly.* (U&A *10/13/1862)*
>
> *The Express packages sent to the regiment while at Harrison's Landing have at last arrived* [almost nine weeks later], *half the contents all spoiled and all the original packages taken out. Dr. Little received several boxes, not more than half the contents of any use.* (U&A *10/20/1862)*
>
> *The mails come—like angels visits—few and far between.* (U&A *10/27/1862)*

AFTERLIFE OF THE 13TH

The 13th did have an afterlife of sorts. Colonel Marshal was authorized on May 29, 1863, to reorganize the 13th as the 14th New York Heavy Artillery Regiment. He sought to recruit members of the 13th for his new unit. My research discovered six Brockporters from the 13th and five other Brockporters who served in the 14th NYHA. The Davis report says that 15 Town of Sweden men served in the 14th, but I have been unable to identify them. Phisterer says that the 14th "contained many men who had served in two years' organizations," but they were recruited very widely over New York State. Phisterer lists 100 communities where "companies were recruited principally." Brockport, Clarkson, and Hamlin are not among them. (1476–77) Although the *BR* predicted that "the old Thirteenth may be speedily filled up," (5/28/1863) the first companies were not mustered in until August 29, 1862, and the last on January 17, 1864. (1476)

The 14th did not see action until the Battle of the Wilderness, May 5–7, 1864, but then fought in 15 engagements between then and April 2, 1865, in all of which it suffered casualties. In fact, it suffered 1,073 casualties in all, including six officers and 209 enlisted men who were killed in action or died of wounds with a roster of 3,914—a much higher casualty rate than was suffered by the 13th. (Phisterer 1477) At least two Brockporters were among the casualties. Robert J. Gordon of Brockport was wounded at Petersburg and Joseph Parker of Hamlin was captured in the last few days of the war.

At least 87 Brockporters from the 13th did serve in other regiments later in the war and two had seen service in other regiments before joining the 13th. This is more than half of the 139 Brockporters I have identified in the 13th. This seems to be an extraordinary phenomenon, that so many men who had suffered through two years of hardship and mortal danger would voluntarily go back into service. Some of them may have aspired to officer status. The ones who succeeded are mentioned in the "Officers" section of this chapter.

Thirty-two men served in ten NY Cavalry regiments, including the 13 members of Company G. They were: two men in the 14th, five in the 22nd, three in the 8th, 17 in the 3rd, and one each in the 21st, 24th, 10th, 4th Provisional, and 1st and 2nd Veteran Regiments. Twenty-six served in ten other NYVI regiments. They included two men in the 25th, four in the 105th, eight in the 108th, six in the 140th, and one each in the 33rd, 49th, 81st, 151st, 160th, and 5th Veteran Regiments. Twenty-six men served in ten artillery regiments, including 13 men in the 14th Heavy Artillery, four in the 8th HA, one each in the 4th and 7th HA, and the 3rd, 4th, 18th, 22nd, 24th, and 25th Light Artillery Regiments. Finally, two men served in the 1st Mounted Rifles and one each in the 7th Veteran Reserve Corps and the 50th Engineers Regiments.

Part III

SEVEN BROCKPORT COMPANIES AT WAR

Company K of the 13th NYVI was only the first Union Army company to be recruited in Brockport. Seven others followed. (Actually, several other companies recruited in Brockport, but the Brockport area was not their recruitment base. So few Brockporters enlisted in them that they are not included in Part III, but are the subject of Part IV.) The purpose of Part II was to give an in-depth view of life in a Brockport company. This Part provides a less exhaustive overview of the war effort by the other seven companies. Their action will be described, unit-by-unit, in the chronological order of their recruitment. The order will be Company H of the 8th NY Cavalry, Company F of the 105th NYVI (that merged with Company F of the 94th NYVI), Company H of the 108th NYVI, Company M of the 3rd NY Cavalry, Company A of the 140th NYVI, Company C of the 22nd NY Cavalry, and Company B of the 24th Light Artillery. Standard sources will be used to describe the actions of the regiments in which the Brockport companies served. Excerpts from the published letters of their Brockport members will be incorporated in the text where appropriate.

Chapter 15

Company H, 8th NY Cavalry

Recruitment

Four months after Company K of the 13th NYVI was organized, recruiting drives were undertaken for two companies for the 8th NYV Cavalry that was being formed by Colonel Samuel J. Crooks, a 34-year-old Rochester lawyer. Phisterer says that Company H was "recruited principally" at Rochester, Brockport, Bergen, Clarkson, Fairport, and Hamlin. It seems likely that the Bergen, Clarkson, and Hamlin recruitment was part of the effort based in Brockport. Also, at least three of the original members of Company H give Spencerport as their recruitment site and one gives Webster. Company K was recruited principally in nine communities, including Brockport, but not Clarkson or Hamlin. The two companies were later merged. Therefore, they count as only one Brockport company.

Two Barry brothers, George H., age 34, and Frederick H., age 28, undertook to organize Company H. In the 1864 Brockport directory, Frederick is listed as a speculator and in the 1870 census as a "produce merchant." Frederick's wife, Fannie, was the same age as he and gave her occupation as "housekeeper." Also, in their household were a 16-year-old servant girl and a 28-year-old seamstress. In 1870, his wife was Mary F., housekeeper, seven years younger than he, and they had a five-year-old daughter. George's occupation in the 1860 census was "produce merchant." His 33-year-old wife, Mary, was a housekeeper and they had two small children. He does not appear in the 1870 census or the 1869 Brockport directory.

The *BR* reported on September 26, 1861, that "Messrs. George H. and Frederick H. Barry…have opened a recruiting office at Harrison's corner, desiring to raise a cavalry company." On October 10, 1861, it relayed George H. Barry's claim that "This morning…he has in different places about fifty recruits." In fact, the NY Adjutant General's records show only 18 Brockport area soldiers enlisted in Company H by that date. The *BR* reported on October 24, 1861, that his company "numbering thirty-two men was accepted and sworn into service yesterday." By November 28, Company H had seven more Brockporters. Of course, that was far short of the required number for a company. However, 24 other men had been recruited elsewhere for Company H—ten in Rochester, seven in Batavia, and seven elsewhere in the state. They were also joined by forty men who had been recruited for a Chenango County company. Even with the addition of the Chenango County men, Company H was not large enough. (The Davis Report says that 50 Town of Sweden residents served in Company H.)

George Guenther and Charles Warren were the Brockport recruiters for Company K. Guenther is listed in the 1860 census as a 31-year-old resident of Brockport with an occupation dealing with marble (the second word in his occupation listing is illegible). His birthplace is illegible on the census page, but Heritage Quest gives it as "HCAS." The *BR* says he was a native of England, though his name is German. His wife was Mary, a 28-year-old housekeeper born in Canada, and they had two children. He does not appear in the 1870 census or in the Brockport directories for 1864 or 1869. Warren appears in the 1869 village directory as a "drayman prop. sale stable Clinton St." In the 1870 census he is listed as a 37-year-old truckman with a 29-year-old wife, Catherine, and two children. (For other details of this recruitment effort, see pages 44–46.)

Neither of the two companies had reached full strength by the time they were accepted into service, even with the addition of the Chenango men. Therefore, once they reached Washington in December, the Company K men were transferred to Company H, which now had a full complement of 102 members. As a result neither Guenther nor Warren were commissioned. Guenther enlisted as a private in Company K, but, according to the ACWRD, was not transferred to Company H and was discharged on January 19, 1862. Later, he enlisted in Company L of the 2nd New York Veteran Cavalry on August 8, 1863, and was mustered out on November 8, 1865. Sweden cemetery records list Warren as a second lieutenant, but the ACWRD says that he was mustered into the 8th as a private, but not assigned to a company and deserted on January 11, 1862.

Although Frederick H. Barry lost the first lieutenant's commission that he had expected, on August 18, 1862, he was commissioned a captain and undertook a recruitment effort to muster a replacement company for the 8th. The *BR* (8/21/1862) carried a recruitment advertisement for "Capt. F.H. Barry's 8th New York Cavalry" on August 21, 1862. Prospective recruits were instructed to report to "No. 1 Main Street Bridge, Rochester." A week later, the *BR* said that Barry "who holds forth at the tent recently occupied by Capt. Pond, recruiting for the 8th N.Y. Cavalry reports this morning between forty and fifty men. A few of them were obtained here." On October 24, it announced that 32 men were signed up for Barry's company and the regiment was "accepted and sworn into service."

I can identify only four Brockporters who responded to Barry's call, all of them enlisting in Rochester. However, because Brockporters were required to enlist in Rochester, I may not have been able to identify all of them. Those that I know of are:

- Benjamin F. Chappell, who was wounded at Five Forks, Virginia, on April 1, 1865, after having been promoted to second lieutenant on February 11, 1865.
- Monroe M. Copps, who deserted, was arrested, court-martialed, and sentenced to three years imprisonment. Earlier, he had signed up for the 13th NYVI, but failed to take the oath.
- Sylvester Edwards, who was discharged for disability on May 13, 1865.
- John Grunwell, who was discharged for disability on January 16, 1864.

According to Phisterer (879, 881), Barry served as captain only "in August 1862" and "no service recorded; not commissioned." Once the Brockporters in Companies H and K were mustered there came the problem of keeping them in the service. Desertions were rife. Eleven Brockporters deserted by the time the regiment saw action in May 1862. Also, by the end of 1861, one had died and another was discharged for disability.

OFFICERS

The merger of the three groups raised the question of who were to be Company H's officers among the three putative captains and the three aspiring first lieutenants. Elections were held and George Barry emerged as captain, Alfred S. Kinney, the leader of the Chenango group, became first lieutenant, and Daniel Sackett of Chenango was second lieutenant. Frederick Barry became first lieutenant, but was busted back to quartermaster sergeant on November 28, 1861.

George H. Barry commanded the company until October 12, 1863, when he was wounded near Culpeper, Va., and was discharged for disability from wounds, February 9, 1864. Neither Barry is listed in the Town Clerk's Certificates of either Sweden or Clarkson. In addition to the Barrys, a surprising number of Brockporters became officers in or through the 8th Cavalry. I count at least five others.

James B. Vanderhoef of Brockport became a non-commissioned officer in Company H and an officer in the regiment. He was a 38-year-old carpenter who enlisted as a private on October 14, 1861. He was promoted to quartermaster sergeant in February 1862, and commissioned first lieutenant of Company F on December 6, 1862. He was "discharged, May 25, 1863, for disability by reason of being wounded in the right hand." (Phisterer, STCR) After the war, he returned to his trade as a carpenter and builder and lived at 26 Mechanic Street (now Park Avenue), just down the street from George Barry at 9. (1864 and 1869 directories)

Benjamin F. Chappell, age 25, enlisted at Rochester as a private on August 30, 1862, as part of Frederick Barry's effort to recruit a replacement company M. He became Commissary Sergeant on October 14, 1862, and was commissioned a second lieutenant on February 11, 1865, but did not serve in that grade. He was wounded at the Battle of Five Forks on April 1, 1865, and died April 21. (Phisterer) The 1860 census lists him as a 22-year-old merchant living in the home of his parents, Guy, farmer, and Clarissa, housekeeper, Chappell in Brockport. His father was a leading Brockport citizen and real estate developer for whom Chappell Street is named.

Charles G. Hampton, age 19, enrolled as a private in Company H, September 28, 1861. He received three promotions in two years—corporal February 14, 1862, sergeant August 11, 1863, and second lieutenant in Company D of the 15th NY Cavalry October 5, 1863. He was captured at Winchester May 25, 1862, imprisoned for about four months, and returned to the regiment. (Norton 149) He was wounded and captured again in action near Upperville, Virginia, February 20, 1864, paroled March 1, 1865, and returned to active service as a captain in Company G of the 15th NY Cavalry on April 11, 1865, two days after Lee's surrender. (Phisterer 1005) In the 1860 census, Hampton was an 18-year-old laborer in the household of Israel Starks, father of Major Milo Starks of the 140th NYVI. After the war, Hampton married Milo's sister Emma, and they settled in Michigan.

Second Lieutenant Benjamin Chedell Efner, thirty-four, former Brockport resident, served in the 8th New York Cavalry and died of wounds suffered at Beverly Ford, Virginia. *Photo courtesy of New York State Military Museum © Historical Data Systems, Inc.*

Dwight Hamilton, age 21, of Spencerport, enlisted as a private in Company H, was promoted to corporal, December 31, 1861, sergeant May 1, 1862, second lieutenant of Company A on August 14, 1863, and to captain on October 31, 1864. After the war, he was promoted to major by brevet, September 88, 1866, "for gallant and meritorious services in the war." (Phisterer 336)

The most distinguished officer in Company H may have been Morton A. Read, Brockport's only Congressional Medal of Honor recipient, awarded for his capture of the regimental flag of the 1st Texas infantry at the Battle of Appomattox Station, April 8, 1865. He had enlisted in Company H as a private at age 18 on October 14, 1861, became corporal June 16, 1863, sergeant August 1, 1863, and first sergeant April 9, 1864. On November 1, 1864, he transferred to Company D, where he was commissioned a first lieutenant February 6, 1865, then transferred to Company L on February 25, 1865.

A former Brockport resident, Benjamin Chedell Efner, was an officer in the regiment, as second lieutenant in Company M from October 14, 1862, until April 17, 1863, and in Company I until he died of his wounds after being shot in the slaughter at Beverly Ford, Va., on June 9, 1863. He was promoted to captain posthumously. His mother lived in Brockport during the war (*U&A* 6/11/1863) and he was buried in Brockport's High Street cemetery.

Besides Warren, another example of retrospective promotion is the case of Hiel Brockway III, grandson of the co-founder of Brockport. The AJ's report says that he enlisted September 23, was mustered on October 14, and deserted the same day. The Sweden cemetery record says that he was a second lieutenant in September 1861, and Charles Bush's genealogy of the Brockway family agrees.

WAR SERVICE

Bibliographical note: The narrative in this account is based mainly on five sources. Henry Norton was a member of Company H and wrote a 207-page regimental history in 1889, *Deeds of Daring, or History of the Eighth N.Y. Volunteer Cavalry*, Chenango Telegraph Printing House, Norwich, N.Y. Robert Marcotte, *Where They Fell*, Q Publishing, 2001, includes the 8th among the Monroe County regiments whose histories he recounts. The third and fourth are, of course, Phisterer and the ACWRD. The fifth is Colonel William L. Markell, Historical Sketch of the 8th Cavalry on the NYS Military Museum website. Markell was one of the regiment's commanders.

SLOW START

Although the 8th Cavalry became a crack fighting unit, one of the best in the Union Army, it got off to a rocky start. For one thing, it lost its first commanding officer in less than three months. Colonel Samuel J. Crooks was an effective recruiter by virtue of his talent as an orator, but apparently was not a competent leader of a military unit. He took command on November 28, 1861, and resigned February 21, 1862. The regiment's incompetent surgeon went with him. (Marcotte 85, Phisterer 885) Lieutenant Colonel Charles R. Babbitt was acting commander until Colonel Benjamin F. Davis, a Regular Army West Pointer, was appointed on July 11, 1862.

Another set of problems that plagued the 8th was similar to the start-up difficulties encountered by the 13th NYVI, as recounted in Chapter 2: poor living conditions and inadequate arms and supplies. The former prevailed at the first stop for the Brockporters, Camp Hillhouse on the fairgrounds on the outskirts of Rochester. One of their Chenango County comrades described life for the new soldiers:

> *They had barracks built for the men...The nights were quite cool at that time of the year. There were coal stoves in the barracks, and bunks, built three tiers high. We had blankets dealt out to us, and had to get along the best we could until morning...There was not much sleep for the boys that night; some of them stayed close to the stove. I think some of them did not lie down that night...In the morning, the first thing was to get ready for breakfast. They had men detailed to cook. They would put two or three*

> *bushels of potatoes into a big kettle and cook them with skins on. They had a table made by driving posts into the ground and nailing boards on to them about three feet high. Every man had to stand up to eat. They had tin plates, tin cups, knives and forks. Each one got so much—two or three potatoes, a piece of meat, a chunk of bread and a cup of coffee, enough for a good meal* [but no milk in your coffee and no butter]...*My appetite was poor...I saw that all of the boys did not eat much, but never said anything...There was not much going on from that time until we went to Washington. There was a camp guard around the camp to keep the boys in, and we used to have quite a time running the guard and going down town. Some of the boys had a leave of absence for a few days to go home again. (Norton 13–15)*

The Brockport soldiers underwent those conditions from their arrival on October 24 until the regiment shipped out to Washington, D.C., on November 28, 1861. (Markell, *BR* 11/28/1861) They formed part of the defense of the capital until March 9, 1862, when they were assigned guard duty along the railroad from Harpers Ferry to Winchester, Virginia.

Winchester

The problem of inadequate arms and supplies afflicted them in their baptism of fire. On May 24, Company H was one of four (*RDA* 6/17/1862) companies detached to reinforce General Nathaniel Banks's army as it retreated during the Shenandoah Valley campaign. They were attacked in the streets of Winchester by a much larger Confederate force. They had not yet received their mounts, were armed with obsolete muskets, and were ignored and abandoned by Banks. They escaped from the town hastily. A member of Company H reported to a Rochester newspaper: "We held the post of honor. We covered the retreat of the whole division, and the enemy were all firing on us. Our company was the last to leave the village...We kept our ranks closed until the rest of them were about a quarter of a mile ahead, when we ran. (*U&A* 5/31/1862) Brockporter John McFarland of Company H was killed and Brockporters Randall J. Beadle, Nathan Bowen, and Charles Hampton were among the six members of Company H who were captured.

RENEWED

The 8th was then posted to picket duty at Maryland Heights until June 23, when it was sent to Relay House, Md. There, it finally received its mounts, new equipment and uniforms, and Davis replaced the long departed and unlamented Samuel Crooks. By August 29, when the regiment departed for Harpers Ferry for scouting duty, he had whipped his troops into shape with rigorous discipline and training.

The troops were delighted with their new status, but they may not have realized what life as a cavalryman really entailed. Much later, one member of Company H described it:

> *I will tell you what a cavalryman has to do when in camp. The first thing after he gets up is to attend to his horse. He feeds his horse grain, consisting of oats and corn mixed together, which is drawn from the government…While he is eating we have to groom him one hour. Not fifty-nine minutes, but sixty full minutes, and keep busy all the time. There is an officer watching you all this time, and if you stop he yells out: "Keep to work there!" After that the boys get their breakfast, having to cook it themselves. Then comes watering horses. Sometimes a man has to go quite a ways. Guard mounting for camp guard follows. Then your equipments have to be kept clean. A cavalryman has more equipments than any other branch of the service; a saber, carbine and revolver. The cavalry is the hardest branch there is in the service. When it comes night we have our horses to water and feed again. In fact, a cavalryman is kept busy all day long…When a soldier is on duty some one is detailed to take care of his horse, so that most every man has two horses to take care of. This is when soldiers are in camp. When we are at the front, or on the march, or fighting the rebels, it is different. There is not so much red tape then. (Norton 106–08)*

HARPERS FERRY

On September 14–15, 1862, the 8th was part of one of the most extraordinary cavalry operations. They were stationed at Harpers Ferry, Virginia, which was completely surrounded by Stonewall Jackson's troops. Colonel Davis decided, against the wishes of the brigade commander, to escape from the trap. Under cover of darkness, he led a double file of some 1,600 troops out of the besieged town, across a pontoon bridge, and through the lines of Longstreet's Confederate corps, virtually undetected. Besides the 8th Cavalry, there were five other units. (Marcotte 86) Taking back roads and crossing fields, they eluded the enemy. On the way, they overtook and captured a Confederate ammunition train of some 75 wagons, 300 horses and mules, and "five or six hundred cavalry and a few infantry," including a brigadier general. (Norton 32)

Company H was near the rear of the file, some ten miles behind the leaders. As they were passing one of the captive rebel wagons, a teamster asked a member of the company the identity of his unit. "The Eighth New York." "The hell you say?" was the startled response.

No less surprised was Stonewall Jackson when he learned that his prey had escaped. Historian James Murfin has called the exploit, "one of the most spectacular cavalry deeds of the war." (Marcotte 87). Moreover, the capture of that amount of Confederate ammunition may have contributed to the decision to order McClellan to attack Lee at Antietam and to the Union victory in that bloody battle. However, the 8th did not participate in that engagement but was kept in reserve. After the battle, as Lee retreated, the 8th was sent after him to pick up and imprison rebel stragglers, of whom there were a great number.

CONTINUOUS COMBAT

After a quiet period from September 20 until October 26, 1862, came a month of almost continuous combat in which the 8th performed aggressively and "gallantly" according to General McClellan. On occasion, Davis singled out Company H for especially risky skirmishing. In one such instance, at Unionville, Virginia, Brockporter Nicholas Wiler lost his horse to an enemy sniper. (Norton 41–42) In the Battle of Barbee's Cross Roads, the 8th was outnumbered five to one, but beat back the rebels, taking fifty prisoners and killing and wounding a large number of the enemy. Company H was one of four companies that charged a full regiment. "The enemy turned and fled to their reserve." (*U&A* 11/29/1862) During December 1862, the 8th was assigned picket and guard duties and spent the Battle of Fredericksburg in reserve.

During the first five months of 1863, the 8th was engaged in 14 battles, losing 45 men, killed, wounded, or missing. No Brockporters were among those casualties, though Thomas Dwyer of Bergen was discharged for disability on March 31, 1863. (ACWRD) The regiment sat on the sidelines again during the Battle of Chancellorsville (April 27–May 4, 1863). General Davis, who had been promoted to a brigade command, was killed on June 9 in the great cavalry battle at Beverly's Ford in which the 8th won "much glory." A non-Brockport member of Company H was killed and two other non-Brockporters in the company were wounded. (Norton 65–67) William L. Markell was promoted from lieutenant colonel to replace Davis. (Markell) The regiment was in almost continuous combat from then until the Battle of Gettysburg in early July.

The 8th was part of a much larger force that played an important role at Gettysburg. One member of Company H made this claim:

> *The first division of cavalry* [composed of thirteen regiments including the 8th] *and the first corps of infantry were the troops that saved the battle of Gettysburg. The cavalry kept the rebels in check for two hours, so the first corps could get into position. The first corps kept the rebels in check for four hours. By that time reinforcements came. At 2 o'clock, the Union troops fell back to Cemetery Hill. If the rebels had got in possession of Cemetery Hill, Round Top, and Little Round Top the first day, history would be different than it is now. (Norton 68)*

After Gettysburg, the 8th pursued Lee's retreating army until late November, harassing and punishing it at every opportunity. During 26 different "frequent and severe" skirmishes and cavalry fights, it suffered some 150 casualties. (Markell) Among the troops recruited in Brockport, they included Edward A. Miner of Brockport, wounded July 9 at Boonesboro, Md.; Captain George Barry of Brockport and Daniel Kehoe of Adams Basin, wounded October 11 at Stevensburg; Nicholas Wiler of Hamlin, wounded and lost an arm September 19 at Raccoon Ford; and William Leonard Conklin of Hamlin, captured August 1 at Brandy Station.

Campany H was frequently in the thick of things during that autumn 1863 campaign. Besides many regimental engagements, it was sometimes engaged on its own. For instance, on July 14 at Falling Waters, Va., it was deployed on its own "as skirmishers and…captured one gun [and] took a large number of prisoners." On September 19, Companies H and G took four prisoners on a scouting foray. (Norton 71, 73–74)

On November 27, the 8th was brigaded and assigned picketing and scouting duties, participating in only two major engagements until April

1864. During that time, on February 27, Markell resigned and the 8th got its fourth commander, Lieutenant Colonel William H. Benjamin. Cavalry was not much used in the Battle of the Wilderness, May 5–20, 1864, so the 8th engaged in raids at the rear of Lee's army, and "distinguished itself by many gallant acts." (Markell). It was in combat virtually every day. Pitched battles at White Oak Bridge and Riddle's Shop, Va., on June 12 cost the regiment three killed and 15 wounded. Among the wounded was Sgt. Morton A. Read of Brockport.

June 22–30, 1864, the 8th was part of Wilson's raid, which destroyed a railroad that was a vital part of Lee's supply line, but with heavy casualties. In the five major engagements, the 8th lost nine men and officers killed or died of wounds. Six others were wounded, and 102 missing and presumed captured. Among Company H's casualties were: George Camp of Bergen, wounded and taken prisoner; and James Bennett and Darwin Pierce, both of Brockport, captured. (Norton 83) Pierce died in Andersonville.

From August through October, 1864, the 8th was "prominent in all the gallant engagements under Sheridan" and "won special mention from both the division and corps commanders." (Markell) On October 9 at Mt. Olive, Virginia, the 8th, with its partner regiment, the 22nd NY Cavalry (which also had a Brockport company), and a Pennsylvania regiment routed the enemy in a fierce fight, taking 350 prisoners, 11 artillery pieces, and much other equipment. Brevet Major General George A. Custer crowed, "Never since the opening of this war had there been witnessed such a complete and decisive overthrow of the enemy's cavalry." (Marcotte 247)

Reorganization

Then, between November 1, 1864 and April 30, 1865, the regiment underwent complete reorganization. On October 29, the three-year enlistments expired and some soldiers went home. For those who remained, the regiment was reorganized on November 1. Fourteen Brockporters were transferred from Company H to Company D, one from Company K to Company H, and three from other companies into Company G. Then, on February 14, 1865, Benjamin resigned and the regiment received its fifth commander, Colonel Edmund M. Pope, who remained with them until the end of the war. Finally, on April 30, new recruits were formed into four new companies.

The End

The 8th was almost continuously engaged during November and December of 1864 in the Shenandoah Valley campaign, searching for rebel troops, chasing them, or fighting them. January and most of February was spent in camp. On February 27, they resumed their pursuit and, on March 2nd, performed what one member of Company H called "its greatest feat." It "charged over the enemy's breastworks, mounted" at Waynesboro, Va., "captured eight hundred prisoners, which was nearly twice their number, five pieces of artillery," much other equipment and "many hundred horses and mules…something that was never done by the same number of men during the rebellion." John Kehoe of Adams Basin was wounded in that battle. He had been wounded earlier, November 12, 1864, at Middle Road, Va. On December 13, he had rejoined the company, together with Brockporters Randall Beadle and Nathan Bowen, who had been released from a Confederate prison. (Norton 100, 109)

On April 1, as the war was drawing to a close, the 8th caught up with the rebels again at Five Forks, Va., and, after being repulsed twice, routed the enemy, with a loss of seven killed or died of their wounds. Among those killed was Brockporter Nathan Bowen, the regimental color-bearer, who had been captured at Winchester and later released. (Norton 113)

Three dramatic events brought the career of the 8th NY Cavalry with its Brockport company to a close. First, Confederate General Lee's flag of truce was delivered to it on April 9. Second, in the victory parade down Pennsylvania Avenue in Washington on May 23, it "was awarded the post of honor at the great review, they being the advance regiment in that great march." Third, General George A. Custer, their division commander saluted them with this accolade: "Men of the Eighth New York, you are the best soldiers I ever saw." (Norton 119)

Phisterer lists 135 engagements in which the 8th participated. They suffered casualties in 67 of them. In addition, he lists 57 casualties on picket or other minor affairs. His totals are 13 officers and 93 enlisted men killed or died of wounds, 12 other officers and 273 other enlisted men wounded, and 11 officers and 393 men missing for a total of 794 casualties from a roster of 2,183. Also, six officers and 213 enlisted men died of other causes, including three officers and 70 enlisted men who died in captivity. My roster lists 58 Brockporters, excluding those who left the company before it saw armed action. Twenty-one of the 58 were casualties. They included one killed, three dead of wounds and two dead in prison, eight others wounded, and seven captured, two after having been wounded. Also, 15 were discharged for disabilities, died of disease, or were transferred to the Veterans Reserve Corps.

After its slow start, the 8th, including Company H, compiled an enviable record. From May 24, 1862, until Appomattox Court House, nearly 35 months later, it was in action almost continuously. The only significant breaks were the summer of 1862 and the winters of 1863–64 and 1864–65—a total of seven months. At Harpers Ferry and Waynesboro, they pulled off some of the most spectacular cavalry feats of the war and they were repeatedly cited for gallantry. One historian includes it among the "300 hardest fighting regiments of the Union army." (Marcotte 88) Perhaps the most sincere compliment came from Confederate General Jubal Early after the 8th and its companion regiments routed his troops at Cedar Creek: "I found it impossible to rally the troops. They would not listen to entreaties, threats, or appeals of any kind. A terror of the enemy's cavalry had seized them, and there was no holding them." (Marcotte 149)

Chapter 16

Company F, 105th NYVI

Recruitment

Recruitment of Company F of the 105th New York Volunteer Infantry was pursued in Brockport almost simultaneously with that of the companies for the 8th Cavalry. In its issue of December 12, 1861, the *BR* published this brief announcement: "RECRUITING.—We understand that Capt. Maxon has enlisted in this village and vicinity, nearly forty men for Colonel Fuller's regiment. About twenty recruits have been obtained here by Capt. T.G. Murphy for the Irish regiment."

In keeping with its usual standards of reliability, the *BR* made a few mistakes. The recruiter for Colonel Fuller was Abram (or Abraham) Moore. Also, according to Phisterer (3233), the regiment was recruited "between November, 1861, and March, 1862." Finally, the roster I have compiled for the Brockport "vicinity" members of the 105th numbers only 12 names enlisted by that date in Co. F and four in Company I. (The Davis Report lists 15 Sweden men in the regiment.)

Like the 8th Cavalry, the 105th was an amalgam of proto-regiments. In fact, the two companies mentioned in the *BR* article came from two different sources to form parts of the 105th. One of the incipient companies was to be recruited in LeRoy, but failed to fill. So the recruiter, the Reverend James M. Fuller, a prominent Methodist clergyman, spread his net much wider, including Brockport. The Brockport men became Company F, among the nine LeRoy companies that were consolidated into seven when the 105th was formally organized.

The other incipient regiment was supposed to be Irish. Irish volunteers in the Union army, being overwhelmingly Catholic, resented being placed in the charge of Protestant chaplains. In response, an Irish-born civil engineer, Howard Carroll, undertook to raise a regiment composed of Catholics, presumably Irish. In fact, the only chaplain the regiment ever had was a Free-Will Baptist minister, and he served only March 13–September 10, 1862. The six companies that had been recruited for the Irish regiment became three in the 105th.

Eleven of the Brockport recruits for Company F resided in Clarkson; 11 were Sweden residents, including Brockport, one of whom was an orphan from a "House of Refuge" in Rochester; and six were from Hamlin. The other fifteen were from towns contiguous to those three. Three from Brockport do not appear on any official records, but are named in the John T. Farnham diaries (11/9/1863) as Brockporters in the 105th, two in Company E and one in Company B. Six of the Brockport recruits joined Company I (for Irish). All of the Brockport recruits in Company I had been born in Ireland.

Companies F and I were a long time forming. The first man enlisted on November 11, 1861, and the last one on March 16, 1862, the day after the regiment was formally organized in LeRoy. As the men enlisted, they gathered at staging areas in Rochester (for the Irish) and in LeRoy (for Colonel Fuller's recruits). On January 25, 1862, the *U&A* reported that 445 soldiers were barracked in a large industrial building in LeRoy that had been taken over for the purpose on November 16 and renamed "Camp Upham" after its owner, Alonzo S. Upham. (Marcotte 78) Captain Moore's company was said to have 52 men. *U&A* reported that "much experience in drilling is gained while this regiment remains in its present quarters…Another company of 50 men was expected to arrive to-day." However, the same issue also reported that Moore was still "recruiting his ranks with good men…Men can go at once into clean quarters, have good clothing, fare, and have an opportunity to learn the manual of arms. Those who want to enlist…may apply to him at Latta's shoe store, in Brockport, to Lieut. Clark at Clarkson, or to Orderly Dayton at Camp Upham."

The tedium and rigor of the training was relieved somewhat for the Brockporters when, "From seventy-five to one hundred visitors from Brockport, friends of Captain Moore,…came to visit him and his company…with generous feelings and smiling countenances [and] plenty of provisions with which to astonish the appetite of our soldiers." They also presented Moore "with a splendid sword, sash, belt and one of Colt's improved revolvers." (*U&A* 3/21/1862) Plenty of other pastimes seem to have enlivened the lives of the recruits, including story-telling, checkers, backgammon and dominoes. They danced with one another to accordion, flute, and violin music. (*U&A* 1/17/1862) There were also dress parades, much speechifying, presentations of swords to officers, and other groups of visitors from the respective hometowns, sometimes numbering in the hundreds.

By the time the regiment left the area on April 1, it had enlisted 1,079 members, 59 of them recruits from the Brockport vicinity, including 43 in Company F. However, the regiment had already suffered considerable shrinkage. There had been 63 desertions, 63 soldiers discharged or mustered out, one transfer to another regiment, and eight deaths. So 944 remained in the regiment. Company F had four desertions, including one Brockport recruit—William H. Black of Spencerport—and four discharges, none of them Brockporters. Thus, 58 of the Brockport recruits remained, including 42 in Company F. The desertion rate for the regiment by April 1 was 5.8 percent, for Company F it was 3.9 percent, and for Brockporters it was 1.7 percent. On the other hand, 20 percent of the 135 members of the Irish Company I had deserted by that date. During their training in LeRoy, the Brockport recruits in Company F were joined by 53 other soldiers who had enlisted elsewhere in western New York for a total roster of 99.

Officers

The regimental commander, March 26–August 2, 1862, was Colonel James M. Fuller. When he resigned, Major John W. Shedd, another LeRoy resident, succeeded him. Howard Carroll, the organizer of the Irish group, was the lieutenant colonel until he was mortally wounded at Antietam, September 17, 1862. Richard Whiteside, of Wyoming, NY, succeeded Carroll. No Brockporters served as regimental officers. Even the support staff (adjutants, quartermasters, surgeons) was dominated by LeRoy and Rochester men.

Apparently, Fuller resigned to resume his position as Presiding Elder of the Genesee District of the Methodist Episcopal Church. Nearly a year later, he was arrested (*BR* 6/25/1863) and released on bail, on charges that he had conspired with a food supplier to defraud the government of $4,000 by billing it for feeding more soldiers than were actually present at camp. His defense was that Governor Morgan and Adjutant General Hillhouse had authorized his action in the case of men "who were only on furlough of ten days." The case never went to trial.

Brockporter Abram Moore commanded Company F throughout its existence. In the 1860 census, Moore was a 36-year-old "speculator," born in New York State, who headed a household that included his 32-year-old wife Martha, two children, his 66-year-old farmer father, and a 22-year-old male farmer with the Moore surname. His real property was worth a substantial $8,000 and his personal property $500. Sixty-two years after the war, James P. Cornes said that Moore had been a small farmer about half a mile east of Brockport and part owner of a tannery. (*BR* 1/12/28) William Clark of Clarkson was first lieutenant until he was discharged for disability on September 12, 1862. Clark does not appear in the 1860 census, but his father, Nathaniel was a 78-year-old farmer with $3,000 in real property and $400 in personal property. Clark was succeeded by Second Lieutenant William Knowles of Lyons. Lucius F. Rolfe of Bethany succeeded Knowles as second lieutenant and was followed on January 3, 1863, by Brockporter Edwin A. Dayton. Those were the only officers Company F ever had.

Dayton was the only Brockporter to rise from the ranks in the 105th to become an officer in the 105th and had a most unusual military career. In the 1860 census, he was a 27-year-old clerk living in a Brockport hotel with 18 other tenants. On April 22, 1861, he enrolled in Company K (the Brockport company) of the 13th NYVI and was commissioned a second lieutenant on May 14, 1861, but was cashiered October 15, 1861. Then he joined Company F of the 105th as a private on December 17, 1861, was promoted to first sergeant on January 6, 1862, to regimental sergeant major on March 26, 1862, and to second lieutenant January 3, 1863. At the conclusion of his service with the 105th, Capt. Moore, commander of his company, called him "an officer you have all learned to love, for his gentlemanly conduct, his ability as an officer and his coolness and bravery on the battlefield." (*BR* 4/9/1863) He transferred to Company F of the 94th NYVI when the regiments merged and was promoted to captain on May 1, 1863, but was dismissed again on October 24, 1863. Seemingly unperturbed, he tried again with the 22nd NY Cavalry, starting over as a private on December 21, 1863. He became regimental sergeant major on April 30, 1864. On August 13, 1864, he was commissioned second lieutenant in his company, but was not mustered in at that rank. Instead, he returned again to the regiment as sergeant major on February 1, 1865. Finally, three months after the war had ended, he was re-commissioned a second lieutenant. After the war, he disappeared. He does not show up in any later censuses and the STCR has the notation "could not obtain any other facts" with respect to his whereabouts after 1865.

WAR SERVICE, HEADED FOR THE FRONT

On March 31, 1862, "Just before taking the cars for New York City, Capt. Abraham Moore, in behalf of the seven companies at LeRoy, presented to Colonel J.M. Fuller a splendid Black Hawk and Henry Clay black stallion" which had cost $300. (*U&A* 4/4/1862) The Rochester group and the ones from LeRoy met in Avon. Their meeting was not auspicious. The Irish resented being forced into cohabitation with "LeRoy Methodists" and attacked their putative comrades-in-arms. (Marcotte 78)

Peace was soon restored and the regiment traveled by the Buffalo, New York and Erie Railroad to New York City. There, they were quartered in the Park Barracks. (*U&A* 4/5/1862) The *New York Tribune* reported that "the regiment cost the government less than any other corps that has been sent to the seat of war from this State" and that it numbered "1,000 well drilled and effective men" (*U&A* 4/3/1862), and the *New York Herald* called the 105th "as fine a body of men as we have yet seen the Empire State produce." (*U&A* 4/4/1862)

The regiment traveled on to Washington on April 4, where it was stationed for a month. Then it moved to the Shenandoah Valley where it participated in rigorous and exhausting but fruitless efforts to corner Stonewall Jackson. (Marcotte 79) The men endured forced marches "over the worst of roads, lying out three or four nights in the most drenching rain" without tents or baggage. (*U&A* 6/26/1862)

RAPPAHANNOCK

The regiment had its first taste of combat in the Battle of Cedar Mountain, Virginia, on August 9, 1862. According to the official records, the regiment suffered non-fatal wounds to one officer and seven enlisted men. However, Brockport recruit Company F's Lewis Rice of Clarkson was wounded "date and place not stated" and died of wounds on September 7, 1862, at Alexandria, Va. It seems likely that he was one of the enlisted men wounded at Cedar Mountain.

Cedar Mountain was the beginning of an intensive month of fighting by the regiment. It was the initial engagement in General Pope's Rappahannock campaign of August 9–September 2, 1862, that culminated in the Second Battle of Bull Run. At Cedar Mountain, a Confederate force of 20,000 repulsed 8,000

Union troops. The entire campaign, including eight armed engagements, cost the regiment 74 casualties, including the wounding of Brockport recruit Miles Buell of Murray on August 30 in the Second Battle of Bull Run.

Three Major Battles

Two weeks after Second Bull Run the 105th took part in two major battles, South Mountain on September 14 and Antietam on the 17th. At South Mountain, one enlisted man in the regiment was killed and two were mortally wounded, but none of them were Brockporters. The story was different at Antietam, the bloodiest one-day battle in American history. The 105th was among the first three regiments to enter the infamous cornfield, the bloodiest corner of the bloodiest battle and bore the brunt of the enemy's deadly fire, before withdrawing, having suffered—in a half-hour combat—74 casualties out of 236 men engaged. (Marcotte 79) James Bogan of Clarkson was killed and Oscar Chase of Brockport and Charles Embling of Riga were wounded, but recovered.

The last battle for the 105th was at Fredericksburg, December 11–15, 1862. The brigade of which the 105th was a part undertook a flanking attack on Confederate forces south of the town and achieved some initial success, including the capture of some 200 prisoners. The company's response to Captain Moore's farewell speech to his men included this tribute: "at Fredericksburgh, when our comrades were falling thick and fast, and the command of the regiment falling upon you, you ordered us to charge as our only safety, and you bravely led us on, and the enemy were driven from their cover." (*BR* 4/9/1863) However, they were not supported and were forced to retreat, as part of the great Union defeat. The regiment entered the fight with 172 men (Marcotte 92) and suffered 78 casualties, including Brockport recruits Thomas Close of Byron, Nathan Tompkins of Hamlin, and Orrin W. Doty of Brockport among the wounded.

The End of the 105th

The 105th participated in no more armed combat. Its ranks had been greatly depleted. Desertions numbered 196, discharges and mustering outs 335, deaths from disease and accidents 47, killed in action or deaths from wounds or prison 61, an aggregate of 639 from 1,079 enlisted, a shrinkage rate of 59.2 percent. The corresponding figures for the Brockporters were nine desertions, 15 wounded, two disease deaths and one killed in action, a 45.8 percentage. Also, AWOLs were an epidemic. General Pope's headquarters reported 187 from the regiment in the summer of 1862 already. (*U&A* 8/23/1862)

The regiment had been so reduced that it could no longer be considered a fighting force. Captain Moore said that it had shrunk "to about two hundred and fifty men in the field for duty" and another "two hundred wounded and diseased under treatment." (*BR* 4/9/1863) Its officers decided to merge it with the 94th NYVI. The unit had served from March 26, 1862 until March 9, 1863, less than a year. It had seen its first combat August 9, 1862, and its last December 15, 1862, just over four months. But those four months had been intensive. It took part in four of the most important battles of the war—Second Bull Run, South Mountain, Antietam, and Fredericksburg—as well as Duryea's Shenandoah and Pope's Rappahannock campaigns.

Brockporter Captain Abram Moore, commander of Company F, addressed his men at the time of the merger. He said, "You have shown... that you are possessed of the courage and bravery worthy to be called the best of soldiers." He explained that he was resigning, that he was to have been the major in the consolidated regiment, but that another officer of the 94th "had but recently been promoted, and was desirous to remain as Major of the consolidated regiment." Therefore, Moore deferred to him. The response to Moore's valedictory, which was signed by thirty members of the company, said, for "your ability as an officer to command, exemplary conduct, courage and bravery, you are not excelled." (*BR* 4/9/1863)

The Brockporters' length of service in the 105th and amount of armed action could not compare with that of their counterparts in either the 13th or the 8th Cavalry. Yet, they and their regiment had performed admirably and well. Edson W. Hoyt of Sweden said it best, "The old 105th has won no great name, but it has seen as hard service as any regiment...and lost nearly as many men in battle...They were a noble band...and the few who yet remain are unflinching true and brave." By the 1870 census, Moore, his wife, and a 15-year-old daughter were living in New York City, and he gave his occupation as "produce dealer." In the 1870 census, William Clark was a farmer in Clarkson, heading a household of his wife, two grown children and his 88-year-old father.

TRANSFER TO THE 94TH NYVI

On March 10, 1863, 418 soldiers from the 105th were transferred to the 94th NYVI. The remaining 22 after deducting the 639 shrinkage and the 418 transfers from the 1,079 enlistees are unaccounted for by the official records. Those 418 included 16 Brockporters who were transferred to Company F and one each to Companies G, H, and I. The 58 in April 1862 were reduced by two-thirds. Those 16 Brockporters constituted only 21 percent of the enlistment roster of their new company. There was no more Brockport company. This section, then deals with only a fragment of the original group. We are concerned mainly with a few individual soldiers.

WAR SERVICE

The 94th had been organized in Jefferson County, far from Rochester, but its war service before the merger had closely paralleled that of the 105th. It had been mustered in only two weeks earlier and it, too, had fought at Cedar Mountain, the Rappahannock campaign, 2nd Bull Run, South Mountain, Antietam, and Fredericksburg. It had suffered similarly heavy casualties. The Brockporters were joining comrades-in-arms when they transferred to the 94th.

After the Brockporters joined the 94th, the regiment engaged in 14 fights, including Chancellorsville, Gettysburg, Petersburg, the Weldon Railroad raid, and the Appomatttox campaign. At Gettysburg, the 94th suffered 245 casualties. One Brockporter was wounded, one was missing, and one deserted. One Brockporter was missing at the Battle of Petersburg. Another Brockporter died of disease eight days after the transfer. Four Brockporters in Company F were captured in the disastrous Weldon Railroad operation, one of whom died in prison and another died later of disease. Two were dismissed, including the infamous Edwin A. Dayton. The other dismissal was George H. Ostrom of Hamlin, who had been promoted to 1st lieutenant on May 8, 1863 and was dismissed January 1, 1864. One soldier, who had enlisted at age 15 was discharged for minority. Another was transferred to Battery H Company of the 1st NY Light Artillery. As a result, only seven of the 59 soldiers recruited through Brockport in November 1861 to April 1862, survived in the service to be mustered out of the 94th at the end of the war.

Chapter 17

Company H, 108th NYVI

Recruitment

More than six months elapsed after the 105th was recruited before another company was formed in the Brockport area. Eugene P. Fuller, late of the 13th NYVI, began enlisting men in the towns of Sweden, Clarkson, Hamlin, and Henrietta. By July 31, 1862, the *BR* was reporting that he had signed up "between fifty and sixty men...and that his prospects for a full company soon are flattering." However, not until October 9 did it publish a list of the 88 men and 13 officers who formed the completed unit. Eight of the names do not appear on the ACWRD roster. (The Davis Report says that there were 81 Sweden men in Company H.)

Unlike the 13th NYVI, 8th NY Cavalry, and 105th NYVI, the 108th did not enlist its members in the towns where they were recruited. All but one of the Brockporters was recorded as having enlisted in Rochester. This required a great deal of cross-checking with census records, local directories, cemetery records, and the town clerks' reports. Even so, I may not have identified all of the Brockporters in the company. My roster of men from the Brockport area in the 108th has 56 names, 55 in the original regiment and one joined later. Company H has 34, Company G has 8 men from Clarkson and one from Sweden, and the other 13 are scattered among six companies. The total number listed for Company H in the ACWRD who had enlisted by August 20 was 99. Therefore, the Brockporters constituted 34.3 percent of the company personnel. Twenty-two Company H members were from the Town of Sweden, three from Clarkson, four from Hamlin, and five from Ogden. Eight of the Brockporters in other companies were from Clarkson, seven were from Sweden, and six were from Hamlin.

The regiment departed Rochester's Camp Fitz John Porter on August 20 for Washington via New York. (*U&A* 8/20/1862), where they were housed temporarily in the Park Barracks. (*U&A* 8/22/1862). There they received their "arms a very handsome Springfield rifled musket." (*U&A* 8/29/1862) They arrived in Washington on the 22nd, where they were part of its defense force until September 6. (Phisterer) After departing Washington, en route to Antietam, the regiment suffered its first casualty. On September 7, Levi Lewis, a member of Company H from Hamlin, was shot dead by Benjamin D. Potter, a drunken soldier from Company A. Potter was arrested and charged with manslaughter, but escaped in 1863 before his trial and was mustered out with the regiment on May 28, 1865. Washburn has no record of him after the war, but a Benjamin Potter, age 50, was reported by the 1870 census in the Monroe County Poor House.

OFFICERS

Although Colonel John W. Williams received the authorization to recruit the 108th, he served as its commander for less than three weeks. He was succeeded on July 28, 1862, by Colonel Oliver H. Palmer, a 47-year-old Rochester lawyer and prominent Republican. When he resigned March 2, 1863, because of ill health, Charles J. Powers was promoted from lieutenant-colonel to succeed him and Francis E. Pierce became lieutenant-colonel. The only Brockporter to serve as a regimental officer was Franklin B. Hutchinson, a 48-year-old grocer from Brockport. He served as quartermaster, April 23, 1864–May 28, 1865, after having served as second lieutenant and first lieutenant of Company H.

Brockporter Captain Eugene P. Fuller organized Company H and was its commander until June 3, 1863. He had earlier commanded the Brockport Company K in the 13th NYVI. He was succeeded by Patrick C. Kavanagh of Rochester and, on January 1, 1865, by Andrew Boyd of Brockport, who had worked his way up through the ranks from sergeant, despite having been wounded at Laurel Hill while first sergeant. He was the son of a laborer, Thomas C. Boyd. Andrew, 24, his parents, and three of his four siblings had been born in Ireland. His youngest sibling had been born in Canada. After the war, he and his brother, Henry, formed a partnership with Judah Gridley to manufacture carriages and sleighs on Clinton Street. Therefore, though Brockporters constituted only a third of the company's personnel, they occupied the captaincy nearly half the time, the first lieutenancy about four-fifths of the time, and the second lieutenancy half the time. So, Brockporters dominated the leadership of the company.

Another Brockporter, 35-year-old John W. Beedle, a farm laborer from Sweden, had an interesting infantry career. On August 20, 1862, he enlisted in Rochester as a private in Company D of the 33rd NYVI and was promoted to first sergeant. Then, on October 1, 1863, he transferred to Company I of the 49th NYVI as first sergeant. Finally, on May 19, 1864, he transferred to Company G of the 108th as first lieutenant and, on August 1, was promoted to captain, but on November 21, 1864, was "dismissed."

WAR SERVICE, ANTIETAM

Phisterer lists 31 engagements in which the 108th was involved. They included Antietam, Fredericksburg, Chancellorsville, Gettysburg, the Wilderness, Petersburg, and the Appomattox campaign—except for the two battles of Bull Run, all the really major battles in the east. Less than a month after they left Rochester, they fought at Antietam. The commander of Company H, Captain Eugene P. Fuller, provided the *BR* with an account, from which the following is extracted:

> *Forward! was the order.—Our ears were soon greeted with the whizzing of bullets and the bursting of shells.—Will the regiment stand fire—will green men who hardly know how to shoulder a rifle, fight—...?...On, the column moved...Crack! Crack! Crack! Went the musketry...A small lane...formed a beautiful rifle pit; behind this was a cornfield—these were occupied by the rebel forces. We were without cover or protection of any kind, save stout arms and brave hearts...Signs of wavering began to manifest itself in the rebel ranks. One poor "gray back" attempted to climb the fence, and reach the cornfield; he was actually pinned to the fence. I saw him after the battle, no less than seventeen bullets had pierced his body... Thus, for two hours, did the battle rage. Our men were falling thick and fast, their cartridges were giving foul, their guns had become so heated and choked, that it was almost impossible to drive the bullet home. The enemy*

> *had been reinforced. Neither regiment or battery had come to our support or relief. Our Major and two Lieutenants had been killed. Is it a wonder that our men began to waver?...They...rallied, and for two more hours, fought with redoubled fury...Bayonets were fixed, and preparations made to charge upon the rifle pit. With a wild shout we rushed down into the midst of the rebels, who threw down their arms and begged piteously for mercy. Nine commissioned officers and 159 non-commissioned officers and privates were taken prisoners. (10/2/1862)*

In his official report, Colonel Palmer credited Fuller with having taken the prisoners under guard to an officer of the Eighth Illinois Cavalry. (OR, Series I. Vol. 19, Part I, Reports. Serial No. 27)

General McClellan was reported to have said that he "never saw raw troops fight so in his life." (*U&A* 9/26/1862) However, the regiment paid a heavy price for its success. It lost three officers and thirty men killed or mortally wounded, two other officers and 107 other men wounded and 43 enlisted men missing for a total number of casualties of 195, nearly one-fifth of the regiment in a single battle. Two Brockporters in Company H (James W. Snow and Daniel Warren of Sweden) were killed and six (Heber Fuller, Patrick Callon, Henry Grunwell, Mathew Hartigan of Sweden and Patrick Sullivan and Charles E. Spring of Clarkson) were wounded. One Brockporter each in Company G (Charles Nicholas Kinney from Clarkson) and Company I (John Hoffman of Clarkson) was wounded. As testament to the ferocity of the struggle in which the 108th was engaged, its regimental flag was pierced seventy times by rebel bullets. (*U&A* 3/12/1863)

One of the wounded in Company H was Charles Spring, a farm boy from Clarkson, who took a bullet in the left forearm. A few days before the battle, he was the Company H drummer, but "exchanged" his "drum for a musket. He would be discharged because of his wound on October 14. 1862. Spring had enlisted at age 16 (though he gave his age as 18). After the war, he became a prosperous farmer in Hamlin.

Fredericksburg

Less than two months later, the 108th was in action again. On the third day at Fredericksburg, December 13, 1862, it was part of the army of plunderers who sacked the city during a day-long orgy of looting and vandalism. The next day, however, they were part of a division that was slaughtered in a futile and disastrous attempt to storm one of the heights surrounding the city. The 108th suffered 92 casualties including three Brockporters in Company H who were wounded, James Hinds of Brockport and David King and Homer H. Hoyt of Hamlin.

CHANCELLORSVILLE

The next battle for the 108th was another Union catastrophe, Chancellorsville, May 1–3, 1863. It was the main victim of "some of the most savage fighting of the war" (Marcotte 105), bearing the brunt of the Confederate attack on the "Chancellorsville salient," a Union force that nearly surrounded the town. After a night-long pounding by the rebel artillery, the brigade of which it was a part was driven out of the salient with "staggering" losses. The 108th suffered 52 casualties. Six Brockporters were wounded, three in company H (John A. Burns, James Hinds, and Thomas Harvey of Brockport), one in Company B (Henry J. Clow of Hamlin) and two in Company I (Mathias Goeden and Frederick Eller of Sweden). Randall Kinney of Clarkson was captured and imprisoned until October 1, 1863.

Arthur G. Newton of Parma, a private in company G, reported this extracurricular incident in a letter dated June 4, 1863:

> *A general spree among officers terminating in a bloodless duel between Capt. Fuller of Brockport and Lieut. Porter of Co. F. Fuller proving himself the coward so out and out that lieut. Porter wouldn't trouble himself to fire at him but denounced Fuller with worst of epithets and oaths for being a coward. Fuller had the cannon on the brain in Antietam and Fredericksburg and some say at Chancellorsville too. (Newton 53)*

En route from Falmouth, Va., to Gettysburg, the regiment halted for rest and dinner near Stafford Court House, Va., on June 11, 1863. Twin brothers, Willard H. and William E. Peck, of Company A, who had been born in Hamlin, but had moved to Penfield, went looking for drinking water. They were captured by guerillas, marched about 1½ miles, ordered to kneel, and were shot in the backs of their heads. William died. Willard was severely wounded, left for dead, and remained unconscious for about 24 hours. Upon recovering, he wandered dazedly in the woods, until discovered by two young ladies, who took him home, where a bullet and five buckshot were removed from his head. He rejoined the regiment, but was deemed unfit for further duty and sent home. After the war he became a Free Methodist minister. (Washburn 297–98)

GETTYSBURG

The fourth major battle in succession for the 108th was the war's climactic conflict at Gettysburg, July 1–3, 1863. In fact, the 108th may have played an important role in the most climactic event of that most climactic battle—the repulse of Pickett's charge, "the high tide of the Confederacy." On July, the 108th was positioned on Cemetery Ridge when the rebels began the cannonading that was preliminary to Pickett's charge. Most of the barrage was frontal, from Seminary Ridge, but Company H's First Sergeant Andrew Boyd (a Brockporter), who was commanding Company H, recalled that they were also subjected to "a cross fire." (Washburn 124)

A member of Company H, 18-year-old Jacob Winslow, a Henrietta farm boy, became terrified by the rain of death from the Confederate barrage and, standing up, engaged the Almighty in conversation. He believed that his predicament was payment for his sinful ways and cried out, "Save me, oh, Lord; and I will serve Thee." Company-mate Robert J. Rider of Clarkson, another farm boy, "rather abruptly" ordered the repentant sinner to protect his head, as they were lying down. No sooner had Winslow obeyed and placed a metal canteen in front of his face than "a bullet crashed through the canteen" and "inflicted a two-inch scalp wound" that "paralyzed" him. Winslow survived, was wounded again at Laurel Hill in May 1864, and was mustered out with the regiment at the end of the war. After the war, he was a student in Lima, Livingston County, and at Oberlin College and Oberlin Theological Seminary in Ohio. Later he served pastorates in Ohio, Nebraska, Kansas, and, finally, Los Angeles. (Washburn 331, GenForum.com)

When Pickett's historic charge began, the 108th and Wayne County's 126th NYVI were on the right end of the front line. Men of the 108th had been needed to drag into position the cannons of Woodruff's Battery, which occupied the same stretch of Cemetery Ridge, because most of the horses had been killed or disabled. Without that artillery and without the withering fire of the two infantry regiments, Pickett might well have succeeded. (Marcotte 134–36)

The 108th paid a heavy price for its share of the victory, 102 casualties, including 16 killed or mortally wounded. One Brockporter was killed (Henry Comstock of Company F from Sweden) and two were wounded (Henry B. Smith, a sergeant in Company H from Ogden, was wounded in fighting in front of Cemetery Ridge on the second day, and Patrick O'Brien of Company H from Sweden was wounded on the third day, the time of Pickett's charge). The Confederates' losses were devastating. An estimated half of the 12,000 troops directly engaged in the fateful charge were casualties.

THE WILDERNESS

From mid-October 1863, through early February 1864, the 108th was involved in a series of five minor engagements interspersed with skirmishing and long, tedious, and grueling marches in bad weather. The most significant engagement for the 108th was Morton's Ford, February 6, 1864, where it "advanced rapidly and without firing a shot to a stone wall occupied by the enemy, when they delivered a volley and with shouts leaped over the wall and were soon in possession of an important position which virtually decided the contest." (ACWRD from The Union Army, II 128) The regiment suffered 25 casualties during that period. Only one Brockporter was on the list. Henry J. Clow, who had been wounded already at Chancellorsville, was shot in the abdomen at Morton's Ford. Five other enlisted men and one officer in the regiment were also wounded there.

Corporal Franklin Cusick, Hamlin farm boy, brother of Henry, served in the 13th and 108th NYVI regiments, wounded and captured in the Battle of the Wilderness. *Photo provided by Mary Smith.*

The 108th next took part in the Battle of the Wilderness, May 5–7, 1864, a confused struggle, fought in a mass of stunted pine and thick underbrush where battle formations were virtually impossible to organize or maintain. The 108th was caught by a rebel counter-attack and fought a pitched battle at 100 yards. It suffered 52 casualties. Among them were Franklin Cusick, a Company H member from Hamlin, who was wounded and captured. Also wounded were Mathias Goeden, a member of Company I from Sweden, who had already been wounded at Chancellorsville; James Hinds of Company H from Brockport, who had already been wounded twice; and Peter D. Bush of Company F, a farm boy from Parma. James Dack of Company H from Sweden, had a close call. He felt a slicing pain through his neck during the battle and immediately suspected the worst. Luckily, only his canteen had been shot off, the force of the bullet severed the canteen straps causing them to jerk violently on his neck.

Spotsylvania

The Wilderness was followed immediately by the 14-day "slugfest" called Spotsylvania, May 8–21, where the two armies battled it out day after day with scarcely any respite. On May 10, the 108th participated in a hopeless assault on Laurel Hill, charging "through a belt of burning woods, 35 to 40 yards wide," but being stopped by an enemy ensconced behind impenetrable breastworks and an "abatis" (felled trees with sharpened limbs pointed outward). (Marcotte 194) On the 12th, it was engaged in an assault that included point blank firing across a breastwork. That campaign cost the 108th 53 casualties. First Sergeant Andrew Boyd of Company H from Brockport and Vincent P. Kelly of Company B from Hamlin were wounded May 10 at Laurel Hill. Boyd was felled by a bullet in the right arm near the shoulder.

Petersburg

The 108th continued to be part of Grant's relentless offensive against Lee. It fought at North Anna, May 22–26; Totopotomoy Creek, May 27–31; and Cold Harbor, June 1–12. Those operations cost it 27 casualties. George Brokaw of Company H from Ogden and Jacob Kaderli of Company G from Clarkson were wounded June 1–3 at Cold Harbor. Grant then focused his attention on the city of Petersburg, Va., reasoning that Richmond was too well protected and that Petersburg was astride Lee's main means of communication. The 108th was part of a five-day assault, June 15–19, that failed to take the city. So Grant resorted to a prolonged siege that lasted over nine months. Kaderli was wounded again on the first day of the siege, June 20. The siege was a miserable experience for the hapless soldiers, but cost the regiment only eight casualties, all wounded enlisted men who recovered—none from the Brockport area.

The Petersburg siege was not, however, a static operation. Units were frequently detached for raids in the area, harassing the enemy, interfering with his communications and supply lines, and attempting to force Lee to abandon Petersburg and Richmond. The 108th was often so engaged. It participated in the Weldon Railroad (June 21–23), Deep Bottom (July 27–29), Strawberry Plains (August 14–18), and Reams Station (August 25) operations, suffering 30 casualties. The only Brockport casualty was the capture of Frederick Frey of Company F from Sweden Center at Reams Station.

At one point in the Reams Station engagement, the 108th was surrounded "and they fought their way out till they got to the clear field" at the rear but once there, they still "had to fight on both sides." Apparently, the panic created by enemy fire in the front, rear, and flank, engulfed the boys from Rochester and swept them out into the open. When this happened, Pierce ordered First Lieutenant Andrew Boyd to form a detail "and save the colors" by removing them from the field.

Each of those operations was thwarted by the Confederates. Yet gradually the Confederate supply lines were severed until only the Southside Railroad and the Boydton Plank Road remained open. (History.com) This set the stage for the Boydton Plank Road raid of October 26–28, 1864.

Boyd commanded the regiment for that operation. He reported that the 108th encountered the enemy at Cedar Creek at 8 a.m. on the 26th, "formed in line of battle and charged through a deep ravine and across the creek, routing the enemy's skirmish line…About 10 a.m., the command was ordered to the… Boydton plank road,…where, at about 3 p.m., it was ordered to charge and take the works in its front, which was done under a severe artillery and musketry fire, in which 1 commissioned officer and 4 enlisted men were wounded. The command remained in the captured works under a severe fire from the enemy until about 10 p.m., when it was relieved and…returned to camp." (ACWRD) One of the wounded was Robert J. Rider, of Company H, a farm laborer from Clarkson. He does not appear in the 1870 census, but in 1880, he is a day laborer in Clarkson, married with two young children.

The Final Drive

After the Boydton raid, the 108th went into winter quarters until February 5–7, 1865, when it took part in the Hatcher's Run engagement, another strike at rebel communications. Then, on March 25, it joined the attack on the Petersburg works, an earthen defense structure that cost the Feds dearly, but tightened the noose some more. The final engagements of the 108th were in the ultimate campaign of the war, March 28–April 9, the drive to Appomattox Court House that culminated in Lee's surrender and the effective end of the fighting. Those struggles were White Oak Ridge (March 28–31), the fall of Petersburg (April 2), High Bridge and Farmville (April 7), and Appomattox Court House (April 9). By then, the Confederates were so dispirited that the 108th suffered only one casualty, a wounded enlisted man, not a Brockporter.

From its entry into combat as the greenest of troops at Antietam until Appomattox, a period just short of 19 months, the 108th, including its Brockporters, was engaged in seven major battles and 24 lesser combats. The regiment suffered 642 casualties, two-thirds of its original roster, including 115 killed in action or died of wounds. The Brockport contingent totaled 55 at the outset, 35 of them in Company H, of whom 20 were casualties—three killed and 17 wounded (one of them three times and one was imprisoned as well). Also, four others were discharged or transferred for disabilities, four deserted, and one was discharged early (Captain Fuller). So far as the official records indicate, only five enlisted men and one officer of the original 35 were not casualties and were mustered out with the regiment on May 28, 1865.

Of the twenty Brockporters in other companies, two were killed, one after being taken captive; seven were wounded; four were prisoners, one of whom died in prison; two died of disease; two were disabled; one transferred to the 21st NY Cavalry; and the fate of two is not known. None of the 20 was mustered out at the end of the war without having been a casualty. Also, Captain Beedle, who was not a member of the original regiment was "dismissed" early.

This means that the Brockporters in the 108th had a casualty rate of 51.7 percent. If to the casualties are added the two who died of disease and the six who were disabled, the rate rises to 66.1 percent, nearly two-thirds. Those who came through unscathed were the four deserters, three of the four officers, and the five enlisted men who were non-casualties and were mustered out with the regiment on May 28, 1865.

Chapter 18

Company M, 3rd NY Cavalry

The 3rd NY Cavalry was known as the Van Alen Cavalry and later the Mix Cavalry after its successive commanders. It was first organized in Rochester in the summer of 1861. A New Jersey unit was incorporated in the regiment as Company M, but was transferred to a New Jersey regiment in April 1862. (Phisterer 779) A new Company M was organized in August–September 1862 in Rochester and Brockport. Phisterer says that Company K was recruited principally at "Elmira, Brockport and Rochester." However, in the ACWRD rosters the only men who joined that company in 1862 were recruited in Syracuse. I could find no Brockporters in that company.

The battle flag of the 3rd New York Cavalry regiment. *Courtesy of the New York State Division of Military and Naval Affairs.*

RECRUITMENT

The recruitment drive for the 108th was not yet finished before that of the 3rd NY Cavalry began, and the 3rd was fully constituted a month before the 108th. All but eight of the 109 men on my roster of Brockporters, based on the ACWRD, enlisted from August 5 through August 26, 1862. Two each enlisted on August 29 and September 9. One enlisted a year later and two more joined the company in March 1864. Finally, Charles B. Armstrong, who is buried in the Town of Sweden cemetery enlisted in Company A of an earlier 3rd NY Cavalry on June 13, 1861, was thrown from a horse and discharged with a disability on September 3, 1861, and was mustered into the new 3rd NY Cavalry on September 10, 1862, as the quartermaster sergeant. Another Brockporter, John Sutphen, also served in the earlier 3rd Cavalry, having been mustered in on August 27, 1861, promoted to commissary sergeant on August 24, 1863, to sergeant on August 31, 1863, and busted back to private on March 1, 1864. He was mustered out on August 29, 1864. His commissary records are in the archives of the College at Brockport.

Commissary Sergeant John Sutphen, Sweden farmer, member of the 3rd New York Cavalry from August 27, 1861–August 29, 1864. *Photo provided by Lorene Wilford.*

The ACWRD lists 83 members of Company M who enlisted in Brockport in August or early September 1862 and 17 who enlisted in Rochester during that time. However, the *BR* (9/4/1862) reported that four of the Rochester recruits were Ogden residents and one each was from Sweden, Kendall, and Clarkson. Two others appear on the STCR and one is in the Clarkson 1869 directory. Five others were buried in Sweden's cemetery and the 1860 census reports one each living in Hamlin and Ogden. Thus, all of the Rochester recruits had some connection with the Brockport area. For a table showing the residences of the recruits see Chapter 3, page 50. (The Davis Report lists 47 Sweden men in Company M.)

Officers

Corporal James Monroe, a forty-two-year-old Brockport broom maker, and his wife. He served in the 3rd New York Cavalry. *Photo courtesy of New York State Military Museum © Historical Data Systems, Inc.*

The principal recruiter for Company M and its commander was Nathan P. Pond. Pond was mustered in on August 8, 1862, as a captain, age 31. He was mustered out on December 8, 1863, for transfer to the 1st U.S. Colored Cavalry and promotion to major. However, he was not actually mustered into that regiment. Rather, on January 10, 1864, he was mustered into the 2nd U.S. Colored Cavalry as a lieutenant-colonel, second in command of the regiment. That regiment participated in a number of engagements in the Peninsular campaign, the sieges of Petersburg and Richmond, the Battle of Fair Oaks, etc. However, its casualties were very light: two men killed and five wounded. After the war, it served as occupation troops in Texas, but Pond had been mustered out on April 14, 1865.

Nathan Patchen Pond was born on September 11, 1832, in Brockport. The 1860 census lists him as a lumber merchant with real estate worth $1,000 and personal property worth $300. His wife was Cornelia, age 24, housekeeper. They had two children ages five and 11 months and an Irish-born maid, age 22. Nathan's parents, Levi, 77, and Clarissa Patchen Pond, 67, lived next door. Levi gave his occupation as "Gentleman" and she was a housekeeper.

Lieutenant Colonel Nathan P. Pond, Brockport businessman, commander of Company M of the 3rd New York Cavalry and of the 1st U.S. Colored Cavalry regiments. *Courtesy of the Rochester Public Library.*

In 1865, Pond had returned to Brockport and gave his occupation as harbormaster. By 1870, he had moved to Rochester and had founded, with Henry Mathews, the Rochester Printing Co., which published the *Rochester Democrat and Chronicle*. He remained co-owner until his death in 1921 at the age of 88. (*Kingston Daily Freeman*, 1/17/21) Pond was an early and longtime leader of the Grand Army of the Republic. He held statewide and national offices, including state commander in 1900. Also, he was instrumental in the effort to erect a monument to Frederick Douglass.

Two other Brockporters were officers in the company. Ira Holmes, 22, was commissioned into the company as a second lieutenant on August 8, 1862. He resigned on February 2, 1863. Holmes was the son of Elias B. Holmes, perhaps Brockport's leading citizen. In the 1860 census, he was age 19, living in a Rochester hotel, gave his occupation as "student at university" and had personal property valued at $5,000. After the war, Holmes moved to Chicago and engaged in banking and real estate businesses. The 1870 census has him living on Michigan Avenue, Chicago's Gold Coast, with banking as his occupation and $100,000 worth of real estate and $100,000 in personal property. His wife, Jennie, was 25 and "keeping house" and they had a five-month-old boy named Elias. By 1880 he was a "real estate dealer" and his wife had changed her name to the, presumably, more dignified Virginia.

The younger Elias had become E. Burton, and they had another son and a daughter. The household also included his mother-in-law and five servants. Burton (1870–1958) became a very well-known traveler, photographer and filmmaker, who coined the term "travelogue."

John A. Carpenter, age 31 in 1862, was the other Brockporter officer. He had enlisted in Company M on September 10, 1862, as a private, was promoted to corporal on November 17, to sergeant on July 10, 1863, to orderly sergeant April 1, 1864, and to first lieutenant October 17, 1864. He was transferred to Company F on January 10, 1865, and back to Company M a month later. He was listed as a harness maker in Brockport in the 1860 census. He does not appear in the 1870 census or the 1869–70 directory.

War Service

The 3rd NY Cavalry, the regiment to which this company belonged, had the longest list of engagements in Phisterer of any regiment with a Brockport company. Before Brockport's Company M joined it in October 1862, it had participated in 21 armed engagements. Thereafter, Phisterer records 105 "engagements, &c." Also, he notes that, in addition, the regiment suffered 18 losses "on picket, scouts and minor affairs." The regiment was engaged in none of the major pitched battles of the war, although it was, for a time, part of the siege forces at Petersburg.

Most of the regiment's engagements were raids. For instance, from December 11–20, it made an "Expedition from New Bern to Goldsboro, N.C." during which it participated in 13 encounters with the enemy. It seems to have been a fairly typical raid and was reported by one of the participants this way:

> *Col. Lewis, of the 3d Cavalry, commanding a force of seventeen companies of cavalry and four mountain howitzers…marched 300 miles, captured 100 prisoner and 300 mules and horses, destroyed the railroad bridge across the Tar river at Rocky Mount, between Weldon and Goldsborough, captured a train of cars having on board 2,000 rounds of artillery ammunition and 50,000 rounds of small ammunition, $100,000 worth of Quartermaster's stores, two railroad depots at Tarboro and Rocky Mount, captured and destroyed a train of 16 baggage wagons, and raised*

the d—l generally. We were cut off several times on our return, which made us march 100 miles out of our way.

At Hookerstown we were attacked both in front and rear, but the rebels were quickly dispersed with canister. They had several pieces of artillery at different points, and used them with pretty good effect. They followed us to within eight miles of Newbern, and while we were waiting for transportation across the river they attacked us. We had a "right smart" skirmish here for two hours, the enemy bringing into action three pieces of artillery, while we used but one. We lost a few prisoners here, and had several wounded—no Rochester boys, I believe. Their cavalry made a charge on one of our guns, but after receiving a well directed canister, returned with considerable loss. The next morning eleven dead horses were found at the point of their repulse.

We lost about thirty men, most of them prisoners, on the march…We marched three days without food or sleep—not halting over six hours in the whole time. Many of the men fell asleep on their horses, and falling from the ranks, were captured by the enemy, who kept close on our rear. The boys all enjoyed the march, and in a few days will be ready for another. It is considered a big thing here…

P.S. Our boys say they would like to make a raid into New York city for a week or two, and fight the damned scoundrels who are trying to sneak out of the draft. (DMNA)

At the time the Brockport company joined the regiment, it was operating in North Carolina, based at New Berne. From November 3, 1863, until May 5, 1864, it seems to have been inactive. By the latter date, it had been transferred to Virginia and was part of the force besieging Petersburg. It remained in Virginia for the remainder of the war. Beginning June 15, it was mainly engaged in raiding behind enemy lines. On one nine-day raid, June 22–30, 1864, on the Southside and Dansville Railroad, it suffered 105 casualties, by far its greatest loss during the war. All told, it suffered 308 casualties after the Brockporters joined it, including 46 officers and enlisted men killed or died of wounds.

The Brockporters suffered relatively few casualties. In fact, more of them were lost to disease (8) and disability (7) than died from enemy action. Only two were killed in action. They were Henry M. Hale of Clarkson, at Core Creek, N.C., April 30, 1863, and Martin C. Vanderpool of Ogden, at Stoney Creek, Va., May 8, 1864. Hale was the only 3rd Cavalry casualty

Private Alonzo Soules of Brockport served in the 3rd New York Cavalry, August 11, 1862–June 7, 1865. *Courtesy of the New York State Division of Military and Naval Affairs.*

at Core Creek and Vanderpool was the only 3rd Cavalry enlisted man to die at Stoney Creek. Two more Brockporters died of wounds. They were George M. Cook of Hamlin, who was wounded at Core Creek, April 30, 1863, and died the next day, and Cornelius B. Davenport, whose hometown is not known, who was wounded at Stoney Creek, Va., May 7, 1864, and died two days later. (Phisterer has no member of the regiment dying of wounds at Core Creek.)

The other casualties suffered by Brockporters included six men who were captured at Reams' Station, June 29, 1864. They were David M. Woodmauer, whose hometown is not known; Peter Lawler and Edward Ebler of Sweden; Charles H. Baker of Ogden; John C. Gascoigne of Hamlin; and Albert N. Barker of Parma. Ebler and Gascoigne were also wounded in that action and Woodmauer died of disease at Andersonville. Other Brockport casualties were wounds suffered by Eli S. Knowlton of Hamlin, May 8, 1864; John Cooper of Brockport, during the Richmond and Danville Railroad raids, May 13, 1864; Jedediah Soules of Brockport, on Darbytown Road, Va., October 7, 1864; and Thomas Sheffield, whose hometown is unknown, at Chapin's Farm, Va., same date. Soules and Sheffield were discharged because of their wounds. Finally, Henry P. B. Starr, hometown unknown, was slightly wounded at Ream's Station and captured in the Battle of the Wilderness, May 8, 1864.

The Ream's Station engagement was part of the Southside and Danville expedition which, in turn, was part of Grant's strategy to cut the transportation routes to Richmond and Petersburg. In that nine-day operation, the regiment lost 80 men to captivity, but Phisterer does not break that figure down by days. Stoney Creek was part of the siege of Petersburg. The regiment suffered its greatest one-day losses in the Darbytown Road engagement. Fifty-two officers and men were casualties, including two officers and 31 men captured.

The company also lost Brockporters for a variety of other reasons. Seven were discharged for disabilities, six were discharged for promotions and transfers, eight men deserted, one became an orderly for a general in another regiment, Holmes resigned, and one soldier was discharged on order of the Secretary of War (reason unknown). Finally, 57 men, including six who had been POWs, served out their enlistments and were mustered out with the regiment in May or June 1865.

Corporal Cornelius B. Davenport, 21, who served in the 3rd New York Cavalry and died of wounds suffered at Stoney Creek. *Photo courtesy of New York State Military Museum © Historical Data Systems, Inc.*

Chapter 19

Company A, 140th NYVI

Recruitment

This company had what was probably the most distinguished record among those recruited in Brockport, although Company H of the 108th is a close second. An account of its recruitment, drawn from the pages of the *BR*, appears in Chapter One, so that will not be repeated here. However, in order to present a statistical analysis of the fate of those recruits, a breakdown of the numbers based on the ACWRD, the SCTCRs, and cemetery records will be presented here. Perfect accuracy in identifying residences is impossible, because the various sources provide conflicting information.

The 140th, like the 108th, was mobilized in response to President Lincoln's call in early July 1862 for 300,000 more volunteers. Milo Starks, a Sweden farm boy, responded by recruiting a company for the 108th. However, the 108th filled up before he was ready and his company became Company A of the 140th. It was officially mustered in on September 13, 1862, at Camp Fitz-John Porter, in the southwest corner of the city between Plymouth Avenue and the Genesee River, and left for Washington on September 19. Company A had the honor of providing the color-bearer, Sgt. John H. Wright of Hamlin. (B. Bennett 63)

After six days in the Washington area, the regiment traveled by train to Frederick, Md. In the haste to leave Washington, no provision was made for feeding the troops. So, upon arriving in Frederick, a foraging party under First Lieutenant Joseph M. Leeper of Company A requisitioned 36 bushels of Secesh potatoes. (B. Bennett 80) Then they moved on to Sandy Hook near Harpers Ferry for a month of training. (B. Bennett 76–95)

Company A was the only one of the ten in the 140th that was composed almost entirely of rural residents. The 104 members of Company A at the time of its formation included 47 residents of Sweden (including 15 from Brockport), 48 of Clarkson, four of Hamlin, one each from Ogden, Fairport, and Rochester, and two whose residences could not be identified. Also, four residents of Sweden enlisted in other companies of the 140th.

Thus, in contrast to the regiments described so far in this chapter, it was remarkably homogeneous. Sweden and Clarkson provided 93.1 percent of the troops whose residence is known, and the three towns provided 97.1 percent. One of the soldiers with an unidentified residence was Henry A. Genett, the tent-mate of a Clarkson man, and the other, Donain Richards was one of his closest buddies. So, they may also have been Clarkson boys, though I cannot document that. (The Fairport soldier, Auranah Mosely, had a sister, Hattie, who was a student in the Brockport Collegiate Institute in 1859, which may explain his connection to Brockport. Also, the Rochester recruit was Graham R. Scott. I have been unable to trace him, but Elizabeth Scott of Clarkson was a student at the BCI in 1850, perhaps another connection.) The Davis Report says that 37 Sweden men were in Company A.

Unlike the other regiments described above, the 140th received two substantial later infusions of soldiers from other regiments. In June 1863, the three years men remaining in the 13th NYVI and in October 1864, the veterans and recruits of the 44th NYVI were enrolled in the 140th. Five men from the 13th and 31 from the 44th joined Company A. None of the names of the transfers appears on the S/CTCRs, but one of them, Edgar Wadhams, who came from Brockport's old Company K of the 13th, was a resident of Holley, (B. Bennett 216), and is listed as a 29-year-old blacksmith in Clarkson in the 1870 census. So, I am adding him to the roster of Brockporters.

Officers

The 140th had serious troubles keeping a commander. Two were killed in action and a third was severely wounded. Irish-born Colonel Patrick H. O'Rorke of Rochester was the regimental commander until he was killed in action at Gettysburg, July 2, 1863. He was a West Point graduate, class valedictorian, and had been a 2nd lieutenant in the elite U.S. Engineers Corps. (B. Bennett 55). He was succeeded by Colonel George Ryan of Connecticut, another West Pointer, who had been a staff officer of the Fifth Corps and a captain in the 7th U.S. Infantry. (B. Bennett 285) One member of Company A said of him that, "He spares no pains for the welfare of his men, and is desirous of having that degree of perfection in discipline which alone can give us power in the field." (*BR* 5/5/1864) Ryan was killed in action at Laurel Hill, May 8, 1864. (B. Bennett 429) Then Lieutenant Colonel Elwell Stephen Otis, a Rochester attorney, commanded the regiment until he was wounded at Chappel House, Virginia, October 1, 1864, and discharged for disability January 4, 1865. Finally, Colonel William Grantsyn, a Rochester engineer, who had commanded Company H since its formation, took over from January 25, 1865, until the unit was mustered out June 3, 1865.

Milo L. Starks, a farm boy from Sweden, was the main recruiter of Company A and served as its captain from its formation until he was promoted to major on November 17, 1863. August Meyer, a 34-year-old Rochester clerk, the first lieutenant of Company B, succeeded him until May 24, 1864, when he was mortally wounded in the Wilderness. One soldier wrote that, "We have full confidence in him as our leader." (*BR* 5/5/1864) Henry Allen, a 25-year-old Clarkson farmer, assumed command of Company A at that time, but his promotion to captain did not come through until September 19, 1864, one month before he was discharged on October 19 for disability (chronic diarrhea). Allen had enlisted as first sergeant of Company A and advanced through the ranks. He was the company orderly, maintained his tent as a reading room and news depot, and was "the boys' favorite." (*BR* 2/26/1863 5/5/1864) Finally, Lewis B. Courtney of Brockport was captain from December 1, 1864, until the regiment was mustered out June 3, 1865. So, for two periods totaling more than five months, the company lacked a captain. Courtney was a 29-year-old farmer from the Town of Sweden who had enlisted as a private and been promoted to sergeant, second lieutenant, and first lieutenant. According to the 1870 census, he was a married carpenter with no children, living in Brockport.

Four other Brockporters served as officers in the 140th. They were Thaddeus K. Burch, a 23-year-old farm laborer from Clarkson, who enlisted as a private and was promoted to corporal, sergeant, and second lieutenant, all in Company A; Jonah Durward Decker, 27, who lived in Clarkson and practiced law in Brockport and who was the company's second lieutenant until December 13, 1862, when he received a disability discharge because of a lung ailment; Edgar J. Warner, who is listed in the 1860 census as an

18-year-old student in the household of a Clarkson farmer and enlisted as a private, was wounded at Laurel Hill on May 8, 1864, was commissioned a second lieutenant May 21, 1864, but not mustered, and was discharged October 25, 1864, at a hospital in Rochester; John H. Wright, a 25-year-old farmer from Hamlin, enlisted as a sergeant in Company A, became first lieutenant of Company B on September 7, 1864, and captain of Company H on March 5, 1865.

Joseph M. Leeper, was a 27-year-old attorney who enrolled at Brockport as the first lieutenant of Company A. His connection to Brockport is a bit cloudy. In the list of recruits for Company A in the *BR* (9/25/1862) his residence is given as Dutchess County. In the 1860 census, he was a lawyer in Newburgh, Orange County. In the 1870 census, he was a lawyer in Walden, same county. In the 1880 census, there are 18 Joseph Leepers and two Joseph Leipers, but only one is 45, a farmer in Ross County, Kentucky, and his wife and children do not match up. Yet, he is buried in Lakeview Cemetery, Town of Sweden. He had seen prior service with the 1st Kentucky Infantry, enlisting on June 8, 1861, as a first sergeant and being promoted to second lieutenant and first lieutenant. The date of his discharge from the Kentucky regiment is not known. He became captain of Company E of the 140th on December 13, 1862, was wounded in action at Chancellorsville on May 1, 1863, and resigned March 26, 1864, pleading the effects of his wound and his previous service. Later, he served briefly as a captain in the 3rd U.S. Veteran Volunteer regiment, being discharged on May 31, 1865. (regiment's website)

Starks was a member of a devoutly religious Baptist family. His father, Israel, farmed, but listed his occupation in the 1860 census as "colporteur," a peddler of religious books. He was also the deacon of the Baptist church in Brockport. His father, also named Israel, was a similarly devout religious man. Milo's letters and diary exhibit deep spirituality, though perhaps not the same passion. He ran a tree nursery and orchard, as well as a truck and grain farm and, before the war, traveled to the Midwest, selling saplings. Starks was loved and respected by his men and by the other officers. On occasion, he commanded the regiment in the absence of O'Rorke. (*BR* 2/26/1863)

WAR SERVICE, FREDERICKSBURG

After the month of training at Harpers Ferry, the 140th joined the Army of the Potomac on November 1, 1862, and spent the next six weeks on the march before their first baptism of fire at Fredericksburg, December 11–15, 1862. Until Fredericksburg, Company A had lost one member to desertion, one to typhoid fever, and one to a disability discharge. Otherwise, it was intact. However, on the 12th, the commander of Company I was accidentally wounded by one of his men and Lieutenant Leeper was promoted to captain and transferred to that command. Then, the next day, the captain of Company E resigned because of illness and Leeper was moved again. (B. Bennett 119) Company A was left without a first lieutenant until Henry Allen was appointed on October 18, 1863. Also, Patrick Caslon of the Town of Sweden in Company H had deserted in Elmira on September 20, 1862.

The 140th was on the periphery of the Battle of Fredericksburg, mainly held in reserve but subjected to intermittent artillery shelling and left much of the time in a very vulnerable situation. It suffered only five wounded enlisted men who recovered and ten missing men, none in Company A. They had a taste of battle, but suffered more from discomfort and fear than from wounds. However, that taste was more than enough for some of them, as morale in the regiment plummeted. In the aftermath of Fredericksburg, two enlisted members of Company A and Second Lieutenant Decker were discharged for disabilities (B. Bennett 130), and two others deserted. Captain Starks was in poor health, also, and was sent back to Brockport to recuperate. (B. Bennett 133) Also, correspondents to two Rochester newspapers reported that Company A lost an unofficial member, a Mrs. Betsey Morse, who returned home with a case of typhoid fever. She had been a nurse, caring for the sick, not only of Company A, "but those of the whole regiment." (B. Bennett 133; I do not find any Mrs. Betsey Morse in any of the towns represented in Company A in the 1860 or 1870 censuses or by Googling her.)

Two other Brockporters had serious problems with military law during the 4½-month interlude between Fredericksburg and Chancellorsville. Private William Grant, a 41-year-old laborer from Sweden in Company H, forged an officer's signature on a commissary order for food, was court-martialed, and sentenced to forfeiture of pay and some time spent standing on a barrel with an appropriate placard hung around his neck. Private Isaac Blake, a 23-year-old farm laborer from Clarkson, was tried and convicted of desertion and cowardice during the notorious "mud march" of late January. Along with nine other soldiers from other companies, Blake was sentenced to "forfeit all pay and allowances due or to become due to him; have both sides of his head shaved and be drummed through the camp of each regiment in the brigade, be imprisoned at Rip Raps, a fort near

Norfolk, Va.; be kept at hard labor for the balance of his term of enlistment; be only supplied with food and clothing necessary for his subsistence; have the letter D marked on his hip with indelible ink; and when the term was up, be dishonorably discharged from the army" (B. Bennett 165, 148–49) He was discharged August 4, 1863. The 1870 census shows him a farm laborer living in Clarkson with his father, who was a gunsmith, and mother.

Despite the absence of serious fighting during that interlude, Company A suffered a number of losses. Besides the ones mentioned above, five men deserted, five died of typhoid fever, and five were discharged with disabilities.

Chancellorsville

The 140th saw its first really serious combat at Chancellorsville, May 1–3, 1863. On the first day, the brigade that included the 140th underwent some three hours of artillery barrage and then repulsed a Confederate attack in force. Private Barton Perrigo of Clarkson was severely wounded in the bombardment and died of the wound. Lieutenant Leeper was slightly wounded in the attack. Also, Walton Gardner of Rochester in Company E was killed. He had formerly published a weekly newspaper in Brockport, and his mother, Mrs. E.A. Gardner, still lived there. In their first real engagement, the regiment had shown its effectiveness as a fighting force with one of the few successes in that Union disaster and were understandably proud. (B. Bennett 180–84)

The second day at Chancellorsville, the 140th was pretty much spectator to a fiery artillery and rifle duel. Private George T. Hoyt of Clarkson described it in a letter home as "the grandest and most terrible sight I have ever seen… the bright flashes and deep booming of artillery, the bright streaks and the bursting of shells, and the crashing of musketry from our lines and from the rebels." (B. Bennett 188) May 3 was largely a repetition of May 2, with the 140th not directly involved in the combat, but Private Martin W. Haight of Clarkson suffered a wound that led to his discharge four months later. The regiment as a whole lost two enlisted men killed, two who died of wounds, one officer and nine enlisted men who recovered from wounds, and one officer and six enlisted men missing.

In the two months between Chancellorsville and Gettysburg, the 140th was occupied with marches and temporary camps, with no combat activity. Company A had very few personnel changes. It gained two Brockporters by transfer from the 13th.

Gettysburg

That brief interlude proved to be the calm before the biggest storm of the war and the moment of greatest glory for the 140th and Company A. On July 2, the Fifth Corps was ordered to move to the relief of the Third Corps southeast of Cemetery Ridge. The 140th was the rear of the column, marching along the northern slope of Little Round Top. Its unoccupied crest commanded the battlefield where the climactic confrontation took place the next day. Major General Gouverneur K. Warren, former commander of the brigade that had included the 140th, was reconnoitering and discovered that, though the 20th Maine was holding its own on the left end of the battle line, two Texas regiments were fighting their way up the right end of the western slope against the desperately outnumbered 16th Michigan Infantry.

Warren ordered O'Rorke to change direction, move his regiment over Little Round Top, and drive back the Texans. Company A was at the head of the four-abreast column. The men were exhausted and many were bare-footed after the long, arduous two-week forced march to Gettysburg. In the confusion and haste, the two lead companies, A and G, failed to load their muskets or fix their bayonets. The Texans were so startled by the sudden appearance of the 140th that they were thrown into disarray. By the time they recovered, the lead

The boulder-strewn slope of Little Round Top. *Courtesy of House Divided Project, Dickinson College.*

companies had loaded their rifles and drawn up in battle formation. The other eight companies lined up on the right, and a pitched battle ensued.

O'Rorke was shot dead at the outset of the fight and Starks became the de facto regimental commander, as he led Company A and the 140th into the fray. The Union troops drove back the Confederates and helped save Little Round Top for the Federals. Starks was wounded four times, but refused to leave his men until the battle was won. An officer in the 44th NYVI, who was involved in the battle, in a magazine article 25 years later, listed seven men whom he thought saved Little Round Top that day. They included three generals, two colonels, an artillery lieutenant and—Milo Starks. (Lieutenant E. Bennett, *National Tribune*, letter dated Feb. 7, 1888, as relayed to me by Brian Bennett.)

Historians credit the 20th Main for having saved Little Round Top. However, other regiments were also crucial in that effort. Had the Texans succeeded in reaching its summit at their end, they would have outflanked the 16th Michigan and 20th Maine and, very likely, have made their positions untenable. Therefore, the 140th deserves a large share of the credit, also.

One historian explained it this way: "Fighting men of the 20th Maine would have almost certainly been overrun by the tenacity and superior force of the Confederate Texas 4th and 5th troops—from the high ground flank on the Federal right—had it not been for Colonel O'Rorke and his 140th New York's quick and direct action to fight back and repulse the confederate advance on the northwest incline of Little Round Top. Some key observers—including Major Ellis Spear—second-in-command of the 20th Maine on Little Round Top accused Colonel Chamberlain of "historical dishonesty" in his early 20th century writings." (Frederick)

Historian Bruce Catton called the charge of the 140th "as strange a counterattack as the army ever saw…they simply ran straight at their foes, and the only weight their charge had was the weight of their running bodies." A member of Company D wrote to his father; "You had ought to have seen our boys fight after that [O'Rorke's death]—nothing could exceed their bravery. They charged and re-charged, never being in any instance repelled." (James Rennick Campbell in REE 7/3/1863) Edgar Wadhams, of Company A, wrote in his diary: "the fight…was a hard one to but we drove the rebs from their position and cut them all to pecies they broke and run in confusion."

The victory was the more gratifying in that the Texans had the reputation of elite regiments, never having been bested on the battlefield before, and that possession of Little Round Top was so crucial to the outcome of the

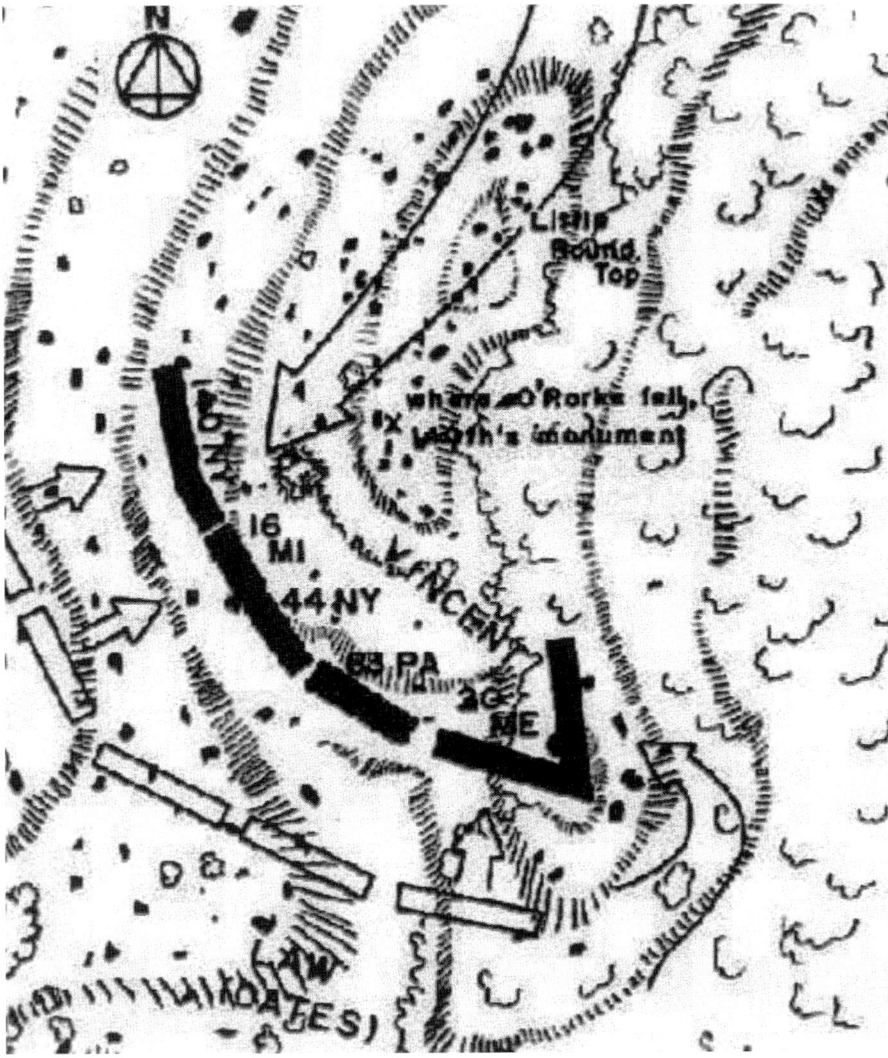

This map shows the lineup of the Union Army regiments at Little Round Top at Gettysburg on July 2, 1863. *Map by John Heiser, provided by Brian Bennett.*

battle the next day. According to historian Allan Nevins the retention of Little Round Top by the Union on the second day at Gettysburg "was pivotal to the Union victory on the third."

As Starks remembered: "In the height of the contest…where our brave men were falling like the leaves of autumn and to us there seemed to be little hope against the odds being thrown against [us]. One of the officers when men were wavering,…cried boys the "Old fifth Corps" never run yet, stand your ground. Twas like an electric shock. To a man they rallied, closed up the broken line and with one Herculanean effort hurled back the foe in confusion."

The regiment and Company A, in particular, paid a heavy price for their heroism. The regiment suffered 133 casualties, including three officers and 34 enlisted men killed or mortally wounded and three other officers and 75 other enlisted men wounded. Eighteen enlisted men became missing in the pursuit of Lee after the battle. Company A lost six men killed, one mortally wounded, and three others wounded, including Starks. Also, one enlisted man deserted and was arrested six days later. The six men who died on the battlefield were buried "in one grave, side by side." (B. Bennett 247)

From Gettysburg until the Wilderness in May 1864, a period of ten months, the 140th did a lot of marching and camping but little else. As part of the army that was pursuing Lee, it was present at the battles of Bristoe Station, Va. (October 14, 1863); and Rappahannock Station, Va. (November 7); and the Mine Run campaign (November 26–December 2), but was never involved in the fighting and suffered no casualties.

"In the winter camp of 1863–64, the regiment was outfitted as Zouaves. These flamboyant uniforms were patterned after elite French army units which had earned military glory in the 1850s, and were 'awarded' to the 140th in recognition of the regiment's seamless record." ("140th New York")

There were, nevertheless, a number of personnel changes among the Brockporters in Company A during that time, Starks was promoted to major, joined the regimental staff, replacing Isaiah Force who had been discharged for disability and Courtney was advanced from non-com status to become the company's second lieutenant. Three privates were promoted to corporal and one to Hospital Steward and one corporal became a sergeant. Private Henry Genet was mustered out for promotion to first lieutenant in the 24th NY Cavalry, where he later became a captain.

The company also lost 16 Brockporters for other reasons. Six were discharged for disabilities or wounds and six others were sent to the Veteran Reserve Corps for the same reason. Two were discharged with no reason recorded, one was transferred, and one died of typhoid. Finally, John Dean, who had disappeared at Gettysburg and was presumed dead or captured reappeared with a bizarre story of having been impressed into the navy.

In April 1864, the *BR* correspondent reported that Company A had left Rochester with 97 men and received by transfers and recruits 26 men, but 11 had deserted, 12 had died, and 30 had been discharged or transferred, so that only 70 remained. ("Zouave" in *BR* 5/5/1864)

WILDERNESS

The relative calm ended for the 140th in early May 1864. For nearly a year, it was involved in one campaign after another with devastating casualties. It began with the Battle of the Wilderness (May 5–7). In preparing for the battle that all realized was impending, Starks said to the chaplain, "I hope God will give me the grace to do my duty." (B. Bennett 389) The battle, at a place called Saunder's Field, was another Union disaster. The 140th formed the front line, together with five units of U.S. Regulars, in an assault across an open field against Confederate troops embedded in the woods opposite. The rebels opened up on them even before the charge began, but the Federals were not to fire until they had crossed the field. Yet, "when the order to charge was given, every man in line moved forward with a rush, not a single man hesitated, but each seemed to vie with the others to see which would first reach the woods on the opposite side and attack the enemy." (Cribben 49)

Foolhardy bravery was not enough, however. The regiment was almost destroyed. It sent 529 men into the battle, failed in its attack, was out-flanked and trapped, routed in disorder, and lost 268 soldiers, killed, wounded, or captured—in twenty minutes of fighting. (B. Bennett 411) Among the Brockporters in Company A, two were killed and one was mortally wounded, 12 others were wounded, of whom three were also captured, and six others were captured, of whom two died in prison. Of the 53 Brockporters who remained in Company A at the outset of the battle, only 32 survived unscathed, a forty percent casualty rate in twenty minutes. None of the five Brockporters who had enlisted in other companies of the 140th were still with them by this time. Also, August Meyer, who had been first lieutenant of the German company, B, and was promoted and transferred to take command of Company A when Starks had been promoted, was mortally wounded and expired 16 days later. Starks himself narrowly escaped. He was helping to organize the retreat, when a lieutenant at his side was shot in the leg. (Cribben 54)

After the Battle of Saunders Field, Starks, now a major, wrote his last letter:

> *Dear Folks at home—By the kindness of a kind Providence my life and health are still spared. Our regiment charged the enemy on Thursday afternoon and in the fight lost ten officers and two hundred and fifty-eight men* [of 529]. *Co. A had 31 killed, wounded, and missing...Our charge was made over an open field from one-quarter to a half mile. The enemy*

James S. Lowery of Clarkson, wounded in the Battle of the Wilderness, captured, and starved to death in prison. *Photo provided by Ron Erwin.*

> *were across the field in a piece of woods. We charged through the field under a most galling fire, and reached the first position of the enemy without a falter. Then the battle became terrific and lasted about twenty minutes, when heavy lines of the enemy were thrown upon each flank and far to our rear. Seeing this, our remaining few were ordered to fall back, which was done, though very much to the surprise of the commanding Generals, who... little expected to see the 140th again. But, thank God, about half of us are still permitted to face the enemies of our country, and through His aid and support hope soon to strike the death blow to this rebellion. Good bye.*

The next two days, May 6–7, saw some skirmishing and shelling that involved the 140th only peripherally and Company A suffered no casualties. Despite the humiliation and carnage of May 5, Starks remained hopeful. He wrote to a Rochester newspaper, "But, thank God, about half of us are still permitted to face the enemies of our country, and through His aid and support hope soon to strike the death blow to this rebellion." (B. Bennett 413)

SPOTSYLVANIA COURT HOUSE CAMPAIGN

The day after the conclusion of the Wilderness battle, the 140th was in action again with the beginning of the Spotsylvania Court House campaign (May 8–21, 1864). The regiment participated in three engagements: Laurel Hill (May 10), Salient (May 12), and Gayle's House (May 14). Grant's strategy had been to occupy a crossroads known as Spotsylvania Court House, separating Lee from Richmond and forcing him to fight in a disadvantageous position. (Phisterer lists the Piney Branch Church engagement and gives casualty figures, but neither Bennett nor Johnson and Buel mention it and no members of Company A were among the casualties.)

Lee reached the location first and was entrenched on a slight rise called Laurel Hill. The Federals had spent the previous sleepless, foodless night marching and were exhausted and suffering from extreme heat despite the early hour. They attacked the rebels in a hasty, disorganized fashion, some still bearing their knapsacks. Twice the Federals attacked and twice were driven back. Colonel George Ryan, who had replaced O'Rorke after Gettysburg, rallied his troops for a third try. He led them to within three rods of the enemy when he was shot dead. As Bennett says, "Major Starks managed to dismount and was trying to lead the regiment on foot when a bullet hit him in the forehead and crashed through his brain, killing him instantly."

Deacon Starks, his grieving father, wrote of Colonel Ryan and his son that they "now sleep beneath Virginia soil…My son has fought his last battle—his work on earth is done; and although I had calculated that he would be my stay and staff in old age, I freely give him up for my country. In my affliction I have much to comfort me…I think my soldier died like a soldier and a Christian, beloved not only in his native town, but in the army."

First Lieutenant Henry Allen of Brockport had commanded Company A after Meyer was wounded at the Wilderness. He and two enlisted men attempted to drag Ryan off the field, but both enlisted men were shot, one mortally, and Allen's hat was pierced by a rebel bullet, shaving some of his hair. He wrote to his family that his hair "was short enough before" but that "I went away without paying the barber that time." He later found three more rebel bullets in his trousers. Without his helpers, Allen was forced to leave Ryan where he lay. (B. Bennett 427) Bennett does not name the wounded soldiers, but Brockporter Graham R. Scott was wounded at Laurel Hill that day and died of wounds ten days later, and Edgar J. Warner was wounded and recovered but was discharged on October 26, 1864, at Rochester.

Another Brockporter was killed at Laurel Hill, two days later. Private Thomas Hewitt was detailed as cook for the officers. He brought some coffee to them at the front lines and, unthinkingly, stood erect with his head above the breastworks. He was picked off by a rebel sniper and died on the spot. (B. Bennett 435)

Starks's father, Deacon Israel Starks, traveled to Virginia to recover his son's body and assist the wounded as an agent of the U.S. Christian Commission. He assisted in tending the wounded in the Fifth Corps Hospital, where Company A's musician, Private Byron S. Blake, of Clarkson, was a hospital steward. (B. Bennett 450)

During the next phase of the Spotsylvania campaign (May 10–14), Grant tried one assault after another in a relentless, but ultimately unsuccessful, attempt to break through the rebel lines and separate Lee from Richmond. The 140th was much involved in that drive and suffered 60 casualties, including 20 deaths. No Brockporters were among them.

Grant's strategy finally achieved some success in its North Anna phase (May 22–31). Through luck and audacity, a substantial part of his army crossed the North Anna River, seriously compromising Lee's position. Those operations were relatively costless. Only nine men were wounded, none mortally, including no Brockporters.

Lee was not always the passive subject of Union attacks. Sometimes his troops took the offensive. The 140th, including Company A, was the victim of such an attack when three rebel divisions surprised the Union line at Bethesda Church on June 2, 1864. They were repulsed, but the regiment lost two men mortally wounded, ten others wounded, and 48 captured. Only about 200 men remained in service in the 140th. Robert Stickle and Henry E. Kincaid of Company A were wounded. Anson J. Seeley was captured and died of disease in Andersonville Prison on September 15, 1864. All three were Clarkson residents. The day prior to that engagement, Brockporter Lewis B. Courtney was promoted to first lieutenant.

PETERSBURG

Grant now turned his attention to the rail center Petersburg, believing that by cutting off the supplies that reached Richmond through that hub, he could starve the Confederate capital into submission. The 140th was part of the 100,000-man force that converged on Petersburg on June 16, 1864. However, through bad luck and miscalculations, they failed to capitalize on their surprise maneuver and did not take the city when it had been virtually undefended. The abortive attack on June 16–19 cost the 140th 22 casualties, including one officer killed and three enlisted men mortally wounded, none of them Brockporters. So, the massive force settled in for a long siege.

While the siege dragged on until the final week of the war in April 1865, forces were dispatched from time to time on forays out from Petersburg to disrupt further the rebels' transportation system. The 140th took part in one of those sallies, to capture the Weldon Railroad south of Petersburg on August 18–21, 1864. The engagement began badly with the Confederates trapping and capturing a large number of Union troops, including 51 members of the 140th. However, the Federals counter-attacked and gained and kept possession of that vital supply line for Lee's army and the Confederate capital and "seriously aggravated the already dire Confederate meat and forage shortages in Virginia." (Marcotte 219) Two Brockporters—Charles H. Stickle and Charles A. Bellinger, both of Clarkson—were among the prisoners and two others—Patrick Flynn and George A. Wright, both from the village—were wounded.

APPOMATTOX

Timothy Farrell, Sweden farmer, 19, of the 140th NYVI, was wounded three times, at the Wilderness, Spotsylvania, and White Oak Ridge. *Courtesy of the 140th NYVI Living History Organization.*

The 140th participated in other raids against the rebels' lines of communication during the fall of 1864 and suffered some 35 casualties, but no Brockporters were among them. During that time, Henry Allen's official promotion to captain finally came through on September 19, 1864. He had been commanding Company A since May 8, 1864. He was discharged a month later for disability and 31-year-old Lewis Courtney of Brockport succeeded him. On March 13, 1865, Courtney was promoted to captain in the U.S. Volunteers by brevet and cited for "gallant and meritorious services at the battles of the Wilderness and of the Weldon Railroad." (Phisterer 379) Thaddeus K. Burch, a 25-year-old farm laborer from Clarkson, was also promoted during that period, first to sergeant on September 1, 1864, and then commissioned a second lieutenant on March 7, 1865, with rank from February 14. Francis T. Clark, a 25-year-old Sweden farmer was promoted to corporal on May 7, 1865, and Alexander Shaw Jr., was promoted to sergeant on May 1, 1865.

Grant launched his final offensive in late March 1865. In an engagement on March 31 at White Oak Ridge, the rebels had some early success and captured a number of 140th soldiers, including George A. Wright of Brockport and George W. Estes of Clarkson. Both of them had been wounded in earlier action, Wright at Weldon Railroad and Estes in the Wilderness. In that same action, Timothy Farrell of Hamlin was wounded. He, too, had been wounded in the Wilderness. But, then, reinforcements arrived and the rebels were pushed back. The 140th was part of the Army of the Potomac that rolled over the grossly outnumbered Confederates in the final days of the war and were present for Lee's surrender at Appomattox Court House on April 9.

Mustering Out

Using the official records as reported by ACWRD, rather than the local sources used on page 47 of Chapter 3, 105 Brockporters appear on the roster of Company A. Twenty of them were mustered out with the regiment on June 3, 1865, at Alexandria, Virginia. Three of them had been POWs and two had been wounded. So, only 15 Brockporters survived with the company to the end unscathed. Nine others were mustered out in Rochester between June 21 and August 30, 1865. All of them had been wounded or captured or both. Four more were mustered out at other places at the war's end. Two of them had been wounded. Finally, no mustering out information is provided on two others. Of the six Brockporters in other companies of the 140th, only one remained at the war's end and he was mustered out from a hospital. Therefore, of the 111 Brockporters in the 140th only 17 were mustered out with the regiment at the end of the war without having been wounded or captured.

The Brockporters in Company A had a 23 percent mortality rate. Ten were killed, five died of wounds, two died in prison, and seven died of typhoid fever, for a total of 24. Nineteen others were wounded, five of whom were also captured and two of whom were wounded twice. So, of the 105, 41 percent were casualties. Twenty-one others were discharged or transferred with disabilities and five others were discharged without disabilities. Ten deserted. Leaving aside the deserters, those discharged without disabilities, and those mustered out without having been wounded or captured, 71 of the 105 were casualties of one sort or another. Of the six Brockporters in other companies, two were killed, two deserted, one was discharged with a disability, and one was mustered out from a hospital.

As to the regiment as a whole, it lost 384 men in the 39-day Wilderness campaign. Only 245 men on its roster of 1,648 answered to its final muster. ("140th New York")

For the most part, the Brockporters in the 140th fought heroically. They engaged in every major battle in the East from Chancellorsville to Appomattox and many lesser ones. Their role at Gettysburg was crucial to the success of the Union in that decisive battle. They suffered accordingly, as the casualty lists amply document. As officers and leaders, Milo Starks, Henry Allen, and Lewis Courtney, especially, stood out for their performance and were recognized for it. But the ordinary foot soldiers who followed them deserve equal credit.

Postscript

As with many other Civil War regiments, the members held periodic reunions for many years after the war. In 1894, the 140th met in Brockport. These Brockporters attended: Martin W. Haight, Henry Allen, Charles Bellinger, Aaron Hamill, Myron Hoy, John Mansler, Donain Richards, George Estes, Arthur S. Lewis, Joseph Leeper, John Lynd, Charles A. Perry, Charles W. Root, James Minot, John Clancy, A.D. Mosley, John Wilson, and Edgar Wadhams—18 of the 111. None of the deserters showed his face. Leeper made one of the three speeches. Henry Allen was elected vice president and M. W. Haight secretary. Richards and Bellinger were among the five at-large members of the executive committee.

Chapter 20

Company C, 22nd NY Cavalry

Recruitment

The recruitment process for this company was described in some detail in Chapter One and need not be repeated here. Also, that reference includes some personal information about Captain Franklin Edwards, the company recruiter and commander and Colonel Samuel J. Crooks, the regimental recruiter and commander. Either Edwards or Crooks or both must have had some kind of connection with Churchville, because 17 of the recruits came from there, including the other two company officers.

The personnel table on page 23 of Chapter 1 is based on the report in the *BR* of January 21, 1864, and differs considerably from the information in ACWRD. By analyzing and combining data from those sources and from Polk's letter in the *BD* June 5, 1885, the composition of the company by residence looks like this; Sweden had 27 recruits, including three who can be identified with Brockport; Clarkson had 13, and Hamlin had four. Apart from the three core towns, Churchville had 17, and Kendall and Murray had two each. Twenty-seven came from Rochester or outside Monroe County. Nine were recruited in Brockport but their residences are unknown. None of the recruits from Churchville or Rochester appear on the roster of graduates from the Brockport Collegiate Institute, so no previous connection to Brockport is evident. According to the *BR* (1/7/1864) Edwards had recruited all members of the company "by his own exertions," presumably including those outside the three-town area. Also, on March 25, 1864, three members of Company K

The battle flag of the 22nd New York Cavalry. *Courtesy of the New York State Division of Military and Naval Affairs.*

transferred to Company C. At least one of them was a Brockporter, James P. Cornes of Brockport. Then, on November 20, 1864, Sgt. Charles E. Spring of Clarkson, also transferred from Company K to Company C and was reduced in grade to private. (The Davis Report lists 24 Sweden men in company C.)

The recruitment process of the 22nd produced a phenomenon not seen with any of the other regiments reviewed so far in this book. Eleven men are identified in the ACWRD as having been mustered into Company C on various dates in November and December 1863 and then "rejected (date not stated)." No reason or explanation is given, except that Henry Shipp was "under age." None of those rejected is on the *BR* list, suggesting that they were rejected before that list was published on January 21, 1864. All of them were mustered as privates, ten in Brockport and one in Riga. One each was a resident of Sweden, Clarkson, Hamlin, and Rochester. I have been unable to identify the residences of the other seven. That accounts for most of the nine mentioned above. Subtracting those 11 from the 101 leaves 90, which compares closely to the 86 on the *BR* list. Also, it reduces the ACWRD roster for Brockport area recruits from 65 to 62.

The 22nd differed from the 8th NY Cavalry in one important respect. About half of the enlisted men and several of the officers were veterans of other regiments. Among the Brockporters in Company C, eight men had previous service, including five in the 13th NYVI and one each in the 1st and 17th NYVI regiments. Edwin A. Dayton had been a captain in the 94th NYVI before signing up as a private in the 22nd. However, they had all been infantrymen without cavalry experience.

OFFICERS

Franklin Edwards, the primary Brockport recruiter, became the company commander. He was a 25-year-old house painter from Brockport, who had earlier been rejected for service in the 13th NYVI. The other two officers were First Lieutenant Christopher C. Bruton, 22, and Second Lieutenant Franklin A. Collister, 28, both of Riga. Bruton was promoted to captain, August 1, 1864, though Edwards remained at that rank until he was discharged for disability March 29, 1865. Apparently the company had two captains at the same time. Bruton was awarded a Congressional Medal of Honor for having captured General Jubal A. Early's headquarters flag on March 2, 1865, and was promoted to major by brevet on March 13, 1865.

Here is a contemporary newspaper account of a ceremony of presentations of captured battle flags involving Bruton: "Captain Christopher C. Bruton, of company C, 22d New York cavalry, an aide-de-camp of General Custar, presented a Confederate national Standard, also used as General Early's headquarters flag. Captain Bruton stated that the flag had been presented to General Early the morning of its capture; that he saw it passing over the mountains, and followed it nearly three miles before he was able to secure it. He believed that Major Compson either captured or killed the bearer. The captain is a resident of Rochester, Monroe County, New York." (DMNA, from the *Washington Chronicle*, March 22, 1865)

Brockporter Henry C. Hammond portrays Captain Bruton a bit differently, describing a scene when Company C had charged across an open field against heavy enemy fire and taken temporary shelter behind an embankment:

> *While lying under the brow of this protective hill, Captain Bruton… complained of not feeling well, (which disease was hereditary with him when in close quarters) as he grew worse he unbuckled his sword belt and laid it down beside him. During the first lull in the firing by the Rebs, up*

> *jumped the Captain, and to the rear he ran with such swiftness that his coat tail spread out in the breeze and was flapping about his body with such force that the members of his company thought it might impede his progress, and hellowed to him to take it off, that he might better and quicker reach the goal he was trying so hard to accomplish.* (Crumb 51)

Collister was promoted to first lieutenant on January 12, 1865, after George Sperry, a transfer from an Illinois regiment, had held that office briefly. Those were the only officers the company had during the war. Edwin A. Dayton of Brockport, who had been an officer in the 94th NYVI, was commissioned a second lieutenant on July 24, 1864, but was not mustered at that rank and does not appear among the list of company officers in Phisterer. ACWRD says that he was commissioned a second lieutenant on that date, but was reduced in rank to private on August 13, 1864, and promoted to regimental sergeant major on February 1, 1865.

James Polk Cornes of Brockport deserves special mention. He was the son of Thomas Cornes, a leading Brockport citizen (see pages 43–44). He mustered in as a Commissary Sergeant in Company K. While still in training, he transferred to Company C on March 25, 1864. Then, on December 2, 1864, he was commissioned a second lieutenant, but not mustered and his commission was revoked. On February 1, 1865, he was re-commissioned a second lieutenant and on May 10, 1865, was transferred back to Company K. In 1885–87, he published a series of "Reminiscences of the War" in the *BD*. Fifty-seven have survived. In 1859, he had been a student at the Brockport Collegiate Institute. According to an article in the *Rochester Democrat & Chronicle* (5/25/30), brought to my attention by Carol Hannan, Cornes was court-martialed in July 1865 and convicted of insulting a guard. He did not learn of that action until three years later and did not get the conviction reversed until 64 years later.

Although only one of the company commissioned officers was from one of the three core towns, residents from Sweden and Clarkson dominated the ranks of the non-commissioned officers. Using the ACWRD roster, eight of the 14 men who held the rank of sergeant at some time came from Sweden and three each were from Clarkson and Riga. Four of the nine corporals were from Sweden, one from Clarkson and four from Riga. All four of the soldiers who held functional non-com titles (farrier, wagoner, or trumpeter) were from Sweden. Of the total number of 27 non-coms, twenty came from the two towns.

War Service, Training

The military career of the 22nd was closely parallel to that of the 8th NY Cavalry as described in Chapter 15. It began very poorly, even more poorly than the 8th, but, eventually, the 22nd became an effective fighting force, though it did not acquire the distinction of the 8th. Phisterer lists 47 "engagements, etc." in which "it or portions of it took part." One of its officers wrote twenty years later that it became "known as among the best fighting cavalry regiments in the service and gained words of praise and commendation for steadiness upon the field of battle." (Polk *BD* 6/5/85)

The 22nd began its training on foot in Rochester on January 5, 1864, and traveled to the Giesboro Point Cavalry Depot on the Potomac just outside Washington, on March 6, 1864, for its horsemanship training in preparation for its entry into combat. That period of time was not happy. The regiment was undisciplined and morale was low. At one point, they narrowly missed having their horses taken away and becoming an infantry unit. Henry W. Halleck, general-in-chief of the Union armies, called the regiment "undisciplined and unfit for the field." (Marcotte 190)

The Brockporters in Company C did not fare well during this period. Four of them died of disease, and James Caldwell of Clarkson was killed by another soldier in a fight. (*BD* 6/5/85) Also, while boarding the train to leave Rochester, "some of the boys in Company C became engaged in a dispute through some misunderstanding with Captain Frank Edwards, when the said Edwards drew his saber and striking right and left soon quelled the disturbance, but with the loss of his saber, which was broken short off at the hilt." (*BD* 6/12/85) Three Brockporters deserted. On the other hand, three Brockporters were promoted from privates during this period, Dayton to regimental sergeant major, Henry C. Hammond of Brockport to sergeant, and Charles M. Webb of Sweden to corporal.

Wilderness

On May 5, the 22nd saw its first action, in the Wilderness. It was an inauspicious beginning. Colonel Crooks mistook a Union cavalry regiment for the enemy and was removed from his command and arrested "for sending false information in relation to the enemy." (Marcotte 190) Part of the regiment was routed in confusion by rebels in the Wilderness on the

7th and again en route to Spotsylvania on the 8th. Their new commander, Major Peter McLennan, was called "stupid" by Major General Winfield Scott Hancock, his corps commander. In those two days, the regiment lost three men killed, eight wounded, and 97 missing; 27 horses killed, 241 horses missing, and four others died. (Marcotte 191)

Cornes reported, in his 1885 articles that:

> *The 22d New York cavalry came finely in position facing the Rebels who now began to show themselves on the edge of the woods fronting us. The rebel batteries were shelling the area, but without effect. Suddenly came the unexpected order, from no one knew to retreat in haste not a shot fired. The regiment stampeded about two miles before being stopped by another cavalry unit and ordered to return to the field from which it had just fled. However, Company C was separated from the rest and given a picketing assignment. No sooner had Captain Edwards begun to place the pickets than we received a volley from Stuart's cavalry. Again, Edwards ordered a retreat and, when Cornes and Brockporter Henry Hammond stopped and began returning the fire, he threatened that if they did not immediately join the command...he would place us under arrest.*

As a result of that retreat, Company C became separated from the rest of the regiment. Cornes alleged that Captain Edwards "had lost his head." He blamed the unwillingness of Edwards to confront the enemy on his cowardice. At least twice Edwards had given orders to retreat that were unwarranted by the situation, and now he sent a non-com riding ahead of the company with a flag of truce and orders to surrender the company "without striking a blow" if he encountered a force of rebels. (*BD* 10/2/85, 10/9/85) Cornes claimed that, "We were all angry and every man, without an exception, was talking of turning and fighting our way back to the regiment the way we came."

Next, Edwards sent Cornes, David H. Mowers of Sweden, and James Leak of Scottsville on a scouting assignment to find a Union regiment to join. While they were gone, the company departed the rendezvous site and eventually rejoined the regiment. The three scouts were left on their own. Leak caught up with the regiment, but Cornes and Mowers became lost. They wandered across the Virginia countryside in search of their regiment. They were captured by rebels three times, but managed to escape by one means or another each time. When they finally found a Union regiment, they were thrown in prison, first as deserters and later as stragglers. By July 9, more than two months away from their regiment, they had not yet been returned to it. There his story ends, as later copies of the *BD* have not survived.

The official records for the three of them contain no mention of their absence. They are not reported as captured or deserted. Evidently, they did return to their regiment. Cornes's subsequent career is reported above. Mowers was promoted to corporal on March 10, 1865, and to sergeant, July 12, 1865, long after Appomattox.

Six Brockporters in Company C are listed as having been captured by the rebels "(date and place not stated)." So, it cannot be determined if they became prisoners on those two days or later. However, the regiment lost 84 men and officers missing during May 5–22, 1864, and 125 during June 22–30, 1864, and only 47 during all the rest of its campaigning. So, it seems likely that they were lost in one of those two periods. One of the captives, Edward H. Billington of Sweden, is listed in the official records as having become a "POW (date and place not stated)" and "Deserted while a prisoner and enlisted in the Rebel Army." He had enlisted as a corporal, but had later been reduced in rank to private. Thomas Joice of Clarkson died of disease in Andersonville on July 27, 1864, so he certainly was captured in May or June. William Sager of Sweden also died in prison at Florence, South Carolina, but the date is not given. Henry C. Hammond of Brockport was promoted to first sergeant on June 16, 1864. So, presumably, his capture post-dated that. The official record for Thomas H. Black of Clarkson states that he was "released (date and place not stated)." Of the six, only Hammond and William Caldwell of Clarkson seem to have remained in prison until the end of the war.

SPOTSYLVANIA AND PETERSBURG

For the three weeks following the Wilderness battle, the regiment was assigned to guard Fredericksburg, (Marcotte 191) although Phisterer reports its engagement at Spotsylvania Court House (May 8–21), North Anna (May 22–26), and Totopotomoy (May 27–31). Then, in June, according to Phisterer, it fought at Cold Harbor (June 1–2), Long Bridge (6/12), Chickahominy and White Oak Swamp (6/13), Malvern Hill (6/14), and the siege of Petersburg (June 16–July 30). Side skirmishes during the siege were Kings and Queens Court House (6/18) and five skirmishes during the raid on the Southside Railroad (June 22–30). During that raid, the 22nd (and the 8th NY Cavalry, see above) participated fully in the destruction of key parts of the principal transportation connection between Lee and Richmond. No Brockporter was wounded or killed during those operations. However, the *BR* published a report from Major Dayton that Company C had been reduced to seven men because of captures and hospitalizations. (7/21/1864)

The Shenandoah Campaign

From August 1 through December 1864, the 22nd was part of General Philip Sheridan's campaign to clear the Confederates out of the Shenandoah Valley and to destroy its utility as a source of provisions for the rebel army. The Shenandoah had been the avenue used by Confederate armies under Lee and Jubal Early to invade Pennsylvania, Maryland, and Washington, and the base for raids by such forces as Mosby's cavalry. Sheridan and, later Custer, were ordered by Grant to stop that. The 8th and 22nd NY Cavalries were at the core of the Union troops.

In those operations, the 22nd finally came into its own as a fighting force. Phisterer lists 23 engagements in which the 22nd was involved between August 17 and December 21, 1864. The regiment was almost constantly on the move, chasing rebels and being chased by them, fighting them in skirmishes and pitched battles, scouting and picketing, patrolling the roads, and burning and otherwise destroying crops, stores, livestock, and anything else that the rebels might use.

About August 20, Company C was detached with two other companies to defend a covered bridge over the Opequan River. The squadron commander reported the action thirty years later:

> *Our 30 men...killed 5 and wounded 12 more, with a loss of only 3 wounded and not leaving the bridge until we were surrounded, the enemy having crossed above and below thereby exposing us to a cross fire while getting back to our supports which were 80 rods in the rear and who had hardly time to get into position before the advance was upon them. For an hour it was a hand to hand contest. Capt. Lloyd was shot through the body and fell from his horse. Shots were exchanged muzzle to muzzle with Cavalry and this was not all; throughout the day as we fell back it was one continuous fight both as dismounted and on horseback. (Crumb 19–20)*

In one engagement, at Tom's Brook, on October 9, they captured all of the enemy's artillery and wagons and 100 soldiers. (Burns 17) At Cedar Creek on October 19, they captured 45 artillery pieces, 32 caissons, 184 horses, 156 mules, 46 wagons, five battle flags, and 672 prisoners. (Burns 18) After retiring to winter quarters from January 26 until February 26, 1865, the 22nd attacked a rebel force at Waynesboro, Va., at the beginning of March and captured 11 artillery pieces, more than 100 wagons, and nearly 1,300 prisoners. (Burns 22) One of the soldiers reported to a Rochester newspaper on the Waynesboro battle, probably the high point of the military career of the 22nd:

> *So we started on a raid up the Valley, and travelled for four days before we came across the Johnnies. Our regiment was on the lead at the time, and we had a splendid opportunity of showing Gen. Custar what the "two two's" of New York was made of. The enemy was strongly entrenched at Waynesboro, and we lay in a piece of woods and let them shell us for an hour. Gen. Custar then dismounted two regiments and sent them on the right flank. He then sounded the bugle for the 22d to "charge," and charge we did, with a yell that completely astonished the rebs. We were inside their breast works before they were aware, and they never fired a shot. Our regiment captured over 900 of them—took two pieces of artillery and four battle flags. There was captured all-together 1,340 men, 8 cannon and 6 flags. (DMNA website)*

The 22nd suffered 49 casualties during the Shenandoah campaign, including one officer and eight enlisted men killed or mortally wounded, one other officer and 15 other enlisted men wounded, and two officers and 22 enlisted men captive. No Brockporters died or were wounded. However, Brockporters Henry Bond of Ogden, Heber Fuller of Brockport, and John Johnson of Riga died of disease during this time and Willard Sanford died of disease on an unknown date. Also, Hiram Murch of Hamlin deserted, Henry Neil of Riga was discharged, and Frank Collister, also of Riga, was discharged for disability on September 8, 1864, but his disability was "removed" and he returned to the company and was promoted from second lieutenant to first lieutenant on November 19, 1864.

THE END

Phisterer lists four engagements for the 22nd in February and March 1865, with only one casualty, a wounded enlisted man. With the end of the war, the regiment was mustered out. The mustering out process took place in stages. This was partly because the war continued through skirmishing in the Shenandoah Valley for some weeks after Lee's surrender on April 9. One Brockporter had been mustered out already in October 1864 and two more on May 18, 1865. Also, Captain Edwards was discharged for disability on March 29, 1865. Four more joined them in June and one in July. The remaining 34 members were mustered out on August 1. The mustering out dates of three are not known, but were probably after the war ended. So, a total of 44 Brockporters survived with the company until the end of the war of the 64 on my original roster, a shrinkage of 31 percent.

What is most striking about the combat experience of the 22nd as a whole and the Brockporters of Company C in particular is the low rate of casualties. The regiment had a total of 342 casualties, 248 of which were "missing." Thus, there were 94 killed or wounded. By contrast, the 140th had 736 casualties, including 457 killed or wounded, the 108th had 642 and 520, the 105th/94th had 941 and 503, and the 8th artillery had 1,202 and 953. Thus, the 22nd had only about one-quarter or less

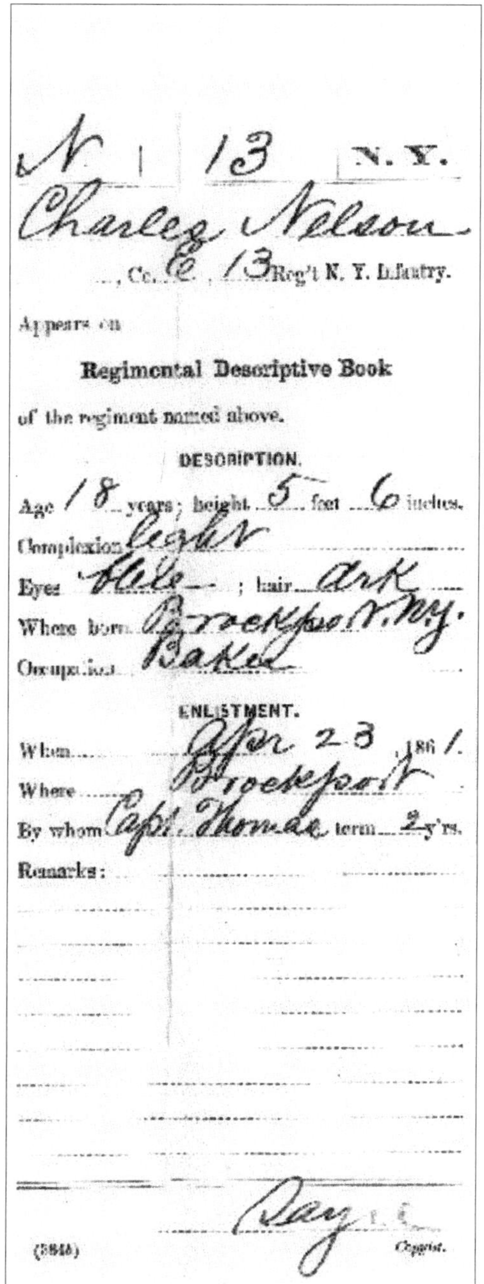

N | 13 N.Y.

Charles Nelson

Co. C, 13 Reg't N. Y. Infantry.

Appears on

Regimental Descriptive Book

of the regiment named above.

DESCRIPTION.

Age 18 years; height 5 feet 6 inches.

Complexion Light

Eyes Hale ; hair dark

Where born Brockport N.Y.

Occupation Baker

ENLISTMENT.

When Apr 23, 1861.

Where Brockport

By whom Capt. Thomas term 2 y'rs.

Remarks:

Day

(5848) Copyist.

The "Descriptive Book" entry for Charles Nelson, 19, Sweden farm boy who served in the 13th NYVI and the 22nd New York Cavalry.

the number of killed and wounded as any of the other regiments in which Brockport companies served.

Brockporters were similarly spared the losses of their counterparts in other regiments. None of them were killed. Only Charles Nelson was wounded and the six prisoners make for a total of eight casualties among the 64 Brockporters, a casualty rate of 12.5 percent. Brockporters had a 40.5 percent casualty rate in the 140th, 51.7 percent in the 108th, 23.7 percent in the 105th/94th, and 36.2 percent in the 8th artillery. Thus, the Brockporters in the 22nd had a casualty rate from one-fourth to one-half the rate of the Brockporters in the other regiments.

Besides those casualties, however, there were a number of other shrinkage factors. Eleven soldiers died of disease, one was killed accidentally, and two died in prison. The two who died as POWs were the only Brockporters who died as a result of enemy action. So, six times as many Brockporters died of disease or accident as were killed by the rebels. Also, five Brockporters deserted, two were discharged for disabilities, and one was discharged early with no reason given. Those total 22 of the 64 original Brockporters in the company.

The record of the 22nd is a bit of a mixed bag. The records of the early months of their service were not very creditable. However, they seem to have performed well on the Wilson Raid and were a very important part of the Union successes in the Shenandoah Valley campaign.

Chapter 21

Company B, 24th NY Independent Battery, Light Artillery

Recruitment

This unit, originally Company B of the Rocket Battalion of Artillery, had one of the most unfortunate experiences of any unit in the Union Army. The original roster included 213 names. Most (114) of the men were recruited from an area within ten miles of Perry, Wyoming County: Perry 74, Leicester 21, Mt. Morris 10, Gainesville 4, Castile 3, and Warsaw 2. However, a Monroe County contingent provided 34 men, 16 from Hamlin, 8 from Clarkson, and 10 from Rochester. The other 65 men came from places all across the state. (This section draws heavily on Julian Whedon Merrill, *Records of the 24th Independent Battery*, Ladies Cemetery Association of Perry, 1870, 280 +22p., reprint.)

The Hamlin-Clarkson group was recruited by Aaron Lester Cady, a 26-year-old Hamlin farmer with a 25-year-old wife and a two-year-old daughter. He seems to have been relatively prosperous, as his real estate was valued at $3,200 and his personal property at $725 in 1860. Cady was commissioned a second lieutenant when the unit was formed on October 5, 1861, but was promoted to first lieutenant on October 26. He became the captain on June 13, 1863, upon the resignation of Jay E. Lee, a former Hamlin resident who had moved to Perry and was the first unit commander. Besides the 24 men recruited by Cady in 1861, seven men from Hamlin and Clarkson joined the battery in 1864.

Cady was an exemplary officer. A sergeant, commanding one of his detachments, wrote of him after the war:

> *He participated in every battle in which the Battery was engaged, evincing the qualities of the good soldier. In entering the army he was actuated by a noble patriotism that led him to make great personal and domestic sacrifices, with cheerful alacrity, thoroughly comprehending the mighty issues of the long struggle; he always had a staunch faith in the integrity of the cause; and an unwavering confidence in its ultimate triumph.*
>
> *He was a faithful and diligent officer with a quick appreciation of the fidelity of the humblest member of the Battery; and a just pride in the intelligence, good discipline and splendid appearance of his command. (Merrill 24–25)*

As an example of his enterprise as a leader, while the unit was stationed at Newport Barracks, he organized and ran a sawmill operation that produced 15,000 board feet of lumber that was used to build quarters in New Berne.

At the Battle of Plymouth, Cady "was stunned by the discharge of a cannon and picked up for dead. Later he regained consciousness and was taken prisoner by the Confederates." (*BR* 9/16/09) After more than five months in prison, he and several other Union officers escaped on October 5, 1864, by jumping from a moving train into a swamp while being transferred from Charleston to Columbia, South Carolina. (Cooper) "After a weary experience in the swamps, forests, and mountains of the South, he reached the Union lines at Strawberry Plains, East Tennessee." (Merrill 25) The ordeal, however, destroyed his health and he resigned from the army January 13, 1865. He returned to Brockport, moved to Waterport, and died November 8, 1865. Forty-four years later, his widow received his captain's commission certificate that had been found in the basement of the Richmond, Virginia, post office, marked on the back "Taken from the body of a Yankee Captain at the capture of Plymouth, N.C." (*BR* 9/16/09)

Lee, a "young and successful lawyer" (Merrill 20), was the primary recruiter in the Perry area, planning to recruit a company to join an artillery regiment that he believed was being organized by a G. D. Bailey in Buffalo. The *BR*, however, believed initially that the company was planning to join a cavalry regiment. (10/24/1861) Only 20 men traveled from Perry to Buffalo, where they met twenty more from Monroe County. Somehow, their number increased to 56 by the time they left for Albany the middle of November. Merrill (141) says simply, "A consolidation of several squads of recruits, occupying the barracks

Officers of the 24th Light Artillery, including Captain Aaron Lester Cady of Hamlin, commander of Company B, not identified individually. *Courtesy of the Civil War Plymouth Pilgrims Descendants Society.*

at Albany, then formed" the Rocket Battalion, which, at that time "consisted of 160 men, equally divided between the two companies."

TRAINING AND PREPARATIONS

While at Albany, the unit became the Rocket Battalion under the command of Major Thomas W. Lion, a former British army officer and inventor of a military rocket, with which the battalion was to be equipped. The Battalion traveled from Albany to Washington via New York City, December 7–10, 1861. Extravagant claims were made for the rocket's ability to "throw forward a flame...sufficiently large to frighten horses" (145) to discharge "bombs, balls and percussion shot as well as rockets," to set fire to "buildings behind which the enemy may seek shelter," and to be able to launch "a ball of fire fifteen feet in diameter...over three miles."

When the fearsome weapons finally arrived in late March 1862, however, they were discovered to have another, less endearing propensity. The trajectory of the missiles was unpredictable. They were as likely to inflict death and destruction on the Rocket Battalion as on the enemy. The experiment was abandoned and the Rocket Battalion was converted to light artillery.

The six-month delay in getting properly equipped and the monotonous camp life resulted in low morale, much sickness, one death, much bickering, jealousy, charges and counter-charges of favoritism, injustice, insubordination, inefficiency, and courts-martial. (152)

Service in the Combat Zone

Finally, on April 26, 1862, the Battery left by steamer for the war front at Newport Barracks near New Berne, North Carolina, arriving there May 12. Still, their troubles were far from over. Major Lion was dismissed for incompetence. Their captain was "sick and unable to attend to his official duties" and "inefficient and given to intoxication." (159) The state of indiscipline in the Battery reached such a point that all its non-commissioned officers resigned, complaining of "want of discipline and of acts of injustice, deception, unredeemed promises and various minor difficulties." (160)

Then, on June 27, the commander of Company A attempted to combine the two units. Every member of Company B refused. As a result, Company A became the nucleus of the 23rd NY Independent Battery, Light Artillery, and Company B became the nucleus of the 24th NY Independent Battery, Light Artillery. To fill up the ranks, another recruitment drive was made in Perry, resulting in 58 recruits from the Perry area who were mustered into service in Buffalo on September 6, 1862.

By the time the new recruits had joined the unit and it was officially organized on November 4, 1862, only 19 of the Brockport area men remained. Edward Lawler of Hamlin had deserted on December 7, 1861, Henry Whitbeck of Hamlin had died in a hospital on February 3, 1862, and John Shell of Clarkson on April 24, 1862, and Michael Harrington of Clarkson on June 5, 1862 had been discharged for disabilities.

The reconstituted Battery now had five officers, 196 enlisted men, four artillery pieces, a few horses, and good food and shelter. (174) Quite naturally, the Perry contingent dominated the ranks of officers and non-coms. Cady was the only Brockport area man among the commissioned officers and Battery-level non-coms. The Battery was organized into six detachments headed by sergeants. Only one of the sergeants, Rufus C. Ainsworth of Hamlin of the First Detachment, was a Brockporter. Each detachment had a non-com designated "gunner." Two of them were Brockporters, Franklin D. Otis of Hamlin of the First Detachment and B. Franklin Corbin of Hamlin of the Fifth Detachment. Finally, four of the detachments had caisson corporals, one of whom was George G. Wright of Hamlin.

November 5th, the Battery had its baptism of fire when two detachments went on a scouting expedition with several other units under Captain Lee's command and returned with 12 prisoners. Brockporters Harlo Cook and Sylvanus King of Hamlin and Hiram Root of Clarkson were among the scouts.

On December 10, 1862, after five months at Newport Barracks, the Battery moved to New Berne itself and its First and Third Detachments were part of a force of some 10,000–15,000 troops that conducted a ten-day, 200-mile railroad-destroying expedition to Kingston, Whitehall, and Goldsboro, North Carolina. The Federals lost 90 killed and 478 wounded, but the 24th had only one casualty. Robert Turner of Owego was killed at Whitehall. Except for two minor skirmishes in July 1863 in which it suffered no casualties, the 24th saw no further action until a disaster at Plymouth, North Carolina.

Plymouth

On April 1, 1863, the Battery was posted to the defense of the Federal redoubt at Plymouth, N.C. It remained there for more than a year. On June 13, 1863, Captain Lee was discharged for disability and Cady was promoted to captain and given command of the Battery. He reorganized the unit, forming three Sections of two Detachments each. Each Section was headed by a lieutenant and each Detachment by a sergeant, a gunner, and a caisson corporal. He also appointed a second lieutenant as Chief of Caissons and the non-com ranks included an orderly sergeant, a quartermaster sergeant, three artificers, two buglers, a wagoner, and two cooks.

By now, only 15 Brockporters remained in the Battery. Joseph Wayne of Hamlin and Harlo Cook had been discharged for disability in January 1863, Franklin Otis died of disease on April 5, 1863, and Solon Rowel[l] of Clarkson was discharged for disability on April 7, 1863. Robert Bullock, of Hamlin inexplicably, does not appear on the reorganized roster. Rufus Ainsworth remained a sergeant and Corbin a gunner, and Wright and Samuel

Nichols of Sweden were promoted to gunners. No other Brockporters were non-coms.

The peaceful sojourn in Plymouth was disrupted violently on the morning of April 17, 1864, when a large Confederate force attacked. The 1,900-man garrison resisted the assaults of the 12,000–15,000-man Confederate force for three days, but, finally was overwhelmed and surrendered. The casualty report for the 24th shows that three enlisted men were killed or died of their wounds, five others were wounded, and one officer and 113 enlisted men were captured.

Of the 15 Brockporters in the company at the time, 13 were captured. Rufus Ainsworth had been arrested for desertion and was sent under guard to New Berne for court-martial at the time of the battle. Because all the witnesses to his desertion were captured, the court-martial was canceled. Talk about lucky! Also, Oliver G. Parmelee of Hamlin had not yet returned from re-enlistment furlough and was not with the unit when it was captured. Of the 13 who were captured, seven died in prison or soon after release from the effects of imprisonment. Of the six Brockporters who survived prison, Bullock and Cady were permanently disabled.

So, of the 23 Brockporters in the original company, one deserted (Rufus Ainsworth was restored to his rank as sergeant, so apparently his desertion was forgiven), five were discharged for disability, two died of disease unrelated to prison, seven died in prison, two were permanently disabled by prison, four survived prison without disability, and two were mustered out without having been imprisoned. None were killed or wounded from enemy action.

In March 1864, Captain Cady had returned to Brockport to recruit more men for his company. Although the *BR* reported (3/17/1864) that he was "quite successful," I can identify only two Brockporters, Philemon Farrell and Andrew J. Secor, both of Hamlin, who enlisted at that time. They had not arrived at Plymouth before the battle and, therefore, escaped imprisonment. Five others, Hiram Root, Charles W. Otis (brother of Franklin, who had died of disease at Plymouth 18 months earlier), William H. Hinton of Parma, John Corkwell of Clarkson, and Wallace E. Hughson and Lewis (or Louis) P. Thayer, both of Hamlin, enlisted in the reconstituted Battery in September or October 1864. None of them saw any combat and all were transferred to Company L of the 3rd NY Light Artillery in May 1865 after the war had ended.

Part IV

Brockporters in Other Units

Chapter 22

Other Brockport Soldiers and Sailors

Research Note

My most unexpected discovery in researching and writing this book has been the number of soldiers and (a few) sailors who served in units that were not recruited in Brockport. My original plan did not include them, but I noticed so many that I decided that no portrayal of Brockport's Civil War experience would be complete without them. The number and identities of Brockporters in the companies recruited in Brockport are relatively easy to discover. The *BR* reported on them extensively and the ACWRD has them nicely packaged. However, the Brockport area men who enlisted in units that were not recruited in the Brockport area are much more difficult to locate. Some are mentioned in the *BR*, others show up in cemetery records, the STCR and CTCR and the 1865 New York census. Some of my sources were postwar. Therefore, I included only men whose names appeared in the 1860 census for the Brockport area, unless I had persuasive independent information. After much thought, I decided to include men who served both in units recruited in Brockport and, also, in non-Brockport units, because all of their experiences are part of the history of the Brockport area in the Civil War.

The research problem is complicated by difficulties with the spelling of names. Everything was hand-written (military records, census sheets, letters, etc.) and the orthography was not always very good. Thus, a lot of names were misspelled in one place or another. For instance, the same man is listed as James Read, Reed, Reid, and Ready in different sources. Therefore, I am quite certain that the list of men that follows is incomplete.

AN OVERVIEW

My list has the names of 233 men from the Brockport area (or who were otherwise credited to the Town of Sweden) who served in 113 different army units plus the United States Navy, the U.S. Medical Corps, and the numerous sub-units of the Veterans Reserve Corps. Twelve units were U.S. Regular Army regiments, including five for "colored troops." Six were Illinois regiments, five were from Michigan, two each from New Hampshire and Indiana and one each from Kentucky, Wisconsin, Rhode Island, Ohio, and Pennsylvania. The other 81 were non-Brockport New York State units. In addition, I have identified six recruits from Sacketts Harbor credited to the Town of Sweden who served in five different units. This does not include 22 men who were recruited at Sacketts Harbor, credited to the Town of Sweden, and assigned to the Navy, but probably never served.

I have been able to identify 23 Brockporters who served in the regiments of other states, 17 who served in the United States Army, and five who served in the United States Navy. The other 188 served in New York State units that did not have Brockport as a recruitment base. Not included are the Brockporters who transferred from the 105th to the 94th (see page 199). Also, I do not include the 24 who were transferred to the Veterans Reserve Corps from other units.

The most popular non-Brockport units were the 8th NY Heavy Artillery (21 Brockporters), the 21st NY Cavalry (16), and the 1st NY Sharpshooters (15). All of them were recruited in Brockport though that was not their recruitment base. A case apart is the Veterans Reserve Corps to which 24 Brockporters transferred. This was a unit for soldiers unfit for combat duty but ineligible for disability discharges. Some soldiers served in more than one non-Brockport unit.

Why so many Brockporters joined non-Brockport units is a bit of a mystery. Some may have moved to the area recently and went to their earlier homes to sign up with their old friends. Others may have gone west to serve with friends whose families had moved there from Brockport. Others such as those in the colored troops, the sharpshooters, the medical corps, and the navy may have preferred their specialized character.

The pages that follow present capsule accounts of the wartime experiences of the units to which Brockport area soldiers (and one sailor) belonged. In their letters and oral reports to their families and friends, they added to the Civil War experience of the Brockport community. The units will be presented in numerical order. That is in numerical order of the designation of the units.

COMPANY K OF THE 1ST MICHIGAN REGIMENT OF CAVALRY

William W. Ransom, sergeant, a married 35-year-old from Hamlin, joined this regiment in April 1861, and died on August 3, 1864, at Finley Hospital in Washington, D.C. During Ransom's service, the 1st engaged in 47 battles and skirmishes. Among them were the Shenandoah Valley campaign, Cedar Mountain, Second Bull Run, Gettysburg, and Cold Harbor. For the entire period of its service, including the last eight months after Ransom's death, the 1st lost 148 officers and enlisted men killed or mortally wounded, 52 died in Confederate prisons, and 174 died of other causes, from a roster of 2,490.

COMPANY B OF THE 1ST NEW YORK DRAGOONS (CAVALRY)

Robert P. Curtis, a recruit from Sacketts Harbor credited to the Town of Sweden, served in this company from September 10, 1864, until mustered out on June 1, 1865. During his term of service, it was engaged in 29 battles and skirmishes in Virginia, including the Appomattox campaign. In those combats, it lost three officers and 33 enlisted men killed or mortally wounded, 11 other officers and 76 other enlisted men wounded, and 17 enlisted men captured.

COMPANIES C, D, F, AND M OF THE 1ST NEW YORK REGIMENT OF VETERAN CAVALRY

These companies, including seven men from the Brockport area, were mustered in on October 10, 1863. The regiment participated in 36 engagements between February 20 and November 22, 1864, serving in the Army of West Virginia and the Army of the Shenandoah, and were mustered out July 20, 1865. The 1,999 men on its roster suffered 281 casualties, including 51 officers and enlisted men killed or died of wounds, 15 other enlisted men wounded and recovered, and 136 officers and enlisted men captured. The Brockporters were:

Frank H. Dodge, a farm laborer from Clarkson. Dodge's age in the 1860 census was 15, but ACWRD gives it as 21 in 1863. Dodge was promoted to corporal and, later, to sergeant of Company D, and was mustered out with the regiment.

Langdon Hovey, a 22-year-old farm boy from the Town of Sweden, who transferred from the 14th NY Heavy Artillery Regiment to Company C of this regiment when it was mustered and was mustered out with it. The 1865 census calls him a laborer. No Langdon Hovey appears in the 1870 census.

George Maxon, a 20-year-old mason from Brockport, who had prior service in B Company of the regular U.S. Army's 14th Infantry regiment. He served in Company F and was wounded on July 6, 1864, at Maryland Heights, Md. In 1870, he was back in Brockport, listing his occupation as "mason, stone and brick."

George H. Soles, age 25 of Brockport transferred from the 14th NY Heavy Artillery to Company C of this regiment on October 10, 1863, as the commissary sergeant, but was reduced to sergeant on February 15, 1864, and mustered out on July 20, 1865.

James H. Snyder, age 18, joined Company M on November 19, 1863, after previous service in the 13th NYVI, was promoted to corporal on December 15, 1864, to sergeant on December 30, 1864, and busted back to private on July 1, 1865. He mustered out on July 20, 1865.

George W. Dudley, 22-year-old laborer from the Town of Sweden, enlisted in Company D as a private on August 14, 1863, after serving in the 29th Ohio Infantry, was promoted to Commissary Sergeant, and mustered out on July 20, 1864.

Peter Guelph, a 26-year-old native of Germany, whose 1860 residence is unknown but who was a saloon keeper in Brockport in 1870. He enlisted in Company C on October 10, 1863, became a corporal on July 1, 1864, and a sergeant on August 1, 1864, was busted to private on September 24, 1864, promoted again to sergeant on December 15, 1864, busted again to private on February 24, 1865, promoted again to sergeant on March 1, 1865, and mustered out on July 20, 1865. Earlier, he had served in the 28th NYVI.

Company I of the 1st United States Regiment of Colored Cavalry

This regiment was organized in December 1863 and first saw combat in May 1864. It took part in the siege of Petersburg and the operations against Richmond. After Lee's surrender, it saw action in Texas until February 1866.

Nathan P. Pond, a 32-year-old Brockport lumber merchant, was commissioned a major in this regiment on December 8, 1864, after serving in the 3rd NY Cavalry. He was promoted to lieutenant colonel on January 10, 1864, and discharged on April 14, 1865. (For his profile, see Chapter 3 above.)

Orville L. Howard, a 19-year-old Town of Sweden farm boy, was commissioned a captain in this regiment on December 22, 1863, at the time it was organized. He had served previously in the 3rd NY Cavalry.

Company F of the 1st Michigan Regiment of Engineers

Samuel Gibbs, a 34-year-old, English-born resident of Sweden, enlisted in this company on December 22, 1863, and was mustered out on September 22, 1865. He does not appear on the 1860 or 1870 censuses for the Brockport area. During Gibbs's service, this regiment built a railroad from Nashville, Tenn., to the Tennessee River, as well as related structures. From June until September 1864, it rebuilt and repaired roads and bridges through eastern Tennessee and Georgia as Sherman advanced on Atlanta. From November 16 to December 11, 1864, it accompanied General Sherman on his march from Atlanta to Savannah, destroying railroad track and bridges and building roads and bridges to facilitate the advance. The regiment was then transferred to the Carolinas performing similar activities. Because it was usually non-combatant, its losses were relatively light: with a roster of 2,920, it lost only six men killed or mortally wounded and two died in Confederate prisons. However, 280 of its men died of disease and another 279 were discharged for disabilities.

Companies E, H, and L of the 1st New York Regiment of Mounted Rifles

George L. Barnes, 32-year-old Brockport carriage-maker, enlisted in Company E on August 5, 1862, and deserted on May 16, 1863. Earlier, the *BR* had reported on April 25, 1861, that Barnes had enlisted in Company G of the 13th New York Volunteer Infantry, but the ACWRD has no record of that. James H. Snyder, an 18-year-old farm laborer from Gaines, enlisted in Company H August 8, 1862. His discharge date is not given. Earlier, he had served in the 13th NYVI. During Barnes's service in the 1st, it took part in 29 battles and skirmishes, mainly in Virginia, including the siege of Suffolk. It lost one officer and 11 enlisted men killed or mortally wounded, 24 other enlisted men wounded, and 15 enlisted men captured. Henry H. Nichols, 25-year-old Hamlin resident, transferred to Company L from the 3rd NY Cavalry on July 4, 1865, and from here to the 4th NY Provisional Cavalry on September 6, 1865. As the war was over by the time of his transfer, his unit saw no combat. In 1870, Snyder was a mason in Knowlesville.

Company E of the 1st New York Regiment of Marine Artillery

Reuben Root, a 24-year-old Town of Sweden blacksmith, enlisted in this regiment on January 14, 1862, as it was being organized. He was promoted to sergeant on February 6, 1862, to quartermaster sergeant on March 1, 1862, and discharged for disability on November 21, 1862. This regiment was raised and organized at New York City for service on gunboats, which were to be provided for it. During Root's service it engaged in combat operations 13 times and lost one officer and 15 enlisted men killed or mortally wounded, 14 other enlisted men wounded, two captured, and one officer and 72 enlisted men died of other causes from a roster of 1,453 men. Root later served in the 22nd NY Cavalry.

COMPANY B OF THE 1ST NEW YORK REGIMENT OF INFANTRY

Henry F. Jacoby, 27-year-old Brockport engineer enlisted as a private on April 22, 1861 (the very beginning of the war), was promoted to sergeant on May 15, 1862, was wounded and taken prisoner at Charles City Cross Roads, Va., on June 30, 1862, during the Seven Days' Battle, was paroled, and was discharged from the hospital for disability on December 11, 1862. During his service, the 1st lost 42 enlisted men killed or mortally wounded, six other officers and 114 other enlisted men wounded, two officers and 65 enlisted men captured, and three officers and 31 enlisted men died of disease and other causes from a roster of 1,267. Later Jacoby served in the 158th NYVI.

BATTERIES C, H, AND L OF THE 1ST NEW YORK REGIMENT OF LIGHT ARTILLERY

William H. Thompson of Brockport was mustered into Battery C on August 18, 1864 after serving in the 140th NYVI. ACWRD says that William H. Peterson, who had been in the 94th NYVI earlier, was transferred to Battery H on December 1, 1863, though ACWRD lists no Battery H for this regiment and no WHP in Batteries A–G. After December 1, 1863, the regiment fought at Totopotomoy, Cold Harbor, White Oak Swamp, and Petersburg. After Thompson joined, it was engaged in the assault on Petersburg, Weldon Road, Hatcher's Run, and the Appomattox campaign. During the first of those periods, it lost six enlisted men killed or mortally wounded, 35 other enlisted men wounded, and one officer and 29 enlisted men captured. During the latter period, it lost three officers and 42 enlisted men killed or mortally wounded, five other officers and 128 other enlisted men wounded, and six officers and 192 enlisted men captured—a very high casualty rate.

COMPANIES E AND G OF THE 1ST KENTUCKY REGIMENT OF VOLUNTEER INFANTRY

Joseph M. Leiper enlisted in Company E as a first sergeant on June 3, 1861, and in Company G as a first lieutenant on June 22, 1862. ACWRD reports that he resigned on June 8, 1863. However, it also reports that he was commissioned a first lieutenant in the 140th NYVI on August 10, 1862, and served in that regiment until he was discharged on March 26, 1864. For a more detailed account of his army career, see Chapter 3 above. This regiment was organized in June 1861, and "performed much valuable service in the early engagements of the war" in West Virginia. In January 1862, Company E was detached as an artillery unit and the regiment "took an active part in the advance on Nashville, Tenn." (The Union Army, ACWRD)

6TH COMPANY OF THE 1ST NEW YORK BATTALION OF SHARPSHOOTERS

This unit was supposed to have been part of a regiment that did not fill up. So, the four companies that were formed were attached to other regiments. The 6th Company was organized on September 13, 1862, and assigned initially to the 108th NYVI. In October 1863, it was transferred to the famous Iron Brigade (Farnham, *BR* 11/5/1863, J. Bennett 48) and mustered out on June 3, 1865. Phisterer does not list the engagements of the individual companies of the Battalion, but only "the battalion, or portions of it." He lists 21 engagements, including the Wilderness campaign, the siege and assault of Petersburg, and the Appomattox campaign. He lists as casualties for the 6th Company ten enlisted men killed in action or mortally wounded, nine other enlisted men died of disease, and four enlisted men died in captivity. These Brockporters served in this unit:

Albert Adams, 25-year-old from Chili, who died a week after being mustered in.

Theron Ainsworth, a 26-year-old Brockport painter was among the 53 members of the Battalion who were captured at Weldon Railroad, was paroled in March 1865, and mustered out with the Battalion. In 1870, he was living in Plainwell, Mich., with a wife and year-old child, plying his trade as a painter again.

Hector A. Butler, 25-year-old painter from Kendall Mills, Hamlin, who was discharged for disability on January 4, 1864.

James S. Edwards, 21-year-old English-born farm laborer from Ogden, who was discharged for disability on August 15, 1863. In 1870, he was a farmer in Belmont, Wisc., with a wife, four children, real estate worth $8,000, and personal property of $1,000.

John T. Farnham, 20-year-old printer from Brockport, who was mustered out with the Battalion. After the war, he resumed his trade as a printer, but he suffered from tuberculosis and died, unmarried, in 1869 at age 27. (I have transcribed six of his wartime diaries.)

George N. Goold, 23-year-old clerk from Brockport, who was killed at Petersburg on June 18, 1864.

William Hughes, a 44-year-old man from Kendall Mills, Hamlin, who mustered out with the Battalion.

M.D. McDougal, a 31-year-old man from Parma, enlisted on August 9, 1862, and on January 15, 1863, was transferred to the Veterans Reserve Corps.

Nelson Miller, 21-year-old from Kendall Mills, Hamlin, who deserted February 5, 1863. In 1870, he was a "boot & shoe maker" in Kendall Mills with a wife, one child, and an estate of $1,500.

John Moore, 32-year-old laborer from Brockport, whose discharge is not recorded.

Henry C. Murray, 31-year-old farm laborer from North Clarkson, Hamlin, who mustered out with the Battalion.

Jackson P. Nichols, 18-year-old farmer from North Clarkson, Hamlin, who was captured in the Battle of the Wilderness on May 5, 1864, and died in Andersonville prison on August 7, 1864.

George W. Raymond, a 30-year-old man from Parma who enrolled on August 9, 1862, and was discharged for disability on February 6, 1863. In 1870, he was a bookkeeper in St. Clair, Mich., with a wife, three children, a housekeeper, and an $1,100 estate.

Samuel G. Robinson, 20-year-old Canadian-born farm laborer from the Town of Sweden, who was promoted to corporal on April 10, 1864, and mustered out with the Battalion. In 1870, he was a laborer in Rochester's 7th ward with a wife and two-year-old child.

John C. Parker, a 24-year-old single machinist from Hamlin, enlisted on August 22, 1862, was captured on August 19, 1864, on the Weldon Railroad raid, spent three months in prison, and was discharged on June 1, 1865. In 1870, he was a married reaper machinist in Brockport.

2nd Illinois Battery

According to the STCR, but not the ACWRD, William McIntyre, earlier in the 13th NYVI, "was mustered into 2nd Ill Battery Oct 1863 as 1st Lieut promoted to Captain Nov 1863 was taken prisoner at Fort Darling in March 1864 was paroled about 14 Nov 1864 discharged about the 15 of December res Bkpt" However, none of the Batteries of the 2nd Illinois saw action in Virginia, where Fort Darling (Drewry's Bluff) was located. Moreover, the Battle of Drewry's Bluff took place in May 1862, before McIntyre's supposed service.

Company E of the 2nd New York Provisional Cavalry Regiment

George Good transferred from the 15th New York Cavalry Regiment on June 17, 1865, (after the war) and was mustered out on August 9, 1865. He is not listed in the 1870 census in New York State.

Company L of the 2nd New York Veteran Cavalry Regiment

This regiment was largely composed of veterans of the 30th NYVI, which had been discharged by reason of the expiration of their terms and whose re-enlistees were converted to a cavalry regiment in August 1863. Its entire term of service was spent in the Deep South. It participated in 40 engagements during 1864, almost all in Louisiana, and eight more in March and April of

1865 in Florida and Alabama. Its casualty rate was relatively light, losing 102 killed, wounded, or captured from a roster of 1,895, an 11 percent rate, but 215 of its members died of other causes, including a large number who drowned when their transport foundered off the coast of Florida. George Guenther, joined this regiment at the time of its conversion and served with it until it was mustered out on November 8, 1865, nearly seven months after the war ended. He was a 36-year-old resident of Brockport in the marble business. Before joining the 2nd, he had served in the 13th NYVI and the 8th NY Cavalry.

COMPANY M OF THE 2ND NEW YORK REGIMENT OF HEAVY ARTILLERY

Henry Loomis transferred here from the 9th New York Regiment of Heavy Artillery on June 27, 1865, and mustered out on September 29, 1865. As the war had ended, he saw no action in this regiment.

COMPANIES B, F, AND G OF THE 2ND UNITED STATES COLORED CAVALRY

This regiment had been organized on December 22, 1863. Enos B. Wood, a farm boy from Parma, age 19, was commissioned into Company G as a second lieutenant on December 28, 1863, promoted to first lieutenant on August 1, 1864, to major by brevet on March 13, 1865, and reverted to captain on October 10, 1865. Thomas S. Hinton of Hamlin, who was 21 in 1862, transferred from the 3rd NY Cavalry to join Company F as a second lieutenant on April 7, 1864, and was mustered out May 11, 1865. Lucius A. Howard, a 24-year-old hack driver who had been living in the American Hotel in Brockport, was appointed to Company B as a second lieutenant on February 23, 1864, but was never mustered. Both had served previously in the 3rd NY Cavalry. During the service of Wood and Hinton, the 2nd took part in 27 engagements, including the capture of Bermuda Hundred, operations in the Petersburg area, and the Richmond campaign and served in Texas from June 1865 until mustered out in February 1866. It lost one enlisted man killed and one wounded. In 1870, Wood was back with his family, now farming in Hamlin, Hinton was a butcher in Parma with a wife and small child, and Howard was farming in Deerfield, Oneida County, with a wife and three small children.

COMPANIES C, F, L, AND M OF THE 2ND NEW YORK REGIMENT OF MOUNTED RIFLES

These companies were mustered in the fall of 1863 and January 1864 and left the state in March 1864. Between May 15, 1864, and April 9, 1865, they saw action in 27 engagements, including the siege and assault of Petersburg and the Appomattox campaign. With 1,686 men on its roster, the regiment lost nine officers and 96 enlisted men killed in action or mortally wounded, one other officer and 112 other enlisted men were wounded, and 112 died of disease, including 20 enlisted men who died as POWs. At least three Brockporters served in the company. Oromel H. Ball, a 39-year-old Sweden resident, enlisted in Company C on January 4, 1864, was promoted to saddler, then regimental saddler and then busted back to private. He was discharged for disability on February 25, 1865. Charles Woodruff, an 18-year-old Hamlin man, enlisted in Company L on October 19, 1863, and was transferred to Company A of the Veteran Reserve Corps on April 1, 1865. John L. Kinney, a 32-year-old Brockport tailor, enlisted in Company M on November 11, 1863, and was mustered out on June 5, 1865. Benjamin Soles, is claimed for the Town of Sweden in the 1865 census, but was a saloon keeper in Schenectady in the 1860 census. He enlisted at age 44 on January 4, 1864, and was killed at Petersburg on July 22, 1864.

COMPANY E OF THE 2ND WISCONSIN REGIMENT OF INFANTRY

Hiram J. Cusick, a single resident of Hamlin, enlisted in this company on December 1, 1861, was wounded at Antietam on September 17, 1862, discharged for disability on December 26, 1862, and enlisted in the 8th Wisconsin Cavalry regiment in March 1864. ACWRD has no listing for an 8th Wisconsin Cavalry and no other listing for a Hiram Cusick to match this one.

Batteries F and L of the 3rd New York Light Artillery (Veteran)

Edwin Loomis, a 19-year-old student from the Town of Sweden, enlisted in Battery F on December 7, 1861, as a musician. He re-enlisted on January 2, 1864 and was mustered out on June 24, 1865. Battery F served in North Carolina from March 1862, in South Carolina from January, 1863; and in Florida from September, 1864. Loomis is not in the 1860 or 1870 censuses. With a roster of 374, Battery F lost one enlisted man killed, eight wounded, and two captured. Philemon Farrell and Andrew J. Secor, two 18-year-old farm boys from Hamlin, joined Battery L on March 24, 1864, and were mustered out on July 7, 1865.

In 1870, Secor was a farmer in the Town of Murray with a wife and two small children. This unit underwent a number of redesignations and reassignments before Farrell and Secor enlisted. During their service, it fought in 14 engagements, including Petersburg and the Appomattox campaign, between May 5, 1864, and April 9, 1865. Gustavus Barker transferred from the 24th NY Light Artillery into Battery L on March 5, 1865. John Corkwell did the same three weeks later (see page 252). With a roster of 408 men, it lost 14 enlisted men killed or mortally wounded, 18 others wounded, eight captured, and four died of other causes. James Johnson a 35-year-old gardener from Parma, enlisted on November 5, 1864, no Battery indicated, and was mustered out on June 24, 1865. He was buried in a Sweden cemetery. James Williams enlisted on September 19, 1864, no Battery listed, as a substitute for John M. Dimick of Brockport. No mustering out date is given.

Companies E and I of the 3rd United States Regiment of Infantry (Regular Army)

Edwin Spitzer, a 22-year-old Town of Sweden laborer in 1865, enlisted as a private on February 15, 1861 (before Fort Sumter) and served for 35 months. He transferred from Company E to Company I at an unknown date. Although this regiment fought in the Peninsular campaign and at Second Bull Run, Chancellorsville, Gettysburg, Antietam, Fredericksburg, and Mine Run, it lost only four men killed, 20 wounded, and eight captured.

3rd United States Veteran Volunteer Regiment of Infantry

Joseph M. Leiper enrolled as a captain in this regiment on January 1, 1865, after having served in the 1st Kentucky Volunteer Infantry and the 140th NYVI and was discharged on May 31, 1865. This regiment was one of ten that were recruited in late 1864 and early 1865 to be elite units. The 3rd was organized in February and March 1865 and served in the defenses of Washington, seeing no combat while Leiper was a member.

Company E of the 4th United States Regiment of Colored Cavalry

Edward W. Bangs, a 20-year-old farm boy from Ogden who had served earlier in the 13th NYVI and the 82nd U.S. Colored Infantry, was commissioned a captain in the 4th on January 20, 1864, and mustered out with the regiment on March 20, 1866. According to ACWRD, the 4th was not organized until April 4, 1864. During its entire service, it was assigned to the defense of New Orleans and other places in Louisiana and Alabama. ACWRD has no casualty record for it.

4th United States Artillery

According to ROEM, Daniel McCarty, a 22-year-old Sweden farmer, enlisted in this regiment, without specifying if it was light or heavy in February 1862 and served for 27 months before being captured and dying in a Confederate prison. ACWRD has no information on a 4th U.S. Heavy Artillery. There were 13 batteries in the 4th U.S. Light Artillery with greatly differing combat experiences. ACWRD has no record of Daniel McCarty in any of them and ROEM does not list a battery. Moreover, the STCR lists a Daniel McCarty as a recruit from Sacketts Harbor.

COMPANIES B AND I OF BATTERY B AND BATTERY H OF THE 4TH UNITED STATES LIGHT ARTILLERY

John Duffy, a 32-year-old Irish-born Town of Sweden farmer, enlisted in February 1862 as a private. He transferred from Company B to Company I. This Battery took part in almost all of the major battles in the East from March 1862 until Lee's surrender, including Fredericksburg, Second Bull Run, Antietam, Chancellorsville, Gettysburg, the Wilderness, Petersburg, Five Forks, and the Appomattox campaign. However, its casualties were very light, only three men killed and nine wounded.

Daniel McArty [or McCarthy], a 19-year-old Irish-born Brockport resident, enlisted in Battery H as a sergeant in February 1862, and was mustered out in February 1865. This Battery fought in the Army of the Ohio and the Army of the Cumberland, mainly in Tennessee, but also in Alabama, Kentucky, and Georgia, including at Shiloh, the siege of Corinth, Chickamauga, and the siege of Chattanooga. Casualty information is not available. (I am unable to determine if there were two Daniel McArtys.)

COMPANY L OF THE 4TH NEW YORK PROVISIONAL CAVALRY

Henry H. Nichols, 25-year-old Hamlin resident, transferred here from the 1st NY Mounted Rifles on September 6, 1865, and was mustered out on November 29, 1865. As the war had ended before his service, he saw no combat in this unit. In the 1870 census, he was living in Otsego, Mich., as a hotel keeper.

BATTERIES C AND K OF THE 4TH NEW YORK REGIMENT OF HEAVY ARTILLERY

Battery K originally had been one of four companies organized as part of the 11th New York Regiment of Heavy Artillery between February 7, 1863, and July 25, 1863. It failed to fill and the four companies were formed into a battalion which took part in the Gettysburg campaign of June and July 1863. On October 16, 1863, they were incorporated into this regiment.

Company C was one of the first eight companies that were organized between November 1862 and February 1863. Initially, the regiment was assigned to the defense of Washington, but later took part in 23 engagements in the Peninsular, Petersburg, and Appomattox campaigns. Also, it helped put down the New York City draft riots of July 13–16, 1862. It lost eight officers and 117 enlisted men killed or mortally wounded, 12 other officers and 293 other enlisted men wounded, eight officers and 341 enlisted men captured, and four officers and 335 enlisted men died of other causes. Most of the captives (322) were taken during the Weldon Railroad raiding expedition at Reams' Station.

Mathew Cusick, a 29-year-old member of a Hamlin family who had removed to Metamora Township, Mich., and had served in a Michigan regiment, returned to New York State to join Battery K, enlisting on April 6, 1863. He was discharged for disability on September 17, 1865. ACWRD has no Mathew Cusick in a Michigan unit, but has one in the 8th United States Army Infantry Regiment.

James B. Root, a 24-year-old Hamlin laborer, enlisted as a private in Company C from August 7, 1862, until October 14, 1863, when he transferred to the 21st NY Cavalry.

Marion Patterson, a 22-year-old Clarendon farmer, enlisted in Battery K on June 21, 1863, was promoted to first sergeant on June 21, 1863, and was discharged on January 4, 1864, no reason given. Earlier, he had served in the 13th NYVI.

Joseph Thompson, a 21-year-old farm laborer from Hamlin who had served previously in the 13th NYVI, joined Battery C on June 21, 1863, and was discharged on August 4, 1865.

COMPANY D OF THE 5TH NEW YORK VETERAN REGIMENT OF INFANTRY

Thomas Rogers was a member of this unit from June 3, 1865, nearly two months after the war ended, until August 21, 1865, when the regiment was mustered out. However, he was AWOL on that date. During his time in the regiment, it performed only routine duties. Rogers was a 22-year-old from Brockport who had deserted from the 13th on December 30, 1861. For punishment, on January 30, 1865, he had been assigned to Company K of the 140th NYVI "to make good time lost by desertion" and was transferred from there to the 5th.

Company H of the 6th New Hampshire Regiment of Infantry

George Williams transferred from the 11th New Hampshire Volunteer Infantry on June 1, 1865, and mustered out on July 17, 1865. Obviously, this unit saw no action in the war. In 1870, Williams was a moulder living as a single man in Brockport.

Company C of the 6th New York Regiment of Cavalry (Veteran)

Alphonso P. Moore, a 21-year-old Clarkson farm laborer, joined this unit on September 23, 1861, and deserted four days later. In 1870, he was a school superintendent in Shelby County, Ohio.

Companies G and I of the 6th United States Regiment of Cavalry

This regiment participated in 11 engagements, including Gettysburg, and lost five killed, 22 wounded, and 20 captured. Brockporters in the regiment were:

Thomas McCoy, a 29-year-old Irish-born miller from Brockport, enlisted on September 5, 1861, and served until September 5, 1864. STCR says he re-enlisted in the "82nd Regiment," but I cannot find that in ACWRD. He spelled his name without the "Mc" gave his occupation as carpenter in the 1860 census and used the "Mc" and gave his occupation as miller in the 1865 and 1870 censuses—same wife and four children.

Edward Maguire, a 23-year-old native of Ireland and resident of the Town of Sweden, enlisted in this regiment in September 1861, and served until mustered out in September 1864. The STCR says he was living in Brockport in 1866, but he does not appear in the 1870 census.

Samuel Tooth, a 26-year-old moulder from Brockport whose enlistment date is unknown.

George Myers, a 46-year-old German-born Clarkson farm laborer, is on the roster of Company G, having enlisted on August 18, 1861, though he is also reported to have enlisted in the 8th NY Cavalry on September 20, 1861, and deserted on October 10, 1861. Perhaps he deserted the U.S. Cavalry to join the NY Cavalry.

Company E of the 7th New York Regiment of Artillery (Heavy)

Henry Cusick, a 21-year-old Hamlin resident, served briefly in this company from February 11, 1863, until he deserted on March 11, 1863. This period coincides with his service in the 13th NYVI and began about two months after he had been wounded at Fredericksburg. I suspect that he took French leave during his recovery and gave a light artillery unit a try, then returned to the 13th where he served out his enlistment. During his brief service, the regiment was assigned to the defenses of Washington and saw no combat or casualties. Later, Cusick served in the 18th and 25th NY Light Artillery regiments.

Company F of the 7th Illinois Regiment of Cavalry

Charles F. Lee, the son of Elon Lee of Clarkson, but resident in Bowling Green, Ill., joined this regiment as a first lieutenant on September 3, 1861, and died of unknown causes on October 12, 1863. Although he was not a Brockport area resident at the time of his commissioning, his experiences were part of Brockport's history as reported in the *BR* (10/29/1863). Edgar Vayo, a 19-year-old farmer from the Town of Sweden, enlisted in this regiment on August 10, 1861, and served three years. Emmet [or Edmond] Crary, a 20-year-old Sweden resident, enlisted as a private on August 10, 1861, was promoted to corporal, re-enlisted on March 30, 1864, and mustered out on November 4, 1865. Their unit participated in several campaigns in Tennessee. It had 28 officers and enlisted men killed in action, 45 wounded, and 85 POWs.

Company F of the 7th Michigan Regiment of Infantry

Thomas Carlysle, a Clarkson butcher, enlisted here on August 9, 1861, and was discharged on February 5, 1864. In 1870, he was again a butcher in Clarkson. His age in 1861 is given as 26, 29, 31, and 35 in various sources. During his service, the 7th fought at Ball's Bluff, in the Peninsular campaign, at Antietam and Bristoe Station, and helped quell the New York City riots. It was commended numerous times for its steadiness under fire, gallantry in action, and stubborn resistance when confronting the enemy. On a roster of 1,375, it lost 183 officers and enlisted men killed in action or mortally wounded, 147 deaths from disease, 17 deaths in Confederate prisons, and 344 disability discharges.

Companies D, E, F, H, I, K, and M of the 8th New York Regiment of Artillery (Heavy)

Twenty-one area men joined seven companies of this regiment on 16 different days. The regiment was organized August 22, 1862, as the 129th NYVI and converted to the 8th NYHA on December 19, 1862. It took part in 14 engagements of the Peninsular campaign between May 17, 1864, and March 25, 1865, and in the Appomattox campaign of March and April 1865. With a roster of 2,956 men, it lost 20 officers and 344 enlisted men killed or mortally wounded, 27 other officers and 562 other enlisted men wounded, one officer and 242 enlisted men captured, and four officers and 302 enlisted men died of other causes, including one officer and 113 enlisted men in captivity, a 45 percent attrition. The Brockport area men were:

Alexander Johnson of Brockport enlisted in Company F on December 27, 1863, was wounded at Petersburg on June 16, 1864, and was transferred to

Private George W. Walker, Hamlin farmer, 19, in Company H of 8th Heavy Artillery, captured and wounded at Cold Harbor, died of wounds in prison. *Photo provided by Mary Smith.*

the Veteran Reserve Corps on March 20, 1865. In 1870, he was a 37-year-old Brockport hotel-keeper with a wife and year-old daughter.

George W. Walker, a 19-year-old farmer from Hamlin, enlisted in Company H on December 28, 1863. He was wounded and taken prisoner at Cold Harbor and died of his wounds on June 11, 1864, at Richmond, Va., Confederate Hospital.

John J. Hard, a 20-year-old Kendall man, enlisted in Company K at Clarendon on August 14, 1862. He was transferred to the Veterans Reserve Corps on April 7, 1864.

George H. Howard, 19-year-old laborer from Clarkson, enlisted in Company M on January 25, 1864, was wounded in the thigh on June 16, 1864, at Petersburg, and transferred to the Veteran Reserve Corps on May 4, 1865.

Luther W. Weirs, a 28-year-old Clarkson farmer, joined Company K on August 14, 1862, and was discharged for disability on June 29, 1864.

Albert Bills, a 32-year-old Kendall farmer, joined Company K on August 20, 1862, and was discharged for disability on March 5, 1864. In 1870, he was a farmer in Blissfield, Mich., with a wife and two children.

Jesse M[ilton?] Crandall, another Kendall farm boy, 21, joined Company K on August 8, 1862. He was wounded at Petersburg on June 16, 1864, and discharged for disability on May 6, 1865. In 1870, he was a farmer in Argentine, Mich., with a wife but no children.

Griffin LaDue, 20, probably also a Kendall farm boy, enlisted in Company K on August 14, 1862, and was captured at an unknown place and date.

Henry Hunt, a 19-year-old of Clarkson, enlisted in Company K on July 30, 1862, took sick immediately, and died in a military hospital in Baltimore on November 20, 1862. The 1860 census says he was a 17-year-old farmer, but the CTCR calls him a laborer.

George Myers joined Company K on September 20, 1861, and deserted on October 10, 1861.

Lucius M. Stafford, 23-year-old student from Brockport and older brother of Stephen R. Stafford, joined Company I on August 7, 1862, and died of disease on November 25, 1862.

Simon P. Webster, a 30-year-old lawyer from Kendall, was commissioned the second lieutenant of Company K on August 17, 1862, was promoted to first lieutenant on February 22, 1864, to captain on December 12, 1864, and mustered out on June 5, 1865. In 1870, he had given up his law practice and was in the "sash and blinds" business in Lockport with a wife and one child.

Captain Simon P. Webster of Kendall, 30, commander of Company K of the 8th New York Heavy Artillery. *Photo provided by Mary Smith.*

Sylvester Edwards, a 43-year-old boatman from Brockport, enlisted on August 30, 1862, was transferred from Company M to Company H on November 1, 1864, and was discharged for disability on May 13, 1865. After the war, he removed to South Chicago, Ill., where he joined the GAR post and died in 1889.

Willard W. Bates a 25-year-old Kendall farmer in 1860, joined this regiment as a lieutenant-colonel on August 10, 1862, was promoted to colonel, June 3, 1864, was wounded at Petersburg June 22, 1864, and died of his wounds 22 days later. He had served previously in the 13th NYVI and the 25th NYVI.

Stephen Randall Stafford was commissioned the second lieutenant of Company I on August 23, 1862, after previous service in the 13th NYVI and the 3rd NY Cavalry. He was promoted to first lieutenant on January 27, 1864, to captain on November 5, 1864, and to major by brevet on March 13, 1865. (See profile in Chapter 2)

Frank Sedgwick joined Company E on August 7, 1862, and deserted (date not stated). He was also listed as arrested for deserting from the 13th NYVI, although his entry in ACWRD for the 13th does not say so. Later he served briefly in the 14th NY Heavy Artillery.

Hiram J. Carpenter, of Clarkson, enlisted in Company D on July 25, 1862, as a corporal, but was busted to private on September 6, 1862. He suffered three wounds, including the loss of one hand. In 1870, he was a farmer in Gaines with a wife and daughter.

Hiram Allen, 28 of Hamlin, enlisted in Company K on July 25, 1862, was wounded at Petersburg on June 16, 1864, and died the next day.

Erastus Stover, 20-year-old, probably from Hamlin, enlisted in Company K on August 7, 1862, at Clarendon, was wounded on June 3, 1864, at Cold Harbor, and discharged for disability on July 6, 1865.

Irving W. Hallock (or Hollock), 19-year-old, probably from Hamlin enlisted in Company K on August 11, 1862 at Clarendon, was promoted to corporal on February 1, 1864, wounded on October 27, 1864, and mustered out on June 5, 1865. In 1870 he was a minister in Barre, Orleans County.

John Holvorson was a 34-year-old Norwegian-born farm laborer in Hamlin who enlisted January 5, 1864, in company K and was discharged for disability on December 5, 1864. In 1870 he was a farmer in Hamlin with 100 acres.

COMPANY D OF THE 8TH MICHIGAN REGIMENT OF INFANTRY

William M. Brown a 42-year-old married man of Sweden, enlisted in this company on August 17, 1861, and died of disease on December 11, 1861 at Hilton Head, SC.

COMPANY F OF THE 8TH UNITED STATES ARMY REGIMENT OF INFANTRY

Mathew Cusick, who also served in the 4th New York Regiment of Heavy Artillery enlisted in this company, date unknown. Cusick enlisted in the 4th New York on June 21, 1863, but, because the dates of his service in the U.S. Army are not known, it is impossible to know what part of the service of the 8th he experienced. The 8th was stationed in Texas at the outbreak of the rebellion, Company F was captured by rebel forces on May 9, 1861, but released in time to reach Washington by July and join in the defense of the capital until March 1862. Then it took part in the Peninsular campaign, Antietam, Fredericksburg, and Chancellorsville before Cusick's service in the 4th NYHA.

COMPANIES A, F, AND L OF THE 9TH NEW YORK REGIMENT OF CAVALRY

Horace R. Howard, a 25-year-old single Hamlin farmer, enlisted in Company L on September 22, 1862, was promoted to corporal July 1, 1863, to sergeant on June 1, 1864, transferred to Company F on November 1, 1864, and mustered out on June 1, 1865. The 1865 census says that he also transferred to the ambulance corps and was wounded in the hip. Herman Wilcox, enlisted in Company A at Rochester (ACWRD) or Sacketts Harbor (STCR) on September 9, 1864 and mustered out on June 30, 1865. After serving as train-guard during the Peninsular campaign, the 9th received their mounts and participated in an extraordinarily large number of engagements. Phisterer lists 140. They included Yorktown, Williamsburg, First Bull Run, the Peninsular campaign, Chancellorsville, Gettysburg, the Wilderness,

Spotsylvania, Cold Harbor, Petersburg, and the Shenandoah Valley and Appomattox campaigns, "gaining a well earned reputation for gallantry and efficiency." (ACWRD) With a roster of 2,620 men, it lost eight officers and 89 enlisted men killed or mortally wounded, 32 other officers and 238 other enlisted men wounded, four officers and 135 enlisted men captured, and five officers and 122 enlisted men died of other causes, including 16 enlisted men who died in captivity.

COMPANIES C, D, AND M OF THE 9TH NEW YORK REGIMENT OF ARTILLERY (HEAVY)

Company M was originally the 22nd New York Independent Battery, Light Artillery, organized on October 28, 1862. It was incorporated into this regiment as Company M on February 5, 1863. Edwin F. Clark, a 31-year-old Clarkson clerk, was commissioned a second lieutenant in Company M when the Battery formed and was mustered out with the regiment on September 4, 1865. Earlier, he had served in the 13th NYVI. Henry Loomis, a 21-year-old (ACWRD says 18) married Sweden farmer, was listed as a draftee by the *BR* on August 13, 1863, and enlisted in Company D on January 25, 1864. He transferred to the 2nd New York Regiment of Heavy Artillery on June 27, 1865. William H. Crampton of Bergen, Genesee County, enlisted in Company M on September 3, 1864 and was reported missing at Cedar Creek, Va., on October 19, 1864. He appears in neither the 1860 nor 1870 censuses, though several other Cramptons lived in Bergen in those years. George M. Rowe, who had served previously in the 12th NYVI, enlisted in Company D on September 14, 1864. He was commissioned a first lieutenant in Company C April 13, 1865, and mustered out on May 3. He served later in the 194th NYVI. The regiment saw combat duty from May 31, 1864, until April 9, 1865, including the Peninsular campaign, the Petersburg operations, and the Appomattox campaign. It lost seven officers and 196 enlisted men killed or mortally wounded, 17 other officers and 491 other enlisted men wounded, one officer and 86 enlisted men captured, and five officers and 244 enlisted men died of other causes, including 38 as captives.

Company F of the 10th New York Regiment of Cavalry (Veteran)

Robert Hopkins, a 19-year-old farm boy from Sweden, served in this unit from November 26, 1861, until May 26, 1862, when he deserted. Earlier, he had agreed to enlist in the 13th when it was forming, but refused to take the oath. Three months after deserting from the 10th, he re-joined the 13th at Rochester, but deserted again six weeks later. While he was in the regiment, it was charged with guarding railroads in the Gettysburg, Pa., area, seeing combat only once with no casualties. In the 1870 census, Hopkins was an unmarried hired farmhand in the Town of Sweden.

Company H of the 11th New Hampshire Volunteer Regiment of Infantry

George Williams, 21-year-old resident of Brockport, enlisted in this unit on December 19, 1863, and transferred to the 6th New Hampshire Volunteer Infantry on June 1, 1865. During Williams's service in the 11th, it joined in the pursuit of Longstreet in Tennessee after the siege of Knoxville and fought in the Battle of the Wilderness after a forced march of 175 miles in 11 days, the assault on Petersburg, and the Appomattox campaign. During Williams's service, the 11th lost 46 officers and men killed, 165 wounded, and 66 captured from a roster of 1,665.

Companies C and I of the 11th New York Regiment of Cavalry

John Myers, German-born 26-year-old Brockport boatman, enlisted in Company I on December 22, 1863, transferred to Company C on July 11, 1865, and mustered out on September 30, 1865. During Myers's service, the 11th participated in 38 engagements during 1864, mainly in Louisiana. Early in 1865, it was transferred to Tennessee and finished the war with eight engagements there. In those operations it lost one officer and 18 enlisted men killed or mortally wounded, one other officer and 57 other enlisted men wounded, and three officers and 107 enlisted men captured.

Companies C and H of the 11th United States Regiment of Infantry

James L. Sholes (or Shoals), a 19-year-old single Hamlin blacksmith, enlisted in Company H in March 1862, transferred to Company C, unknown date, was wounded in the hip at Gettysburg on July 2, 1863, and died in the 2nd Division 5th Corps Hospital that day. Before Gettysburg, the 11th took part in the Peninsular campaign, 2nd Bull Run, Antietam, Fredericksburg, the "mud march," Chancellorsville, the Wilderness, Spotsylvania, Cold Harbor, Petersburg, Hatcher's Run, and a number of other major battles. ACWRD does not provide overall casualty statistics, but it quotes the regimental commander as saying that after the Battle of Gettysburg: "Our loss in this engagement was fearful. Out of 261 enlisted men and 25 officers, the regiment lost 106 enlisted men and 10 commissioned officers."

12th New York Regiment of Cavalry

William Westerfield, a 22-year-old German-born printer from the Town of Sweden, enlisted in this regiment without company assignment on December 29, 1862, and was mustered out with the regiment on July 20, 1865. The regiment had a very active career, seeing action in 70 engagements from June 20, 1863, until April 26, 1865, all in North Carolina. One of its companies was trapped in Plymouth with the 24th NY Light Artillery (see Chapter 21), where it lost eight enlisted men killed or died of wounds, one officer and ten enlisted men wounded, and two officers and 100 enlisted men captured. Overall, it lost three officers 36 enlisted men killed or died of wounds, three other officers and 64 other enlisted men wounded, and seven officers and 314 enlisted men captured. Neither ACWRD nor STCR indicates that he was captured at Plymouth. So, he probably was not a member of that company. After the war, Westerfield lived in Clarendon, Orleans County.

Company I of the 12th New York Regiment of Infantry

George M. Rowe, a 21-year-old Sweden farmer, enlisted on April 23, 1861, and mustered out on May 17, 1863, serving later in the 9th and 194th NYVI. During his service, the regiment fought at Blackburn's Ford and in the siege of Yorktown, Second Bull Run, the Seven Days' battles, General Pope's campaign in Virginia, and at Fredericksburg. It lost three officers and 66 enlisted men killed or mortally wounded, 12 other officers and 190 other enlisted men wounded, and four officers and 136 enlisted men captured.

Company F of the 13th New York Regiment of Cavalry

Michael Comerford, a 22-year-old Sweden farmer, was listed as a draftee by the *BR* on August 13, 1863, enlisted on June 12, 1863, was discharged on October 14, 1863, and confined at Albany, NY, that day for four years for manslaughter. During Comerford's service, the regiment helped suppress the New York City draft riots of July 1863, in which it lost two enlisted men killed, and fought at Fairfax, Va., where seven enlisted men were missing. In 1870, Comerford was still single and farming a three-acre patch in Sweden with his brother, Lawrence.

Companies C, F, and G of the 14th New York Regiment of Artillery (Heavy)

The 14th was organized between August 1863 and January 1864 and joined in 15 engagements between May 5, 1864, and April 2, 1865, including the campaigns around Petersburg. With a roster of 3,914 men, it lost six officers and 204 enlisted men killed or mortally wounded, 18 other officers and 422 other enlisted men wounded, 19 officers and 399 enlisted men captured, and three officers and 309 enlisted men died of other causes, including one officer and 86 enlisted men who died in captivity. (The Davis Report says that 15 Sweden men were in the regiment.) The Brockporters whom I can identify who served in it were:

Langdon Hovey, who later served in the 1st NY Cavalry, enlisted in this regiment on October 10, 1863, without a company assignment and was transferred to the 1st NY Cavalry in November 1863.

Thomas C. Berry, 25-year-old Brockport constable, enlisted in Company F on August 8, 1863, but was not mustered until October 20. ACWRD has no further record of him. In 1870, he was back in Brockport as a molder with a wife and two school-aged children.

George H. Soles, age 25 of Brockport, enlisted in the 14th on July 9, 1863, as a private without company assignment. He transferred to the 1st NY Veteran Cavalry on October 10, 1863. He had served earlier in the 13th NYVI. In 1870, he was living in the Town of Sweden, probably farming.

Joseph Parker of Hamlin, age 27, enlisted in Company F on August 11, 1863, was captured at Fort Stedman on March 25, 1865, and released two days later. Earlier, he had served in the 13th NYVI. He does not appear on either the 1860 or 1870 censuses.

Robert J. Gordon, the 20-year-old son of a Brockport machinist, served in the 13th NYVI and less than two months after being mustered out enlisted in Company B of this regiment. He was wounded at Petersburg on June 17, 1864. Yet, he still mustered out with the regiment on July 21, 1865. In 1870, he was a writing teacher living in a boardinghouse in Brockport.

Frank Sedgwick mustered into Company C on September 11, 1863, and deserted on December 26, 1863. He had served previously in the 13th NYVI and the 8th NY Heavy Artillery.

George W. Hoskins, a 22-year-old student from the Town of Sweden, enrolled in Company F on July 18, 1863, was commissioned a second lieutenant on March 30, 1865, and mustered out with the company on August 26, 1865. He had been a student at the Brockport Collegiate Institute in 1858–59.

Marvin Barrows, a 28-year-old Sweden resident, enlisted in Company G on January 4, 1864, was captured, and died of starvation in Andersonville in August 1864.

According to an obituary in the *BR* (12/5/1935) Clarkson M. Scholes, a 19-year-old Clarkson resident, enlisted—company and date not given—in this regiment and served until mustered out on June 3, 1865. After the war he lived for 52 years in Montana before returning to Clarkson in 1920. He is not listed in the ACWRD or the CTCR.

George Albert Nurse, a 21-year-old machinist from the Town of Sweden, enlisted in Company G on December 9, 1963, was wounded in the foot on May 26, 1864, taken prisoner on March 25, 1865, and paroled on March 30, 1865. He mustered out on June 26, 1865. He does not appear in the 1860 or 1870 censuses.

COMPANY M OF THE 14TH RHODE ISLAND REGIMENT OF ARTILLERY (HEAVY)

The enlisted men in this regiment were African Americans and the officers were white. It served in Louisiana and Texas and was engaged in only one skirmish in which one enlisted man was killed, a "few" wounded and three enlisted men from Company G were captured and executed by the Confederates. (Chenery 61) One Brockporter, William A. Cone, a 23-year-old "mulatto" from Brockport, served in the 14th from January 6, 1864, until mustered out with the unit on October 2, 1865. On June 15, 1864, and again from August 1864 until January 15, 1865, he was assigned to duty as a hospital attendant. The 1860 census listed him as a laborer, but the STCR called him a farmer.

COMPANY B OF THE 14TH U.S. ARMY REGIMENT OF INFANTRY

One Brockporter, George Maxon, who also served in the 1st NY Cavalry served in this regiment. The ACWRD has no further information about his service. The 14th was formed in May 1861 in response to Lincoln's first mobilization call. It fought in the Peninsular campaign, at Antietam, Fredericksburg, Chancellorsville, Gettysburg, the Wilderness, and Petersburg, and six of the other bloodiest battles of the war and was recognized for its valiant service by being assigned the place of honor in the grand parade in Richmond to celebrate the return of peace. In 1870, Maxon was back in Brockport, plying his trade as a mason.

COMPANIES D, E, G, AND H OF THE 15TH NEW YORK CAVALRY

George Good, Town of Sweden farmer, enlisted in Company E on August 12, 1863, and was transferred to Company E of the 2nd New York Provisional Cavalry on June 17, 1865 (after the war). ACWRD gives his age in 1861 as 21, but the 1865 census lists him as 20. Charles G. Hampton 21-year-old farm hand from the Town of Sweden, transferred from the 8th New York Cavalry and was commissioned a second lieutenant in Company H on September 7, 1863, transferred to Company D on October 5, 1863, was wounded and captured on February 20, 1864, returned on March 1, 1865, promoted to captain and transferred to Company G on April 11, 1865, and discharged on May 15, 1865. The 12th NYVI was reorganized as this regiment when its original term of service had expired in August 1863. It fought in 32 engagements in Shenandoah Valley campaigns, then took part in the Appomattox campaign. It lost three officers and 37 enlisted men killed or mortally wounded and four officers and 126 enlisted men died of disease and other causes, of whom 44 died as prisoners.

COMPANY M OF THE 15TH NEW YORK REGIMENT OF ENGINEERS (VETERAN)

This regiment was organized in May 1861 as an infantry unit and was converted to an engineer regiment in October and trained as sappers and miners. Company M was one of seven companies that were added in the fall of 1864. Company M was originally organized for the 175th NYVI. The regiment saw very little combat and suffered few casualties. After Company M was formed, the regiment reported no casualties in five engagements, including Appomattox Court House. Four Brockporters served in this company from September 16, 1864, until June 13, 1865. They were:

Joseph S. Bryant, a 29-year-old farmer from Sweden. In 1865 he was a carpenter.

Edgar B. Fellows, a 37-year-old blacksmith from Brockport, transferred from the 50th NY Engineers. After the war he resumed his blacksmithery in Brockport.

Robert G. Straight, a 25-year-old Sweden farmer. The only Robert Straight in the United States in the 1870 census was a 12-year-old boy in Virginia.

George Hartford, a 36-year-old from Bradford County, Pennsylvania, who was credited to the Town of Sweden as a Sacketts Harbor recruit, and was promoted to Artificer.

Companies F and G of the 17th Indiana Regiment of Infantry

George M. Rowe, a 23-year-old farmer from the Town of Sweden, enlisted as a private in Company G on April 20, 1861, at the very outset of the war. He was the son of Asa Rowe, one of the most prominent residents of the area. He was discharged for disability on September 11, 1862. During his service, the regiment fought at Shiloh, the sieges of Corinth and Chattanooga, and Stone's River, but suffered only one casualty, one member killed. Thomas A. Dooley, 23-year-old cooper from the Town of Sweden, enlisted in Company F on October 27, 1864, and mustered out on August 8, 1865. During his service, the 17th was mounted and operated as a cavalry unit in Tennessee, Alabama, and Georgia, being almost continually engaged in combat operations. It had several notable successes. In a battle at Selma, Ala., it captured 100 prisoners. Then, with only 451 men, it captured the city of Macon, Ga., 3,000 prisoners, including five Confederate generals, 60 artillery pieces, and 3,000 rifles. With a roster of 2,311 men, it lost by death 232 men and by desertion 161. Another 82 were unaccounted for, probably most of them captured.

Company I of the 17th New York Regiment of Infantry

Francis G. Dolph, age 19, enlisted at Newark on May 10, 1861, when it was formed, and was discharged for disability on March 8, 1863. He lived in Newark as a peddler in 1860. His father, John, was a master cooper in Arcadia, Wayne County, in 1860, and a carpenter in Brockport in 1870. Also, his younger brother, John W., enlisted in the 22nd NY Cavalry in Sweden. Francis is listed in STCR, so, apparently, Francis was regarded as a Town of Sweden resident when he enlisted. During his service, the 17th was present at ten engagements, though it was heavily involved only at Second Bull Run, where it "made a valiant assault" and suffered four officers and 33 enlisted men killed or mortally wounded, eight other officers and 92 other enlisted men wounded, and 46 enlisted men captured, and at Fredericksburg. Also, 42 men died of other causes. Later, Dolph served in the 22nd NY Cavalry.

18th New York Independent Battery, Light Artillery

25th New York Independent Battery, Light Artillery

Theophilus Martell, a draftee from Sweden, enlisted on December 14, 1863, and Hiram J. Woodward, a 37-year molder of Sweden, joined five days later. Three men from Hamlin, Henry and James M. Cusick, apparently related, and William Morey joined them on September 19, 1864, and transferred to the 25th on December 20, 1864, along with 114 other members of the 18th. Woodward was mustered out on June 8, 1865, Martell on July 20, 1865, and the Hamlin men on August 1, 1865. James was a 42-year-old farmer from Hamlin with a wife and five children under eight. Morey, who was 19 when he enlisted, Henry Cusick, who was a 24-year-old farm laborer, Martell, and Woodward do not appear in the 1860 or 1870 censuses. Henry had been a member of the 13th NYVI and also had served briefly in the 7th NY Heavy Artillery. (I have in my archives transcripts of letters from H. C. dated June 1, 1864, and April 7, 1865.) Also, Edmond Barker and Lafayette Thompson, recruits from Sacketts Harbor who were credited to the Town of Sweden, served in the 18th from September 19, 1964, until July 20, 1865. Thompson's discharge date is not given. Between the enlistments of Martell and Woodward and the departure of the three Hamlin men, the 18th participated in two engagements in Louisiana in which the Battery suffered no casualties. After their transfer, the 25th was assigned to the defense of New Orleans and nearby areas of Louisiana but was involved in no combat. After the departure of the Hamlin men, the 18th served in three engagements in Alabama in March and April 1865 and lost one enlisted man who was mortally wounded. (The Davis Report lists eight Sweden men in this regiment, but STCR lists only the Cusicks and Morey.)

Company K of the 19th Illinois Regiment of Infantry

Henry D. Stoughton, a 28-year-old Brockport resident served from June 4, 1861, until mustered out on July 8, 1864. He was promoted to corporal. The 19th was one of the very first regiments to be mustered into federal service in Illinois. It took part in 24 skirmishes and battles, mainly in Tennessee, but also in Missouri, Alabama, and Georgia. It lost 36 men killed or mortally wounded, 38 men wounded, seven POWs, and six others missing. Its initial roster contained nearly 1,000 names and it received "a large number of recruits" later, but mustered out with fewer than 350 men.

Company H of the 19th Michigan Regiment of Infantry

Harrison Rockafellow, a 19-year-old who gave his residence as Coldwater, Mich., but was listed in the 1865 census as a resident of Brockport, enlisted on August 4, 1862, and mustered out on June 10, 1865. The 19th was first seriously engaged at Thompson's Station, Tenn., where it first "displayed those qualities of heroism that afterwards distinguished this regiment on many a hard fought field." (ACWRD) After a "sanguinary" five-hour battle, the brigade surrendered. However, the captives were soon paroled, reorganized, and returned to the war. The 19th was part of Sherman's force in the capture of Atlanta and Savannah, and his "march to the sea." With a roster of 1,206, it lost 85 officers and men killed or mortally wounded, 139 died of disease, including seven POWs, and 182 were discharged for wounds or disease.

19th New York Independent Battery, Light Artillery

Theodore D. Hallett, a 36-year-old "peddler of silks, etc." of Brockport, served in this unit. He enlisted on September 2, 1864, and mustered out with the Battery on June 26, 1865. The Battery had been organized on October 26, 1862. After Hallett enlisted, it saw action in seven engagements, including two assaults on Petersburg, the Weldon Railroad expedition, and Hatcher's Run. It suffered casualties only at Fort Stedman, Va., on March 25, 1865, when one enlisted man was killed and two officers and 12 enlisted men, including Hallett, were captured. ACWRD says that Hallett was also wounded in that engagement, though Phisterer lists no men wounded then. Hallett was released five days later. In 1870, he was back in Brockport, peddling his "silk &c" again, with a wife and son.

Unknown Company in 21st New York Battery

Monroe O. Shoals (or Sholes), a 21-year-old Hamlin farmer, enlisted on September 23, 1864, served for eight months and transferred out to an unknown unit. ACWRD has no record of him and he is not listed in the 1860 or 1870 censuses. This battery served in the Reserved Artillery in the Louisiana-Alabama area and saw no combat during his service.

Companies D, G, and H, 21st New York Regiment of Cavalry

Sixteen Brockport area men served in this regiment. It formed in the fall of 1863 and mustered out between June 23 and August 31, 1866, 16 months after the war ended. Except as indicated, the Brockporters all enlisted in Company G on October 14, 1863. The regiment saw action in 56 engagements, largely in the Shenandoah Valley campaign. With a roster of 1,758, it lost three officers and 63 enlisted men killed or mortally wounded, ten other officers and 121 other enlisted men wounded, and three officers and 108 enlisted men captured. One officer and 78 enlisted men died of other causes, including ten enlisted men who died in captivity. The Brockporters were:

David Jewett Butler, a 33-year-old railroad depot laborer from the Town of Ogden, in Company H. He was promoted from private to sergeant on October 15, 1863, and mustered out on June 27, 1865.

Martin Coats, an 18-year-old cartman from Brockport. He transferred to Company D on September 9, 1865, and was mustered out on August 13, 1866.

Charles Gartley, an Irish-born 18-year-old farm boy from Brockport, was promoted from private to corporal February 15, 1864, and to sergeant on April 30, 1865. He mustered out on July 7, 1866. In 1870, he was back in Brockport working as a "truckman" with a wife and son.

James B. Root was a private in the 4th NYHA until he transferred to Company G of this regiment with a captain's commission on October 14, 1863. He was wounded in a charge on a Confederate train at Purcellsville, Va., July 16, 1864, and resigned January 23, 1865. In that raid, four enlisted men were killed or died of wounds, two officers and eight enlisted men were wounded, and ten enlisted men were captured.

Hiram H. Whitcher, a 26-year-old teacher from the Town of Sweden. He enlisted in Company G on July 31, 1863, was promoted to sergeant major on November 29, 1863, and to quartermaster sergeant on March 1, 1865. He mustered out on August 8, 1865.

George A. Nobles, a 30-year-old farm laborer in the Town of Sweden, enlisted in Company H and deserted four days later. Earlier, he had served in the 13th NYVI. In 1870, he was a reaper maker in Brockport.

Charles Thompson was a 25-year-old Clarkson farm laborer who enlisted in Company H and mustered out on June 26, 1866. Earlier, he had served in the 13th NYVI. By 1870, he was back in Brockport, living in the household of the father of Stephen Randall Stafford and was employed as a steward at the Brockport State Normal School.

Michael Tool[e] was a 19-year-old Clarkson laborer living with his tailor father in 1860. After serving in the 13th NYVI, he enlisted in Company H. He served to the end of the war, but, apparently impatient with the mustering out process, deserted June 10, 1865, two months after the war ended.

Stephen Osborn served earlier in the 13th. Osborn had enlisted in Company H on September 21, 1863, was promoted to sergeant in both regiments, and "died on the field of battle," date unknown.

William Henry Joslyn joined Company H as a first lieutenant on October 14, 1863, was promoted to captain on May 11, 1865, and mustered out on October 5, 1865. Earlier, he had been a private in the 13th NYVI. While in the 21st, he was wounded in action on July 17, 1864, at Snicker's Gap, Va., during the Shenandoah Valley operations. Immediately after the war, he returned to Brockport, but later he lived in Denver and Verona, Oneida County. He died in 1909.

James D. Hopkins, a 21-year-old blacksmith from the Town of Sweden, enlisted in Company G on August 12, 1863, was confined at the Dry Tortugas disciplinary camp, and transferred to Company D on September 9, 1865. He was confined at the time of mustering out. His discharge date is unknown.

Henry George Diver, a 27-year-old common laborer from Brockport, was transferred to Company D on September 9, 1865, and discharged on April 10, 1866. In 1870, he was in Brockport, still a common laborer, with an Irish-born wife and five children.

Calvin N. Pomeroy, an 18-year-old single man from the Town of Sweden, enlisted in Company G on August 3, 1863, was captured (date unknown) and died at Andersonville on June 11, 1864.

Charles B. Gage, 18-year-old son of a Clarkson laborer, enlisted in Company G on August 10, 1863, and was killed at Lynchburg, Va., on July 19, 1864.

John E. Knowles, 18-year-old Canadian-born Brockport clerk, enlisted in Company G on August 10, 1863, after serving in the 140th NYVI and 13th NYVI. He transferred to Company D on September 9, 1865, and was mustered out on July 7, 1866. He does not appear in the 1870 census.

George H. Norton, a 26-year-old Brockport baker, was listed as a draftee in the *BR* on August 13, 1863, and joined Company G on August 6, 1863, being mustered in on August 26. His date of discharge is not recorded. In 1870, he was back in Brockport as a baker.

Company D of the 21st New York Regiment of Infantry

George Duer, a 41-year-old laborer from the Town of Sweden, served briefly in this company. He was mustered in on May 9, 1861, and was discharged for disability on July 1, 1861, while the regiment was still in training at Fort Kalorama, D.C.

21st New York Light Artillery Regiment

Menese [?] Shoals [or Sholes] a 21-year-old Hamlin farmer enlisted on September 23, 1864, served eight months, and was transferred to an unknown unit. ACWRD says that "on December 20, 1864, a number of men…were transferred to the 26th Battery." During Shoals's service, the 26th regiment served in Alabama, seeing action three times, but suffering no casualties.

22nd New York Independent Battery, Light Artillery

Edwin F. Clark, a 29-year-old Brockport clerk, who had been living in a hotel, was commissioned a second lieutenant in this battery when it was organized on October 28, 1862, after previous service in the 13th NYVI.

The battery became Company M of the 9th New York Heavy Artillery on February 5, 1863, but Phisterer says that Clark did not join the 9th and his name is not on its roster in the ACWRD. He mustered out of this battery on September 4, 1865. Apparently, it saw no action before the merger, as ACWRD has no information on its service record or casualties.

COMPANIES H AND M OF THE 24TH NEW YORK CAVALRY

This regiment was formed in December 1863 as a reorganized 24th NYVI. It fought in the Peninsular campaign, at Petersburg, and in the Appomattox campaign. "The regiment saw less than a year of active service, but endured much hard combat and suffered severely. It lost 7 officers and 113 men killed and mortally wounded; 1 officer and 133 men died of disease, accidents, in prison etc., a total of 254." (ACWRD Union Army)

William A. (or H.) Welch, an 18-year-old Parma farm laborer, enlisted in Company H on December 15, 1863, was promoted to bugler on March 12, 1864, and died at Camp Stoneman Hospital the same day.

Henry A. Genet[t] transferred to Company M for promotion to first lieutenant from the 140th NYVI on May 28, 1864. He commanded Company M from September 2, 1864, until March 15, 1865, was promoted to captain of Company C on April 22, 1865, and was mustered out as supernumerary on June 24, 1865. He was wounded at Petersburg on June 28, 1864.

John L. Ball enlisted in Company M on January 22, 1864, after service in the 13th NYVI. However, according to ACWRD, he was "rejected (date not stated)."

Charles King, a 30-year-old Hamlin laborer, enlisted on August 5, 1864. In 1870, he was a day laborer in Hamlin with a wife and two small children. (Not in ACWRD)

William Pelo, a 30-year-old Brockport machinist, joined very late, on February 11, 1865, and, presumably saw no combat. (Not in ACWRD)

COMPANIES C AND G OF THE 25TH NEW YORK REGIMENT OF CAVALRY

James Murray enlisted on April 2, 1864, and deserted May 7, while the regiment was still engaged in the defense of Washington. It saw no combat during his service. Earlier, he had served in the 13th NYVI. In 1860, he was a 29-year-old Irish-born single farmer in Ogden. He does not appear in the 1870 census.

COMPANIES C AND E OF THE 25TH NEW YORK REGIMENT OF INFANTRY

Willard W. Bates, Kendall farmer, 25, who served previously in the 13th NYVI, joined Company C as a first lieutenant on November 7, 1861, was promoted to captain on January 20, 1862, and was wounded at Chickahominy, Va., on June 27, 1862. He was discharged for promotion on August 21, 1862, and served in the 8th NY Heavy Artillery. Also, he served as a lieutenant colonel in the 129th NYVI, but data on that unit is not available on ACWRD.

Wesley W. Conner, a 23-year-old Town of Sweden resident who had previously served in the 13th NYVI, enlisted in Company D as a sergeant on November 27, 1861, was transferred to Company E with a second lieutenant's commission the same day, was promoted to first lieutenant on January 4, 1862, and to captain on June 21, 1862. He mustered out with the regiment on July 10, 1863. The regiment participated in the Peninsular campaign of 1862 and fought at Fredericksburg and Chancellorsville. It lost nine officers and 51 enlisted men killed or mortally wounded, 11 other officers and 138 other enlisted men wounded, three officers and 107 enlisted men captured, and three officers and 25 enlisted men died of other causes, including one officer and two enlisted men in captivity. After the war, Conner lived in Rochester.

25TH NEW YORK REGIMENT OF HEAVY ARTILLERY

Henry H. Cusick, a 24-year-old Hamlin farm laborer, who had served previously in the 13th NYVI, 7th NYHA, and 18th NYLA, enlisted here on December 20, 1864, and was mustered out on August 1, 1865. During

Cusick's service it was assigned to the defense of the southern district of Louisiana and suffered no casualties.

COMPANY H OF THE 26TH/94TH UNITED STATES COLORED INFANTRY REGIMENT

The 26th USCT was organized on Riker's Island, NYC, February 27, 1864, and served in South Carolina until October 1864. Its designation was changed to 94th U.S. Colored Troops on April 4, 1864. It was very active in military engagements at Johns and James Island, Honey Hill, Beaufort, and a number of other locations. Two officers and 28 enlisted men were killed or mortally wounded, and three officers and 112 enlisted died from disease. It was mustered out on August 28, 1965. ("26th Regiment") Brockporter Daniel Williams served in this regiment, but ACWRD does not give his dates of service. The STCR gives his birth year as 1820, his occupation as laborer, his residence as Brockport, and his race as colored. In the 1860 census his age is 38, his occupation as carpenter, his residence as Brockport, and his race as white. The 1870 census says that his age is 45, his occupation boating, his residence Brockport and his race white. In the 1860 census he was living in the same household as William A. Cone, who served in the 14th Rhode Island Volunteer Infantry (Colored).

COMPANY E OF THE 26TH NEW YORK REGIMENT OF INFANTRY

This regiment was mustered on May 21, 1861. Valentine Schwab, a 21-year-old Rochesterian who had enlisted in Brockport in the Brockport company of the 13th NYVI, joined it on January 8, 1862, and was mustered out with the regiment on May 28, 1863. During his service, it participated in five major battles or campaigns, General Pope's campaign in Virginia in August and September 1862, South Mountain, Antietam, Fredericksburg, and Chancellorsville. It lost during that time five officers and 103 enlisted men killed or mortally wounded, 12 other officers and 231 other enlisted men wounded, 56 enlisted men captured, and 42 enlisted men died of other causes, including one in captivity.

26th New York Light Artillery

William Kelley (or Kelly), a 20-year-old Canadian-born Brockport resident, who served earlier in the 13th NYVI, enlisted on September 27, 1864 and was mustered out on July 12, 1865 During Kelley's service, the 26th was stationed in Louisiana, especially in the defense of New Orleans. During its entire history, it suffered only one casualty, a wounded enlisted man, none during Kelley's service.

Company F of the 27th New York Regiment of Infantry

James Barry [or Berry], 34-year-old Sweden farmer, enlisted on May 21, 1861, was wounded at Gaines' Mill, Va., on June 27, 1862, and discharged as a consequence on May 1, 1863. During his service, the 27th fought in the Peninsular campaign and at South Mountain, Antietam, and Fredericksburg. It lost two officers and 66 enlisted men killed or mortally wounded, 13 other officers and 144 other enlisted men wounded, 98 enlisted men captured, and one officer and 11 enlisted men died of disease and other causes, of whom seven enlisted men in captivity.

Company G of the 28th New York Regiment of Infantry

Peter Guelph, formerly of the 1st NY Cavalry, Veteran, enlisted on May 22, 1861, was promoted to corporal February 25, 1862, and mustered out on June 2, 1863.

Company A of the 29th Ohio Regiment of Infantry

George W. Dudley, 20-year-old laborer of the Town of Sweden, enlisted on August 14, 1861, and was discharged for disability on January 30, 1863.

During his service, it joined the Army of the Potomac in the battles of Winchester, Port Republic, and Cedar Mountain. He also served in the 1st NY Veteran Cavalry.

32nd New York Battery of Light Artillery

George Marks, who enlisted in the 8th NY Cavalry in Sweden, was detached on March 8, 1862, and tranferred to this unit. His date of discharge is unknown. The 32nd was on artillery reserve in the Washington, D.C., area from March 1862 until June 1863 and in the Harpers Ferry area from then until August 1864. It suffered only four casualties, all wounded enlisted men.

Company G of the 32nd New York Regiment of Infantry

Patrick Gleason, a 19-year-old Irish-born Town of Sweden common laborer, enlisted as a corporal on May 15, 1861, and mustered out with the original enlistees on June 9, 1863. The principal engagements of the regiment were in the Peninsular campaign, Antietam, Fredericksburg, and Chancellorsville. With a roster of 1,040 members, it lost 45 mortally wounded and 54 dead from other causes.

Company D of the 33rd New York Regiment of Infantry

John Beedle, a 35-year-old Town of Sweden farmer, joined this regiment as part of a newly formed company of new recruits on September 22, 1862. He was promoted to first sergeant, date unknown. While he served, the 33rd fought at Fredericksburg, but its principal engagement was at Marye's Heights and Salem Church, Va., where it lost one officer and 26 enlisted men killed or mortally wounded, four other officers and 116 other enlisted men wounded, and one officer and 73 enlisted men captured. He transferred to the 49th NYVI on October 1, 1863.

COMPANY F OF THE 34TH NEW YORK REGIMENT OF INFANTRY

Martin S. Straight, a 21-year-old farm laborer from Sweden, enlisted as a private on May 10, 1861. He was promoted to corporal, wounded at Antietam, and mustered out with the regiment on June 30, 1863. Philip Edwards, a 19-year-old Canadian-born farmer from Hamlin, enlisted on July 25, 1864, company unknown, and served for three months. The regiment fought in the Peninsular and Maryland campaigns, including Antietam, where 154 of its members were killed, wounded, or missing of 311 engaged, a 50 percent casualty rate on one day. Its last two engagements were Fredericksburg and Marye's Heights. Its total casualties were three officers and 91 enlisted men killed or mortally wounded, nine other officers and 184 other enlisted men wounded, two officers and 65 enlisted men captured, and one officer and 67 enlisted men died of other causes.

COMPANY C OF THE 37TH NEW YORK REGIMENT OF INFANTRY

Thomas Myers transferred as a veteran of the 101st NYVI on December 24, 1862, was taken prisoner on May 3, 1863, and paroled on May 14, 1863. During his time with this regiment, it suffered the loss of 222 members killed, wounded, or missing at Chancellorsville in May 1863. He transferred to the 40th NYVI with the other three-year men on May 29, 1863.

COMPANIES A AND K OF THE 40TH NEW YORK REGIMENT OF INFANTRY

Thomas Myers transferred from the 37th NYVI to Company K on May 29, 1863, was taken prisoner (for the third time) on October 15, 1863, paroled on March 15, 1864, and transferred to Company A on July 7, 1864. He mustered out on September 16, 1864. During his time in the regiment, it fought at Gettysburg, Kelly's Ford, Mine Run, in the Wilderness campaign, at Spottsylvania, the Po River, North Anna, Totopotomoy, and Cold Harbor, and in the siege of Petersburg, and lost three officers and 125 enlisted men killed or mortally wounded, 19 other officers and 346 other enlisted men wounded, and two officers and 94 enlisted men captured.

COMPANY B OF THE 42ND ILLINOIS REGIMENT OF INFANTRY

Homer Arnold, the son of Enoch and Sybil Arnold of Hamlin, served in this unit, dying on December 9, 1863, at Bridgeport, Ala. The *BR* (2/2/88) reported that he and Americus Doty, who was a 24-year-old fruit culturer in Hamlin in 1860, served in a Minnesota regiment and that Doty was wounded in the Battle of Chickamaugua on September 20, 1863, and died December 3, 1863, age 27, and that both were buried in Hamlin on the same day. ACWRD has no record of Doty. During their service, the 42nd lost 57 officers and enlisted men killed, 26 wounded, and 12 captured.

COMPANY C OF THE 47TH NEW YORK REGIMENT OF INFANTRY

Joseph Sanford, a 24-year-old Brockport laborer, appeared on the list of draftees in the *BR* of August 13, 1863, and enlisted on October 14, 1863. He mustered out on August 30, 1865. He does not appear on the 1870 census. During his service, the 47th joined in an expedition to Florida in February 1864 that cost it 313 men killed, wounded, or missing. In April 1864, it was posted to Virginia, where it fought at Port Walthall Junction and Cold Harbor, in the final assault of Petersburg and follow-up encounters. During the last few months of the war, it fought in several battles in North Carolina. During that time, it fought in 21 engagements and lost two officers and 86 enlisted men killed or mortally wounded, 12 other officers and 317 other enlisted men wounded, and two officers and 130 enlisted men captured from a roster of 2,345 men.

Company I of the 49th New York Regiment of Infantry

John Beedle transferred to this regiment from the 33rd NYVI on October 1, 1863 and was discharged for promotion as a first lieutenant in the 108th NYVI on May 3, 1864. During his service, the regiment saw very little action. He transferred out two days before its heavy involvement in the Battle of the Wilderness, May 5–7, 1864. In 1870, he was on his father's farm in Sweden.

Companies A and K of the 50th New York Regiment of Engineers (Veteran)

This regiment began on September 20, 1861, as the 50th NYVI, but was converted to an engineering unit a month later and served as such until mustered out in June 1865. Four Brockporters served in 11 combats from May 5, 1864, until April 6, 1865, including the Battle of the Wilderness, Petersburg, and the Appomattox campaign, in which the regiment lost three enlisted men killed or died of wounds and four other enlisted men wounded. All Brockporters were mustered out with the regiment. The Brockporters were:

Henry C. Hammond, a 21-year-old Brockport carpenter, enlisted in Company K on February 22, 1864. In 1870, he was back in the village working as a clerk in a feed store with a wife but no children.

George L. Smith, a 21-year-old farm Clarkson laborer, enlisted in Company K on February 22, 1864. In 1870, he was living in Brockport and working as a "moulder," presumably at one of the foundries.

Edgar Thompson, a 21-year-old Parma farm laborer, enlisted in Company A on February 9, 1864, and was promoted from private to artificer April 22, 1865, after the war had ended.

William C. Webb, a 25-year-old cooper living with his parents and four siblings in the Town of Sweden, enlisted in Company K on March 29, 1864. He was promoted to artificer on July 21, 1864. Earlier, he had served in the 13th NYVI. His father and a brother were also coopers. After the war, he returned to his parents' household and resumed his trade.

COMPANIES C, D, H, AND K OF THE 52ND NEW YORK REGIMENT OF INFANTRY

Alexander White [or Whyte], 31-year-old Scottish-born Brockport butcher enlisted in Company C August 19, 1864, was promoted to sergeant on May 20, 1865, and mustered out on July 1, 1865. The regiment had been formed in November 1861. After White joined it, it fought in four engagements plus the Appomattox campaign. It participated in the final, successful assault on Petersburg. During those eight months, it lost three officers and 11 enlisted men killed, three officers and 51 enlisted men wounded but recovered, and one officer and 41 enlisted men captured. White does not appear in the 1870 census.

Thomas G. Warren, 22-year-old English-born Hamlin farmer was listed among the draftees in *BR* 8/13/1863. He enlisted in company K on August 7, 1863, was wounded in the foot on October 4, 1863, and was discharged for disability on January 15, 1864. (His wound must have resulted from an accident, as the 52nd was not engaged in combat during the time he served.) Later he served in the 3rd NY Cavalry.

Louis Becker and Henry Peachy were reported by the *BR* (8/13/1863) to be draftees. Becker enlisted in Company H on August 9, 1863, transferred to Company D on October 4, 1864, and mustered out on July 1, 1865. Peachy enlisted in Company K on August 14, 1863, and died of "inflammation of the brain" on March 18, 1864. Becker does not appear on the 1860 or 1870 censuses for Monroe County or in the 1869 directory for Sweden.

54TH NEW YORK REGIMENT OF INFANTRY

Willard Sanford, 18-year-old Brockport resident, enlisted in August 1864, for 100 days. When this regiment originated in 1861 its men were entirely of German birth. By the time Sanford joined, however, it had been replenished more diversely. During his service, it operated on James Island, S.C., and on the Santos River and lost four enlisted men killed and 16 wounded.

63RD PENNSYLVANIA REGIMENT OF INFANTRY

Howard Beardsley, a 19-year-old Brockport clerk, enlisted on August 22, 1863. The 63rd was engaged in most of the major battles in the East, including the Peninsular campaign, Second Bull Run, Fredericksburg, Chancellorsville, Gettysburg, the Wilderness, and Petersburg. It suffered its greatest losses at Fair Oaks (27 killed, 40 wounded, three POWs), Chancellorsville (120 killed, wounded, or missing from a roster of 330), and three days in the Wilderness (25 killed, 81 wounded, and three POWs). By September 9, 1864, its ranks were so depleted that it merged with the 98th Pennsylvania Volunteer Infantry. Previously, Beardsley had served in the 3rd NY Light Artillery. He is not listed in the ACWRD.

COMPANIES E AND H OF THE 64TH NEW YORK REGIMENT OF INFANTRY

Byron C. Ketchum, a 23-year-old Hamlin farmer, enlisted in Company H as a sergeant on October 6, 1861. He had been living with his parents and 25-year-old seamstress sister. His farmer father, Abram, had a rather substantial estate of $4,975. Ketchum was commissioned a second lieutenant on September 19, 1862, promoted to first lieutenant on December 24, 1862, and to captain on June 18, 1863. On June 19, 1864, he was wounded at Petersburg and was discharged on October 8, 1864. In 1870, he was a drugstore clerk in Brockport with a wife but no children. David Herman[n], 24, enlisted in Company E on September 14, 1864, at Rochester as a substitute for Brockporter Charles Benedict and deserted to the enemy on December 12, 1864, at Petersburg. He does not appear on the 1860 or 1870 censuses in Monroe County. Another substitute (for George Burrows), William Jacobs, and John Kirby, 21, enlisted at Rochester the same day but were not assigned a company. Their mustering out dates are not given in ACWRD. John Landers, a substitute from Elisha W. Young, is reported by ACWRD as enlisting on September 9, 1864, in Rochester in both this regiment not assigned to a company and in the 71st NYVI, also unassigned. Stephen H. Warren of Brockport (per *BR*) enlisted at Rochester on August 3, 1864, and mustered out on July 14, 1865. The 64th took part in the Peninsular campaign. It played prominent roles at Fair Oaks, Antietam, Fredericksburg, Chancellorsville, and Gettysburg. In 1864–65, it served in

Captain Byron C. Ketchum, Hamlin farmer, 30, commander of Company H of the 64th NYVI, wounded at Petersburg. *Photo provided by Mary Smith.*

the Wilderness, Petersburg, and the Appomattox campaign. Overall, from a roster of 1,313, it lost 182 men killed or mortally wounded and 129 from other causes. Its division "saw the hardest service and suffered the heaviest losses of any in the army and the 64th was one of the finest fighting regiments in the war." (ACWRD Union Army)

Companies C and K of the 76th New York Regiment of Infantry

This regiment was organized on January 16, 1862. Two Brockporters served in it. Hiram Williams a 25-year-old Hamlin farmer, signed up for Company C in the Town of Sweden on August 7, 1863, and James Read (or Reid or Reed), 21, a Hamlin farm laborer, enlisted in Company K in Buffalo five days later. They transferred to the 147th NYVI in January 1865. During their service, the 76th fought in 17 engagements, including the Mine Run campaign, the Battle of the Wilderness, and the siege of and assault on Petersburg. During that time, the 76th lost 41 killed, 167 wounded, and 165 captured. In 1870, Williams was a railroad laborer in Brockport with a wife and daughter.

Company K of the 81st New York Regiment of Infantry

Jules F. Billard, 23, who had served briefly in the 13th NYVI, enlisted on August 26, 1861, was commissioned a first lieutenant on September 14, 1861, and discharged on February 6, 1862. The *BR* identified him as a resident of "this vicinity" (5/2/1861) and "formerly of this village." (2/1/3/1862) The 81st saw no combat action during his service. The 1870 census has him an apothecary in New York City.

Company F of the 82nd United States Regiment of Colored Infantry

Edward W. Bangs had served in the 13th NYVI, until he was commissioned a first lieutenant in the 82nd. ACWRD and Phisterer say that happened on June 23, 1863, but ACWRD says the 82nd was not organized until April 4, 1864, by which date, he had been commissioned a captain in the 4th U.S. Colored Cavalry.

Company D of the 89th New York Regiment of Infantry

The Davis Report says that seven Sweden men served in this regiment. Its Company D recruited 102 members in Rochester. However, the 1860 census lists only William Kelly, who was 18 when he enlisted on February 25, 1864, as a resident of Sweden. After Kelly enlisted, the regiment fought in the operations at Petersburg and Richmond, Cold Harbor, Chaffin's Farm, Fair Oaks, and in the Appomattox campaign. In those actions, it lost four officers and 53 enlisted men killed or mortally wounded, ten other officers and 168 other enlisted men wounded, and three officers and 119 enlisted men captured.

COMPANY I OF THE 91ST NEW YORK REGIMENT OF INFANTRY

James J. Peachy, 26-year-old English-born Hamlin farmer, transferred to the 91st from the 147th NYVI on June 5, 1865, and mustered out on July 3, 1865. As the war had ended, he saw no combat in the 91st.

COMPANY B OF THE 93RD NEW YORK REGIMENT OF INFANTRY

Edson W. Hoyt, a 24-year-old Town of Sweden school teacher who had graduated from the Brockport Collegiate Institute in 1859, enlisted on November 9, 1861, and transferred to the Signal Corps on January 1, 1864. In 1870, he was married and he and his wife were schoolteachers. During Hoyt's service, his company was among those assigned to non-combatant duty at White House, Va., and suffered no casualties.

COMPANY K OF THE 98TH NEW YORK REGIMENT OF INFANTRY (VETERAN)

This regiment was formed by the merger of two incomplete units from Wayne and Cortland Counties on February 5, 1862. Edward S. Smith, 18-year-old Clarkson student, had enlisted in the Wayne County regiment on November 4, 1861. He re-enlisted on January 2, 1864, and mustered out with the regiment on August 31, 1865. The regiment participated in 25 engagements between April 16, 1862, and April 2, 1865, including the siege of Yorktown, Fair Oaks, the operations around Petersburg and Richmond, and the siege, assault, and fall of Petersburg. With a roster of 1,468, it lost four officers and 98 enlisted men killed or mortally wounded, 12 other officers and 265 other enlisted men wounded, 72 enlisted men captured, and four officers and 132 enlisted men died of other causes, including 22 enlisted men who died in captivity—a casualty rate of 40 percent. Smith was wounded on an unknown date, was promoted to sergeant on May 23, 1865, and commissioned a first lieutenant on June 21, 1865. In the 1865 census, he is listed as a jeweler, but in 1870, he lived in Brockport with a wife but no children and plied the trade of cabinetmaker.

COMPANY C OF THE 100TH ILLINOIS REGIMENT OF INFANTRY

Henry M. Starin, a 32-year-old single Clarkson carpenter, enlisted as a corporal on July 29, 1862, was promoted to sergeant, and mustered out on May 22, 1865. The 100th was heavily involved in combat in the area of Charleston, S.C., in the struggle to capture Petersburg and Richmond, and in the Appomattox campaign. Fox included it in his list of "three hundred fighting regiments." (The only regiment with a Brockport company on Fox's list was the 140th NYVI.) During Starin's service, the 100th lost seven officers and 146 enlisted men killed or mortally wounded, 17 other officers and 339 other enlisted men wounded, and six officers and 197 enlisted men captured, with 2,334 men on its roster.

100TH NEW YORK REGIMENT OF INFANTRY

Henry F. Jacoby, after service in the 1st NYVI and the 158th NYVI, was transferred to the 100th on June 30, 1865, after the war had ended. Jacoby was its sergeant major.

COMPANY C OF THE 101ST NEW YORK REGIMENT OF INFANTRY

Thomas Myers, a 34-year-old laborer from the Town of Sweden who had been born in New Brunswick, enlisted on January 26, 1862, was taken prisoner on June 30, 1862, while on picket duty, was paroled on August 5, 1862, and transferred to the 37th NYVI with the regiment on December 24, 1862. During his service, it fought in the Seven Days' battles, Groveton, Second Bull Run, Chantilly, and Fredericksburg. At Second Bull Run, it lost 73 percent of its roster killed, wounded or missing, a percentage exceeded in one battle by only two other Union regiments during the war. Its total losses were one officer and 25 enlisted men killed or mortally wounded, six other officers and 111 enlisted men wounded, and one officer and 37 enlisted men captured.

COMPANY D OF THE 102ND NEW YORK REGIMENT OF INFANTRY

James Myers, 21, of Sweden, enlisted on January 4, 1862, was wounded on May 3, 1863, at Chancellorsville, and died of his wound on May 26, 1863. Before Chancellorsville, the 102nd suffered 115 casualties at Cedar Mountain and 37 at Antietam. At Chancellorsville, one officer and 13 enlisted men were killed or mortally wounded, three other officers and 34 other enlisted men were wounded, and one officer and 38 enlisted men were captured.

COMPANY B OF THE 103RD NEW YORK REGIMENT OF INFANTRY

This regiment was formed on March 1, 1862, by the merger of two pre-existing units and nicknamed the Seward Infantry because Secretary of State William Seward had promoted its formation. It saw action in 22 engagements, including such major battles as South Mountain, Antietam, Fredericksburg, and Petersburg. At Antietam, it suffered 117 casualties. Overall, with a roster of 1,797 men, it lost four officers and 61 enlisted men killed or mortally wounded, six other officers and 107 other enlisted men wounded, 33 enlisted men captured, and three officers and 100 enlisted men died of other causes, including five enlisted men in captivity. James A. Edmonds, a 20-year-old Sweden farmer, joined it on August 20, 1862, was promoted to corporal on November 30, 1864, and mustered out with the regiment on June 12, 1865.

COMPANIES H AND I OF THE 122ND NEW YORK REGIMENT OF INFANTRY

Three Town of Sweden men who enlisted in August 1862 died while serving in this regiment. Carlton Sanders [or Saunders], 25 and married, enlisted in Company H, was shot in his left lung on July 3, 1863, at Gettysburg and died from the wound on July 6. William Hewitt, 16 and single, of Company H was wounded on May 3, 1863, at Marye's Heights, Va., and died from that wound on May 5. Lewis S. Loomis, 20, single, of Company

I, was killed in the Wilderness on May 6, 1864. The regiment fought at Antietam, but suffered no casualties. Marginally engaged at Fredericksburg, only five enlisted men were wounded. Hewitt was the only casualty in the regiment at Marye's Heights. At Gettysburg, ten enlisted men were killed and five mortally wounded, two other officers and 25 other enlisted men were wounded, and two enlisted men were captured. After Gettysburg, at Rappahannock Station, five enlisted men were killed or mortally wounded and one officer and seven other enlisted men were wounded. It suffered its greatest loss in the Wilderness, where one officer and 21 enlisted men were killed or mortally wounded and five other officers and 58 other enlisted men were wounded, and three officers and 31 enlisted men were captured.

Company H of the 122nd Illinois Infantry

Joseph D. Grunwell, a 35-year-old resident of Girard, Ill., who had resided in Brockport in 1860 and served in the 13th NYVI, joined this company as a corporal when it was formed on August 10, 1862. He was mustered out on July 15, 1865. His unit served in Kentucky, Tennessee, Mississippi, and Alabama, engaging in a number of skirmishes and guarding a railroad, and fought in pitched battles at Jackson, Tenn., Town Creek, Ala., Paducah, Ky., and Tupelo, Miss. In a battle at Nashville, Tenn., in December 1864, the regiment captured four pieces of artillery and a battle flag losing 26 men killed or wounded. In early 1865, it assisted in capturing three Confederate fortifications in the Gulf area.

Company D of the 124th New York Regiment of Infantry

Joseph Brown, a 20-year-old Sweden farm laborer was listed as a draftee in the *BR* of August 13, 1863, and enlisted on September 24, 1864. He "deserted to the enemy" on November 7, 1864, at Hancock Station, Va. The only engagements in which the 124th was involved during Brown's short tenure were at Poplar Spring Church and Boynton Plank Road in October. In the latter fight, the regiment lost three enlisted men killed and one officer mortally wounded, four other officers and seven other enlisted men wounded, and two enlisted men missing. Phisterer does not list any engagement of the 124th at Hancock Station. Brown does not appear in the 1870 census or the 1869 directory.

132ND NEW YORK REGIMENT OF INFANTRY

Samuel Ireland, a 22-year-old schoolteacher, and James H. Hickson, 36, both of Clarkson, enlisted on July 10, 1862, and served for 36 months. The 132nd spent almost its entire service in North Carolina. It fought at Pollockeville, Trenton, Young's Cross-roads, New Berne, Blount's Creek, Sandy Ridge, Batchelder's Creek, Southwest Creek, Jackson's Mill, Gardner's Bridge, Foster's Mills, Butler's Bridge, and in the campaign of the Carolinas at Wise's Forks, Snow Hill, and Bennett's House and was mustered out on June 29, 1865. It lost one officer and 13 enlisted men killed or mortally wounded and one officer and 159 enlisted men of disease and other causes, a total of 174, of whom 71 died in captivity.

COMPANY B OF THE 138TH INDIANA REGIMENT OF INFANTRY

John Ruggles, 18 years old, enlisted on May 27, 1864, and was mustered out on September 30, 1864. He is listed in the 1865 census for Clarkson, but his ACWRD record gives his residence as Laporte County, Ind., and his burial site as Douglas County, Wisc. The 138th was one of the "100 days'" regiments that were recruited by the states but were armed, subsisted, clothed, and paid by the Federal government. The 138th was assigned guard duty along Tennessee railroads, "keeping Sherman's lines of communication open for the transportation of supplies to his army." Although the 138th was a non-combatant unit, eight of its men died in that 127-day period and one deserted. (ACWRD Union Army)

144th New York Regiment of Infantry

James Smith, 17, of Hamlin, enlisted September 29, 1864, was killed at Honey Hill on October 30, 1864, and was buried on the battlefield near Hilton Head. During his service, the 144th was engaged in combat operations in South Carolina. In the Honey Hill battle, the regiment lost 108 killed, wounded, or missing from a roster of 1,844.

Companies E, G, and I of the 147th New York Regiment of Infantry

Charles Hilbert, a 27-year-old German-born farm laborer from Sweden, and Oscar Overton, a 22-year-old Brockport sausage maker, enlisted in Company E. James J. Peachy joined Company I at the time of its formation on August 7, 1863. Peachy transferred later to the 91st NYVI. James Read (or Reid or Reed) and Hiram Williams were transferred to the 147th with their company as Company G from the 76th NYVI when it disbanded in January 1865. After the war, Williams resided in Brockport as a railroad laborer. The regiment saw action in 23 engagements, including Chancellorsville, Gettysburg, Mine Run, Wilderness, Petersburg, Hatcher's Run, and the four engagements of the Appomattox campaign that occurred after January 1865. The 147th lost nine officers and 159 enlisted men killed or mortally wounded, 18 other officers and 403 other enlisted men wounded, four officers and 190 enlisted men captured, and two officers and 177 enlisted men died of other causes, of whom 71 enlisted men died in captivity—50 percent of its 1,916-man roster. Only 81 of the casualties occurred after the men from the 76th joined it. Overton and Hilbert were wounded at Five Forks on April 1, 1865, and discharged for wounds on July 24, 1865, and June 29, 1865, respectively. Williams was discharged for disability on June 3, 1865. In 1870, Hilbert was a common laborer in Brockport with an Irish-born wife and four children. Overton was a farm laborer in Brockport, with a wife and daughter.

COMPANY D OF THE 151ST NEW YORK REGIMENT OF INFANTRY

Henry Hunt, 19, of Clarkson, enlisted on August 17, 1862 and Sylvester King joined on October 22, 1862. Hunt died in the service, in unknown circumstances. By December 16, 1863, King was transferred to the Veteran Reserve Corps. During his service in the 151st, it fought in six engagements in the 1863 Virginia campaign and lost one officer and 14 enlisted men killed or mortally wounded, 38 other enlisted men wounded, and seven enlisted men captured. King had signed up for the 13th NYVI as a resident of Hamlin, but may not have served. In 1860, he had been a 35-year-old master carpenter, living in the Orleans County Town of Barre with a wife and four small children. In 1870, he was a store clerk in Barre and in 1880 and 1900 he was the chief of police in the village of Albion.

COMPANY C OF THE 158TH NEW YORK REGIMENT OF INFANTRY

Henry F. Jacoby, after having served in the 1st NYVI, enlisted on December 8, 1863. He was promoted to sergeant on March 1, 1864, and to sergeant major on March 16, 1865. He transferred to the 100th NYVI on June 30, 1865. From December 1863 until the summer of 1864, the 158th performed garrison duty and took part in several raids in North Carolina. Later, it joined in the final assault on Petersburg and fought in the Appomattox campaign. During that time, it lost two officers and 49 enlisted men killed or mortally wounded, five other officers and 84 other enlisted men wounded, eight enlisted men captured, and 83 enlisted men by disease and other causes, including five enlisted men who died in captivity.

160TH NEW YORK REGIMENT OF INFANTRY

Waterman Davis, a 67-year-old(!) mechanic from Brockport, served in the band of this regiment. He enlisted on August 27, 1862, and died of disease on July 30, 1863. He had served earlier as a drum major in the 13th NYVI. At an early war meeting in Brockport he was identified as a veteran of the War of 1812 and said, "There is no such thing as fear when you get there. All you want to do is obey your officers, and all will go right. When you get there, all you have to do is to jump into the fire eaters." (*BR* 4/25/1861) William Putnam, a 39-year-old Brockport Baptist clergyman, was mustered in as field and staff Chaplain on November 21, 1862. He was discharged on March 10, 1864, but enlisted as a private on September 1, 1864 without company assignment and mustered out on May 8, 1865. During Waterman's service, the 160th, participated in ten engagements, all in Louisiana. The 933 men on its roster suffered one officer and 12 enlisted men killed or mortally wounded and four other officers and 33 other enlisted men wounded. When Putnam re-enlisted, it had been transferred to Virginia for the Shenandoah Valley campaign, where it took part in three engagements and lost two officers and 29 enlisted men killed or mortally wounded, six other officers and 82 other enlisted men wounded, and 24 enlisted men captured. In 1870, Putnam was a Baptist preacher in Mason, Mich., with a wife and two small children.

Waterman Davis, Brockport mechanic, 67, drum major in 1812 war and in 160th NYVI, died of disease July 30, 1863. *Courtesy of the New York State Division of Military and Naval Affairs.*

Company C of the 186th New York Regiment of Infantry

Duane and Frederick Cooley, who seem to have been brothers, were recruited at Sacketts Harbor and credited to the Town of Sweden. They enlisted on September 3, 1864, (ACWRD) or September 22, 1864, (STCR) and were mustered out on June 2, 1865. Benjamin Filkins enlisted August 19, 1864 (ACWRD) or September 26, 1864 (STCR) at Sacketts Harbor (STCR) or at Adams, NY (ACWRD), which is near Sacketts Harbor, and was also credited to Sweden. Laconious M. Howard, 28, and Edward Johnson enlisted at Sacketts Harbor (STCR) or Elliburgh, NY (ACWRD] on September 25, 1864. Howard mustered out on June 2, 1865, but Johnson deserted the same day he enlisted. Lyman Randall enlisted September 3, 1864 (ACWRD) or September 26, 1864, (STCR) at Sacketts Harbor (STCR) or Lorraine, near Sackett's Harbor. (ACWRD) Samuel B. Kellogg, 18, enlisted there on September 17, 1864, and George W. Pool did so three days earlier at Sweden and they mustered out the same date as the others. Herbert Webb, 18, enlisted at Sacketts Harbor on September 24, 1864, was wounded at Petersburg April 2, 1865, had his right arm amputated, and died May 1. During their service, the 186th fought at Petersburg and Hatcher's Run in 1864 and during the Appomattox campaign in 1865. With a roster of 1,020, it suffered no losses in 1864, but 48 enlisted men killed or mortally wounded, 11 officers and 115 other enlisted men wounded, and six enlisted men captured in the 1865 Appomattox campaign.

COMPANY K OF THE 188TH NEW YORK REGIMENT OF INFANTRY

Joseph Newell a 39-year-old Brockport boatman, enlisted on September 29, 1864 and mustered out on July 1, 1865. William A. Conradt, a Sacketts Harbor recruit credited to the Town of Sweden, enlisted on September 13, 1864, and was mustered out on July 1, 1865, and Henry Vincent, also from Sacketts Harbor, enlisted on October 7, 1864, and deserted on October 10. The 188th fought at Petersburg, including its fall, and at Hatcher's Run and the Appomattox campaign. It lost one officer and 36 enlisted men killed or mortally wounded, three other officers and 96 other enlisted men wounded, four enlisted men captured one of whom died in captivity, and 53 enlisted men died of disease and other causes. After the war Newell returned to Brockport.

Company E of the 189th New York Regiment of Infantry

George W. Aldrich, a 34-year-old Sweden farmer, was listed as a draftee in the *BR* of August 13, 1863, but did not enlist until August 29, 1864. The 189th entered the war during the Petersburg siege and fought at White Oaks and Five Forks during the Appomattox campaign. It lost one officer and eight enlisted men killed or mortally wounded and one other officer and 28 other enlisted men wounded. Aldrich does not appear in the 1870 census or the 1869 directory. Erastus Aldrich, apparently his younger brother, was on the draftee list at the same time, but does not appear in the ACWRD.

Company A of the 193rd New York Regiment of Infantry

Volney Thayer, a 17-year-old from Hamlin, enlisted on March 27, 1865, in the final weeks of the war and mustered out on January 18, 1866. The regiment saw no combat, but lost 25 enlisted men to deaths from disease. In 1870, he was a farm laborer in Clarkson with a wife and one-year-old son. Charles R. Hinton, also of Hamlin, enlisted on March 1, 1865 at age 15 and mustered out January 18, 1866.

Company C of the 194th New York Regiment of Infantry

Daniel Clark Castleman, a 16-year-old (claiming 18 for enlistment) Hamlin farmer's son, enlisted on March 29, 1865, and was mustered out on May 3, 1865. (The 1865 census lists his father, also Daniel, as a 43-year-old Hamlin farmer who served in the 104th NYVI, but he is not in the ACWRD.) George M. Rowe, who served previously in the 9th and 12th NYVI regiments, was commissioned a 1st lieutenant in this company April 13, 1865, and mustered out three weeks later. This regiment was mustered at the very end of the war and saw no combat. However, seven enlisted men died of disease during its service.

Company E of the New York Regiment of Marine Light Artillery

Reuben Root, a 23-year-old single resident of Sweden, enlisted on January 14, 1862, was promoted to sergeant on February 8, 1862, and to quartermaster sergeant on March 1, 1862. He was discharged for disability on November 21, 1862. Later, he enlisted in the 22nd NY Cavalry on December 21, 1863, and died of disease on April 9, 1864 at Giesboro, D.C. (His ACWRD record for the 22nd says that he had prior service in Company E of the 1st NYVI, but he is not listed on its roster.) The regiment served on gunboats provided to them and took part in these marine engagements in and around North Carolina: Roanoke Island, Elizabeth City, New Berne, Elizabeth, siege of Fort Macon, South Mills, Tranter's Creek, Swift Creek, Neuse River Washington, near Shiloh, Rawle's Mills, expedition to Goldsboro, Kinston and Folly Island, and several minor affairs. It lost one officer and 16 enlisted men killed or mortally wounded, 16 other enlisted men wounded, eight enlisted men captured, and one officer and 72 enlisted men died of other causes, with a roster of 1,453 men.

United States Medical Staff Volunteers

Augustus Clark, a 45-year-old physician in Brockport in the 1860 census, served in this unit. Other details are not available. In 1870, he had retired and was residing in Brockport with a 61-year-old wife and children ages ten and five.

Veterans Reserve Corps

These units were composed of soldiers who were unfit for combat duty but ineligible for disability discharge. Brockporters who were assigned to them included:

George H. Howard of Clarkson transferred from 8th NYHA on May 4, 1865 and was discharged November 16, 1865. (AGNY per Mary Smith)

George H. Washburn of Hamlin transferred from the 108th NYVI January 1, 1865 and was discharged June 19, 1865. (ACWRD)

James R. Van Sickles of Hamlin transferred from the 8th NY Cavalry to VRC May 15, 1864. Date of discharge unknown.

Charles Woodruff of Hamlin transferred from the 2nd NY Mounted Rifles to Company A of the VRC on April 1, 1865, and was discharged on August 9, 1865.

John J. Hard of Kendall transferred from the 8th NY Heavy Artillery to the VRC (Invalid) of the 20th NYVI on April 7, 1864. He died at Point Lookout, Md., October 18, 1865.

George H. (or W.) Howard transferred from the 8th NY Heavy Artillery to Company G of the VRC on May 4, 1865, and was discharged on November 14, 1865.

Sylvester King of Barre transferred from the 151st NYVI to Company C of the 7th VRC on December 16, 1863. He was discharged from a military hospital on June 28, 1865.

M.D. McDougal of Parma transferred from the 1st NY Battalion of Sharpshooters to the VRC on January 15, 1863.

John H. Silliman of Bergen transferred from the 8th NY Cavalry to Company 51 2nd Battery on September 9, 1863.

Alexander Johnson of Brockport transferred from the 8th New York Regiment of Heavy Artillery on March 20, 1865 and was discharged on July 21, 1865.

These six soldiers transferred from the 108th NYVI:

Frederick Eller of Sweden transferred to the 48th Company VRC 2nd Battalion on September 12, 1863, and was discharged on June 26, 1865. CTCR 1866 residence Buffalo.

William A. Haynes of Clarkson transferred to the VRC December 15, 1863. Discharge date unknown.

Charles E. Perry of Clarkson transferred to the 166th Company 2nd Battalion on May 31, 1864, and mustered out on June 27, 1865.

Homer H. Hoytt transferred to Company A 1st Regiment VRC on July 1, 1863, and was discharged on November 15, 1865. In 1870 he was a curtain agent in Grand Rapids, Mich., but had returned to Parma as a carpenter by 1880.

John Barnhar[d]t of Brockport transferred to Company A 3rd Regiment VRC on July 1, 1863 and was discharged on July 6, 1865.

Erastus West of Ogden transferred to the VRC on February 15, 1864. In 1870 he was a laborer in the Town of Ogden.

These eight soldiers transferred from the 140th NYVI:

Franklin Cooley, a Sacketts Harbor recruit credited to Sweden, transferred to the VRC on February 1, 1865, and mustered out on June 26, 1865.

John L. Cooper of Brockport transferred to the VRC on December 21, 1863.

Richard Coward of Sweden transferred to Company F of the VRC, 7th Infantry on October 29, 1863, and was mustered out on June 28, 1865.

Charles Fishbaugh of Clarkson transferred to the 22nd Company of the VRC, 2nd Battalion on October 29, 1863, and was discharged at Douglas Hospital, Washington, D.C., on June 30, 1865.

Thomas M. Clark of Clarkson transferred to the VRC on April 23, 1864. Discharge date unknown.

Alfred S. Lewis of Clarkson transferred to the 102nd Company VRC 2nd Battalion on March 23, 1864, and was mustered out on June 30, 1865.

James S. Mulvaney transferred to the VRC on April 23, 1864. Discharge date unknown.

Robert Stickle of Clarkson transferred to the 22nd Company VRC 2nd Battalion on January 31, 1865, and mustered out on November 21, 1865.

United States Navy

Joseph Pease, a 25-year-old Parma farmer, served in the Western Gulf Blockading Squadron on the frigates Colorado and Lackawana. After the war, he was a physician in Hamlin. (*BR* 2/9/88)

William B. Mann, a 23-year-old Town of Kendall resident who had just completed his medical training, was commissioned an assistant surgeon in the U.S. Navy on September 17, 1861. He was the ranking surgeon on the receiving ship Miami of Admiral Farragut's fleet, when it steamed up the Mississippi to take the city of Vicksburg. Later, he was stationed at Plymouth on the Roanoke River. He resigned his commission on May 12, 1865, settled in Brockport, and established his medical practice. He died in Brockport in 1920.

Frederick Belden, 28-year-old single Brockport resident, was commissioned in the Navy as an Acting Master Mate on November 19, 1862, served on the gunboat USS *Fearnot* in the West Gulf Squadron. The Fearnot was equipped with powerful rifled guns capable of accurately firing 32 pound rounds. During Belden's service, it was assigned blockade duty at New Orleans. ("USS *Fearnot*") Belden died on September 30, 1863, of yellow fever.

Charles Robins, a 25-year-old Canadian-born Brockport turner, enlisted in April 1861 as a common seaman and served on the USS Minnesota for 36 months. The 1865 census reports that he had his "health permanently impaired" being "made permanently very deaf by discharge."

The following 22 men were recruited at Sacketts Harbor, credited to the Town of Sweden's draft quota, and enlisted in the United States Navy. This all happened late in the war and the records are unclear as to whether they actually served: John Cain, Oavin Carroll, Michael Foley, John Conway, James Carter, Eugene Banner, William Gotchens, John Hinds, John Dean, William Pattsham, George Mink, Joseph Pease, Edward Abbott, Patrick Frim, John Gray, John Clark, John Andrews, Richard Fitzgerald, George Kendall, Charles Marrell, John Meyse, and Michael Maloney.

Conclusion

The foregoing chapters have described in detail the involvement of the Brockport area in the Civil War. These conclusions will attempt to summarize that information. This study has treated the Brockport area as a fairly loose-knit community, defined, as well as can be determined at this distance in time, by the circulation area of the *Brockport Republic* newspaper. This is understood to be the three western Monroe County towns of Sweden (including the Village of Brockport), Clarkson, and Hamlin and, to the extent that they supplied men for companies recruited in Brockport, the immediately adjacent towns of Parma, Ogden, Riga, Bergen, Clarendon, Murray, and Kendall. The recruits from the adjacent towns had become, in effect, assimilated members of the Brockport community by joining Brockport companies.

In Part I, the homefront efforts are described. They resulted in more intensive and extensive involvement of civilians in the war than has been the case in any other American war. The recruitment of the fighting units was devolved on the local communities, the counties and, ultimately, the towns. Recruitment offices were a common presence in the towns, war meetings were held frequently and involved many Brockport civilians, and many Brockporters were involved in active efforts to persuade their neighbors to sign up.

Seven companies were recruited in Brockport and one in Hamlin. In addition, some 233 men served in the Union war effort in units that were not recruited in the Brockport area. The total number of names on the rosters of the Brockport units in the ACWRD is 1,265, but, in every case, a large minority of the soldiers were not Brockporters. My composite roster includes 863 names.

Unfortunately, those statistics as well as almost all others in this summary are only approximate. All of the sources from which they were drawn are replete with inaccuracies and omissions. Some names on my composite roster do not belong there and others are missing, but I cannot say which they are. Nevertheless, they provide a pretty accurate picture of the situation.

The homefront did much more than supply Brockporters for the Union Army, of course. The home folks also provided the bonuses that attracted men from elsewhere, especially Canada, to help fill the local draft quotas. The STCR lists the names of 117 men who were not town residents but received enlistment bounties from the town and were credited against Sweden's draft quotas. The CTCR does not include such names and the Hamlin Town Clerk did not submit a report, though both jurisdictions surely engaged in the same practice.

Some historians have treated the Civil War as a "poor man's war" because, they say, the rich could buy substitutes and escape army service, but the poor could not afford to do so. In the case of these three towns, however, that was not the case. True, some well-heeled Brockporters did buy substitutes, but they also paid the taxes that enabled the towns to hire substitutes for their poor neighbors. Only five Brockporters seem actually to have been drafted.

Once their boys went off to war, they were not forgotten by the home folks who sent many parcels of food and other supplies to the camps. Also, they provided relief aid for the families they had left behind. Some family members actually visited their sons and brothers where they were stationed. Besides the letters that flowed copiously between the war theater and the homefront, the *BR* and the Rochester papers published long accounts of army life supplied by their fellow citizens. The *BR* alone published some 189 long dispatches from Brockport soldiers. Because censorship was minimal, the home folks had a very full picture of what the war was like.

Of course, the most intense involvement in the war was experienced by the soldiers themselves. Once on active duty, the Brockport companies underwent virtually every experience encountered by the Union armies in the East. When the service of the men in non-Brockport units is taken into account, almost the whole gamut of Civil War activity is covered, for many of them served in the West. They suffered the shame of the rout at First Bull's Run, the defeats at Chancellorsville, Fredericksburg, and Second Bull's Run, and the failed Peninsular campaign with its long, fruitless siege of Petersburg.

They also tasted success at Antietam, Gettysburg, and, ultimately, victory in the Appomattox campaign.

They suffered through the inconveniences and annoyances of the mustering, training, and traveling to the front. They marched endlessly to and fro in the confusion of army (dis)organization and camped in bad weather and sparse and shoddy equipment. They went hungry or partook of tasteless and monotonous army fare. They suffered sickness and death from disease and accidents. Despite those hardships, among the 863 were at least 90 men who served in more than one regiment and at least ten who served in three regiments. This does not include men who were in units that were transferred as a whole to another regiment or who were consigned to the Veterans Reserve Corps.

Brockporters shared the experiences of soldiers everywhere of forming close buddy-type friendships with their comrades, but also encountering thieves and brutes and scoundrels among them. They served under both incompetent cowards and brilliant heroes. Some of them were cowards themselves and became deserters. Many others behaved gallantly on the battlefield.

Who were these men who went off to war? I have made a statistical analysis of my composite roster and present some information from it with the caveat mentioned above.

First, let's see where they came from. I can identify the residences upon enlistment of 796 men, mostly using 1860 census returns. The three core towns supplied 631 of them (79.3%)—Brockport 204, Sweden 147, Clarkson 147, and Hamlin 133. (In fact, the Davis Report gives a figure of 356 from Sweden, including Brockport.) Some of those credited to Sweden may actually have resided in the village, as the distinction was not always evident. The immediately adjacent towns sent another 104. The Town of Ogden accounted for 45 of those. Rochester was the residence of nine and Riga of eight. The others were scattered, including one from Pennsylvania. This tabulation does not include the Sacketts Harbor recruits.

Occupation-wise, the recruits reflected the very rural environment from which they came. Farmers, farm laborers, and farm boys accounted for 277 of the total of 485 (57.1%) whose occupations are known. Many other of the occupations were part of the farming culture: blacksmith (7), farrier (3) produce dealer (3) wagoners (2) and saddler, harness maker, teamster, gardener, thresher (1 each). Members of the professions were few: lawyers (3), teachers (4) plus a man who combined farming with teaching, physicians (2), engineer and clergy (1 each).

Fewer still were businessmen: produce dealers (3), "speculators" (2), merchants (3), and hotel keeper (1). Craftsmen numbered 54: painters (8), printers (4), machinists (4), carriage makers (3), masons (5), carpenters (10), butchers (4), shoemakers (4), coopers (2), bakers (3) wheel-wrights (2), and tailor, saddler, tinsmith, marble worker, molder, tanner, miller, and turner (1 each). Then there were clerks (16), cartmen (3), students (13), boatmen (5), domestic servants (8), and teamster, hack driver, peddler, and railroad worker (1 each). Finally, 63 of the recruits were identified as "laborers."

Age-wise, they were, of course, young. I list two 14-year-olds and one 15-year-old. Ten were 16 and 19 were 17. The most numerous single age categories on my list were 18 with 56 recruits and 19 with 40. So teenagers accounted for 130 of the 602 total (21.6%) whose ages are known. Those in their 20s numbered 342 (56.8%), the thirtysomes were 93 (15.4%), and the fortysomes were 34 (5.6%). Finally, I found one 50-, one 61- and one 65-year-old (Waterman Davis a veteran drummer from the War of 1812 who died in the service). The median age was 23.

So far as the experiences of Brockport soldiers in the war can be shown statistically, they appear in the following list, as percentages of the 863 on my roster. The remainder completed their terms of service and were mustered out or their fate is not known:

Killed in action or mortally wounded	34 (3.9%)
Others wounded	141 (16.3%)
and recovered	90 (10.4%)
and were given disability discharges	37 (4.3%)
and became POWs	15 (1.7%)
and died of their wounds	2 (0.2%)
and were given disability discharges	2 (0.2%)
Were captured without having been wounded	41 (4.8%)
including those who died in captivity	20 (2.3%)
or deserted to the enemy	1 (0.1%)
Discharged for disabilities	100 (11.6%)
Discharged early for other reasons	12 (1.4%)
Deserted	88 (10.2%)
Died of disease or accidents	50 (5.8%)
Transferred to the Veterans Reserve Corps	24 (2.8%)
Total	490 (56.8% of 863)

To summarize, 217 Brockporters, 25.1% of the 863 on my list were casualties, killed, wounded, or captured. Another 164 (19.0%) were non-combatant casualties, having died of disease or accidents or been discharged with disabilities. (Thomas Myers of Sweden had the distinction of having been captured and paroled three times, each time while serving in a different regiment.) Thus, 484 Brockporters (56.1%), including the deserters and those who refused the oath or were rejected at recruitment, survived the war more or less unscathed. That is, 43.9% did not survive unscathed, a very substantial rate of loss.

In my canvass of Civil War literature, I have been unable to identify a study quite similar to this. The closest I have come is Edmund J. Raus, Jr., *Banners South*, Kent State U.P., 2005, and Nicole Etcheson, *A Generation at War*, U.P. of Kansas, 2011. The former is basically a sociological study of the impact of the war on Cortland, N.Y., and the soldiers it provided. The latter is a history of Putnam County, Ind., from 1850 through Reconstruction. Also, the Civil War series of The History Press, with its 119 volumes, includes at least 19 that recount the experiences of local communities. However, none of them, I believe, describes the experiences of those communities on the homefront and the war front as comprehensively as the effort undertaken in this study.

Because of the lack of comparable studies, I cannot tell how typical was the experience of the Brockport area. I doubt that it was unique, but I suspect that it tended toward the extreme end of the intensity spectrum for similar communities. The fact that Brockport was the only municipality, except Rochester, to respond to Lincoln's first appeal and the sheer number of companies that were formed in the area and the number of men who served suggests that. In any case, I trust that this study has provided new insight into the impact of the Civil War on one community and, by gross extension, on the nation.

Bibliography

My most important sources have been newspapers and public documents. The microfilm file of the *Brockport Republic* (*BR*) has been the single most useful source. Unfortunately, the year October 1864 through September 1865 is missing. I have also drawn information from the *Brockport Democrat* (*BD*), the *Rochester Union and Advertiser* (*U&A*), the *Rochester Daily Democrat* (*RDD*), the *Rochester Evening Express* (*REE*) and the *Rochester Daily Advertiser* (*RDA*). My most important document source has been the American Civil War Research Database website (ACWRD). Most of the data from it that I have used was drawn from the Report of the (New York State) Adjutant-General 1893–1906.

Jim Foltz of the New York State Archives called to my attention the reports by the clerks of the Towns of Sweden (STCR) and Clarkson (CTCR) on the contributions of the municipalities to the Union effort that were required by the NYS legislature for the Bureau of Military Statistics after the war. They have been another valuable source. Unfortunately, no such report for the Town of Hamlin is available. Similarly, I used the "Detailed Account of Aid Afforded by Towns…," (Davis Report) also required by the legislature for the Bureau of Military Statistics (BMS). Only the Town of Sweden is available. Other useful documentary sources in identifying men in the service were the "Register of Officers and Enlisted Men who are now in the military or naval service, Spring 1865" for Clarkson, Hamlin, and Sweden, and the "Return of Officers and Enlisted Men who have been in the Military or Naval Service" (ROEM) for Hamlin and Sweden, both of which were compiled by the NYS Bureau of Military Statistics and provided to me by Jim Foltz.

BOOKS CONSULTED

Andrews, William G. *Early Brockport*. Brockport, NY: Village of Brockport, 2005.

Bennett, Brian A. *Sons of Old Monroe: A Regimental History of Patrick O'Rorke's 140th New York Volunteer Infantry*. Dayton, OH: Press of Morningside, 1999.

Bennett, John E. *No Word of Them: First Battalion New York Sharpshooters 1862–1865*. Raleigh, NC: www.lulu.com, 2007.

Brown, Charles Curtis. *Civil War Letters of Charles Curtis Brown of Rochester, 13th Regt. N.Y. Infantry, 22nd Regt. N.Y. Cavalry*. N.p: University of Rochester Library, n.d.

Burns, Michael G. *From Rochester to Winchester: The Regimental History of the 22nd New York Cavalry 1864–1865*. Westminister, MD: Heritage Books, 2007.

Busey, John W. *These Honored Dead*. Hightstown, NJ: Longstreet House, 1988.

Chenery, William H. *The Fourteenth Regiment Rhode Island Heavy Artillery (Colored) in the War to Preserve the Union (1861–1865)*. 1898. New York: Negro Universities Press, 1969.

Cooper, Alonzo. "Diary of 1st Lieutenant Alonzo Cooper 12th New York Cavalry Company F." Accessed April 29, 2013. http://www.sciway3.net/cmp-csa/cmp_p_diary_cooper_ny.html.

Cribben, Henry. *The Military Memoirs of Captain Henry Cribben of the 140th New York Volunteers*. Ed. J. Clayton Youker. Central Library of Rochester and Monroe County Historic Monographs Collection. [Oak Park, NY]: c1911, 154p.

Crumb, Dewitt. *Historical Addresses, 23d New York Volunteer Cavalry 2d Brigade, 3d Division Cavalry Corps. Civil War.* W.M. Reynolds, printer. South Otselic, NY. 1894. Reprint. Bainbridge, NY: RSG Publishing, 1995.

Etcheson, Nicole. *A Generation at War: The Civil War Era in a Northern Community.* Lawrence: U. Press of Kansas, 2011.

Farnham, John T. *Diaries, 1861–64*. Typescript. Transcribed by W.G. Andrews. N.p., n.d.

Faust, Particial L., ed. *Historical Times Illustrated Encyclopedia of the Civil War*, New York: Harper & Row, 1986.

Fox, William F. *Regimental Losses in the American Civil War*. Albany, NY: Albany Publishing Co., 1889, 604 p.

Frederick, Jared. "Gettysburg Hero Patrick Henry O'Rorke." History Matters. Accessed April 29, 2013. http://jaredfrederick.blogspot.com.

Geary, James W. *We Need Men: The Union Draft in the Civil War.* Dekalb: Northern Illinois U Press, 1991.

Kilmer, George A. "The Army of the Potomac at Harrison's Landing," pp. 427–8, in *The Battles and Leaders of the Civil War*. Robert Underwood

Johnson and Clarence Clough Buell, Eds. Vol. 2. Secaucus, NJ: Castle, n.d., 4 vols. (reprint).

Marcotte, Robert. *Where They Fell: Stories of Rochester Area Soldiers in the Civil War*. Franklin, VA: Q Publishing, 2002.

Merrill, Julian Whedon. *Records of the 24th Independent Battery*. Bibliobazaar, [Charleston], n.d. reprint of 1870 original.

Norton, Henry. *Deeds of Daring: Or, History of the Eighth N.Y. Volunteer Cavalry, containing a Complete Record of the Battles, Skirmishes, Marches, Etc*. Breinigsville, PA: General Books, 2010 reprint of 1889 original.

"140th New York Volunteer Infantry Regiment." Wikipedia. Accessed April 29, 2013.

Raus, Edmund J., Jr. *Banners South: A Northern Community at War.* Kent, OH: Kent State U Press, 2005.

Skinner, Gord. *Wounded at Gettysburg: A Book of 44 Letters Written by a Civil War Soldier to His Family.* Bloomington, IN: Authorhouse, 2007.

Smith, Mary E., and Shirley Cox Husted, eds. *We Remember Brockport.* Rochester, NY: Monroe County Historian's Office, 1979.

Stewart, George R. *Pickett's Charge: A Microhistory of the Final Attack at Gettysburg, July 3, 1863*. Boston: Houghton Mifflin, 1959.

Stilson, Donald A., comp. *Parma N.Y. Resident Arthur G. Newton Civil War Letters 108th Regiment NY Vol. Inf. 1862 to 1864*. [self-published]. n.p., 2009.

"26th Regiment, United States Colored Infantry." Family Search. Accessed April 29, 2013. https://www.familysearch.org/learn/wiki/en/26th_Regiment,_United_States_Colored_Infantry.

United States War Department. *The War of the Rebellion: A Compilation of the Official Records[OR] of the Union and Confederate Armies*. Washington, D.C.: Government Printing Office, 1880.

"USS *Fearnot* (1861)." Wikipedia. Accessed April 29, 2013.

Washburn, George H. *A Complete Military History and Record of the 108th Regiment New York Volunteers: From 1862 to 1894*. Lavergne, TN: Kessinger Publishing's Legacy Reprints, 2011.

Wert, Jeffrey D. "Mutiny in the Army." *Civil War Times Illustrated*, April 1985.

Index

C

D

I

J

K

L

R

S

T

V

W

About the Author

William G. Andrews is professor emeritus of political science at the SUNY College at Brockport and the author of four books on the history of Brockport, NY. He was the founding president of the Brockport Community Museum, the founding vice-president of the Greater Brockport Development Corp., chair of Brockport's Historic Preservation Board for ten years, past secretary of the NYS Archives Partnership Trust Board, and is now a trustee of the Village of Brockport. He is widowed with six children and thirteen grandchildren.